Miriam

A Novel By

Giles de la Bedoyere

For Caroline, Martin and Charlie

First published in Great Britain 2005

Wellwood Publications
Wellwood, North Farm Road,
Tunbridge Wells, Kent TN2 3DR

ISBN 1 84448 149 2

Set by Chris Griffin Associates
Printed by Biddles

A big thank-you is owed to Sophie Kersey for her
enthusiasm, advice and labours.

Kind friends have criticized Christ's referring to his
Father in Heaven as 'Poppa'; but He did, in actuality, use
the Aramaic diminutive 'Abba', equivalent of 'Dad' or
'Papa'. It was this fact, above all, that persuaded me to
employ informal speech throughout.

> She had thereof indignation that her husband was
> taken from her and went and gave herself to all
> delight; but because it was not fitting that the calling
> of St John should be the occasion of her damnation,
> therefore Our Lord mercifully converted her to
> penance, and because he had taken from her
> sovereign delight of the flesh, he replenished her
> with sovereign spiritual delight before all other, that
> is, the love of God.'
>
> THE GOLDEN LEGEND

ONE

I like early morning. Really early, I mean, before the sun comes up over the hills, when the sky's a translucent grey and the earth's still asleep. Not a soul in view, just me and an empty world holding its breath, waiting – for what? God knows, but I feel it too. Waiting to be born again, the grime and vomit and fag-end of despair cast off as a snake sloughs its skin. A new beginning, not only for me but for everyone and everything.

Grass springs under my feet, drenching my ankles in dew. Scented air comes to me across flowered fields from a land beyond the furthest range. Nature seems as it was before men corrupted it, before Eva ate from the tree of knowledge. A linnet's song melts in to the harmony of tiny sounds that accentuate this expectant hush. Light rises from its hidden source in the east to flood heaven's immensity with promise, breathing colour through rock and foliage, stringing jewels along the spider's web close to my wondering eyes. I pass a hand down my thigh to reassure myself that I'm real, all this is real and not some insubstantial dream.

The dawning of a perfect day, a day that will never end. The birth of a perfect self within me who'll never again be touched by pain or evil, who'll love without counting the cost and want for nothing because to be – simply to be – is happiness enough. My heart grows big, hammers upon my breast-bone, becomes one with the universe, enfolding all that lives.

Standing here, I can almost believe that one day it might happen…

Mostly, I used to get such feelings up north where we spent our summers, in a village on the western shore of the Lake. As a kid I was an early riser, couldn't sleep once the first light stole into my room and prised my eyelids apart. I'd slip on my tunic and tiptoe out of the house on my bare soles (did I ever wear sandals in those days?) down to the bright yellow sand where drying nets were tented between dark-green rocks of basalt at the water's edge. I'd sniff the tangy breeze and let it tumble my hair as it ruffled the shimmering lake-surface. Then I'd dance to an inward music, revelling in my aloneness. These were magic moments snatched out of time and I longed for them never to end.

That kind of ecstasy belongs to childhood. The habit of early rising lasted into my teens but by then it had taken on a new purpose. The scenery had become a backcloth to my meetings with Jo and the wavelets whispering through the half-darkness echoed the beating of my pulse. Beyond that headland's curve he and his brother Jim would be hauling in their final catch and the sun, leaping over the Golan Heights, would blacken their purple sail as it hove into sight. I'd watch its silhouette approach, my heart quickening, until its hull scraped over shingle. As soon as the night's catch had been landed and the dragnet examined for damage from the sharp rocks that thrust upward beneath the water, Jo would come to me running and take me in his arms, lean, smoothly tanned arms still crusted with salt. We'd embrace wordlessly, then he'd hold me away from him and stare at me while I feasted my eyes on him. Green eyes gazing into blue, confident that love could never die.

Yuk! What a schmaltzy little idiot I was in those days. I've learnt a whole lot since, I can tell you. You reach an all time high when you feel you're cradling happiness in the palm of your hand but it's quick-silver, you can't hold on to it. Life's a bitch; one minute you're on cloud nine, the next you're crashing. The Lake itself should've taught me that – there's a devil in its depths which suddenly breaks free and lashes its gentle calm into a frenzy, just as the maniacs shipped to the badlands beyond its further shore break free of their chains and writhe in convulsions before exhaustion stills them. If only you were able to anticipate disaster and say, "Let's stop here, at this point in time, and stay as we are for ever." But life goes on happening and no one remains the same, least of all yourself.

Now I lie back, naked between sweaty sheets, my hair spread over a soiled pillow with a stranger beside me, and ask myself whether that starry-eyed girl and the woman I've grown to be are alike in any thing but name, though only a handful of years and a very few miles separate me from her. Tiberias is within an hour's walk of Migdal and the bustle of its streets outside these barrack-walls tells me it's mid-morning, while sunlight presses on my aching eyelids. The enchantment of early memory has passed, leaving me to nurse a god-awful hangover after last evening's boozing with the boys.

"Cass darling, be an angel and mix me one of your specials. I feel bloody terrible."

Cass yawns, stretches, rolls over me off the bed and grumbles his way to the washstand which serves all purposes in this cramped little hut, including bar-counter. All but one, that's to say; our shared mattress provides the rest! I call Cass a stranger because he has not been part of my whole life like Jo but we've known each other for quite a spell now and on pretty intimate terms – if you think sex has anything to do with companionship. No, that's not fair. Apart from being a damn good lay, he's truly affectionate and I'm extremely fond of him. Yet he's not Jo the fisher-lad with his black, dishevelled curls and sea-blue eyes, whose moods matched mine so perfectly and who no longer exists. Oh he's around in the flesh all right, tooling along in the wake of his beloved 'master' through the countryside we used to explore together as children, yet the cord that bound us has snapped. I tell you, people change.

2

"There, honey." Pleasant, gritty voice, appalling accent. "One of my humdingers. That should set you up."

I take the cup from Cass and move over to make room for his muscular body. Aliens sleep naked even when they are alone in bed, one of their barbarous habits that shock our Jewish susceptibilities. Not mine, however. I've had small chance of covering my assets at night, so to speak, since opting for a career on the streets and besides, his battle-hardened limbs give me the right sort of thrill. The potion he's mixed is bringing back my appetite! Sight starts to focus. I turn my head and take in his rugged features; the cropped hair already thinning at his temple, the nose flattened by some tavern-brawler's fist, brown eyes dwelling on me with a doggy fondness and a mouth that smiles above the strong, attractively dimpled chin.

He says, "Guess you were off on one of your trips, Miri. You weren't asleep but so still, as if the real you had slipped away and left a living corpse behind. Not the first time it's happened."

"Sorry, Cass. It's just something that comes over me and I can't fight it. It used to infuriate my sister Mart – she's the practical one. I seem to go into a kind of trance -and become a different person."

"I'm not complaining, baby, just proving that I'm the noticing sort. It suits you, makes you seem more interesting than the normal run of girls. What's more, you sure compensate when you've snapped out of it. Last night was a spell-binder and I bet there's more to come!"

"Any time, Cass. Think I'll lay off the drink but as for loving. I can't get enough of it. And it's a relief going steady with one bloke instead of taking a chance on one-night stands."

"Yeah, same for me, babes. I'm sick of casual lays who perform for a down-payment, love you and leave you. I need a mistress and when she has your looks I know I've fallen on my feet." He chuckles. " Not my favourite position for making love – but perhaps we should try it... No, seriously, it isn't just your stunning hair and creamy skin that turn me on. You put more into the act itself than others do. It's as if you had, I dunno, some great tide of loving inside you which goes way beyond pure sex. As far as you're concerned, I'm your people's enemy, trampling with my big soldier's boots on everything you hold dear; being my girl has floored any hope you had of regaining respectability. Yet whenever we do it together, you make me feel as if I was the only guy you've ever cared for – or ever will. That's not so, is it?"

"Why shouldn't it be, darling?"

"Cos you sleep-talk, my love. Jo, Jo, Jo, always the same. You wouldn't get that worked up over a pet dog. Who is he?"

"He's a boy I used to know. We grew up together - in fact we were engaged. But that means nothing to me now, not since he turned into holy Jo and froze me off."

I can't keep the hurt out of my voice. Cass responds to it with a

3

caress. An Alien he may be, brash and boastful like the rest of them, but he's got a heart which years of soldiering haven't turned to stone.

"Holy Joe – isn't that what you call those poisonous Set-aparts who gripe at our rule and obstruct everything we do? Don't tell me your boy-friend's one of them."

"Of course not. His poppa's in trade and they wouldn't have him even if he wanted in. Besides, his momma's connected with the Sads, the temple priests, and they're deadly rivals of the Set-aparts."

"So what happened to blight your sweet dreams?"

"Barjoseph happened."

"Common enough name in these parts, isn't it? Sons of Joseph all over the shop… What had this one got that your Jo hadn't?"

"You've got me wrong, Cass. Barjoseph happened to him, not me."

"I'm with you. Picked a queer, did you. Miri? Lousy deal."

"I – I'm not so sure. Jo seemed straight enough in the old days though he wasn't a groper. He fancied me as much as I fancied him. Only he had a funny streak, sort of way-out and in the clouds, all mixed up with fantasies about a superman and a fresh creation. It was that side of him Barjoseph got his claws into."

"Hold on." Cass wrinkles his brow. "You don't mean *the* Barjoseph by any chance – the guy who's credited with all those freak cures and is heading a born-again mission hereabouts?"

"That's the one," I reply bitterly. "He's roped in a crowd of weirdos like himself and made them abandon their nearest and dearest for his sake. Like Jo. I loathe the very thought of that man more than I've ever loathed another human being – and I've known a few reptiles in my time." I'm shaking with anger as I recall him and what he's done to me though I've only set eyes on him three times and we've not exchanged a word.

"Cool it, sweetheart. Don't get up-tight, it'll spoil the mood just when I'm getting to know the girl behind the glamour. Look, I'm not on duty for an hour or so and I'm feeling lazy. How's about we swap childhood memories for a bit? It'll take your mind off things."

I ought to put you in the picture, I suppose.

Cass is a centurion seconded to Herod Antipas, Tetrarch of Galil and Transjordan. He came to Palestine with the Twelfth Legion under the orders of the governor, Pilatus. He's not only an Alien by birth but also by calling since we Yehudis have no fighting units of our own and confine our blood-letting to the altar of sacrifice in the Temple. He's proud of having worked his way up through the ranks, proud of the scars and medals he's won the hard way and determined to make 'primus pilus prior' in the first cohort before he retires. That's the top grade open to a legionary who didn't start as a 'patrician faggot', to use his phrase. His men, Syrian recruits, like and respect him; a Roman officer can always overawe provincial troops. Cass brags about his native city a great deal, its temples and

4

triumphal arch, while chewing his eternal mastic gum. It makes him a conversational drag but doesn't detract from his schoolboy charm.

"You've told me a lot about yourself, Cass, and your home-town."

"O.K. So it's your turn, honey. Shoot."

How on earth do I interest him in the doings of a lakeside village? Migdal is a huddle of limestone cottages scattered over parched meadowland like dice flung down by some playful giant. Our place – our holiday villa, Poppa used to term it – was bigger and better than the rest because we were gentry who'd made their pile down south and only 'slummed' in Galil for the sake of his health which couldn't take the breathless summer heat of Judaea. Leisured upper class, you'd call us, with our suburban residence at Bethaniah, east of the city, and this holiday home by the Lake. I shouldn't say it, but Poppa's wretched lungs meant a heaven-sent break for me; I loathed respectable Bethaniah with its city-slickers and Set-aparts. Reuben Benesdra, the lawyer, for instance – man, what a creep!

"As loathsome as Barjoseph?" suggests Cass.

"Certainly not as pious and high-minded once you got beneath the layers of religious pretension. A first-rate hypocrite, like most of his cronies. Young as I was, I knew he had his eye on me all through my teenage years. I seemed to have something that appealed to men even then, and his fingers followed where his eyes led."

"Dirty groper... Can't altogether blame him, though. Auburn hair, big green eyes and a peachy complexion stand out in this country of leather-skinned faces. Even in Latium where the women are big-breasted and luscious, Miri, you'd be a hit. Some day who knows? I may take you back with me and make 'em sit up."

"I bet you say that to all the girls, You won't want a Yehudi slag hanging on your arm and discouraging all comers when you're looking round for a wife of your own race. Anyway you're right. My freak colouring gave me a head-start with most males, old or young. In those days, of course, I wasn't into men and it meant damn-all to me – until Jo singled me out."

Cass steers me away from that topic, asking neutral questions about my childish pranks and adventures, capping them with his own. This is just as well since there are certain memories I'll never repeat to a living soul. Like the day Jo made me his secret proposal and I accepted him. We'd grown up in each other's arms, you might say, our families being closely acquainted. Zabdiah, his poppa, is a self-made fish-merchant who owns most of the fishing rights in Galil and sells its produce, dried and pickled, in the City. He also owns business premises and warehouses there, so we journeyed in company between the north and the south. He's a gruff, bombastic man and his wife, Salome, seems a pale shadow in his presence, so Jo and I preferred our own devices. We were alike in temperament, sharing daydreams which alternated with bursts of wild mischief. I suppose our parents intended us to be wed one day, a matter for their decision not ours – but Poppa died when I was eight and Momma, heart-broken, followed him. That left Lazarus, Martha and me to fend for ourselves. I was by far the youngest: my brother, whom I adored from a distance, had inherited Poppa's wasting disease and Mart attended his every need, so mine came second. If I ventured within range of her or tried to gain Laz's attention, she'd give me the rough edge of her tongue and sometimes her hand. She'd have liked me to act as an unpaid serving-wench under her command but I refused to toe the line. I was mutinous and wayward. Worse, I had the looks that she'd missed out on. She envied me those, plus the popularity they won for me. I got them from Momma while hers were handed down from the masculine line: rat's-tail hair growing to a widow's peak above her myopic eyes, sallow skin and lank figure. The sharp nose was all we had in common. It's my one physical defect and Cass, whose own is far from ideal, enjoys making fun of it. "You can always tell a Yid by her hooter," he reminds me. Whatever the reason, my sister had little time for me, and Laz, absorbed in his illness, limited himself to a fond word now and again.

I'm wandering, aren't I? Cass wants to prevent me brooding over Jo but he can't control my private thoughts. They hark back to the day when Jo became my life's centre. He stood out among the Lakeside young, like his brother, because a prosperous father had hired tutors from the City to educate them, while insisting that they should learn the fishing-trade the hard way until ready for its business administration. I was eleven and he was just thirteen, celebrating his bar-mitzvah. You know how it goes: for a week young Sam or Dave is cock o' the walk. He can do no wrong, make any demand, be as rude and unmannerly as he likes. Most boys take every advantage under the sun and behave insufferably – while a mere girl has to submit to their airs and graces with no prospect of a similar privilege ahead for her. Jo was no exception. At shul, on his birthday, he lapped up the service in his honour, sporting his new tallith and thanking the chief rabbi as though butter wouldn't melt in his mouth. I was relegated to the background and my present (a pocket-knife) was accepted with a condescending nod. It looked ordinary beside the wax tablets and gold-inlaid stylus lavished on him by his poppa. The elder brother, Jim, is an outdoor type, good with his hands but never one for figures or accounts, so Zabdiah's ambition rested with young Johanan.

By the end of his celebration-week, I was fed to the teeth. I could've slapped him for treating me as just one of his many admirers. I took myself off to the lakeside that last evening, wishing to nurse my wounded feelings in solitude. Light had seeped from the sky yet the water radiated a silvery shimmer of its own and there was a mystery in the atmosphere that reminded me of my favourite hour. I squatted on a patch of turf and watched the creature-life, the tiny lizards black-backed to tone with the dark rocks, and the tortoises sidling along the Lake's edge. For distraction, I told myself the story I'd once learnt from Momma of how the witch Fatma had begged a crust from some baker's wife and, being refused, had condemned the poor woman to carry her oven on her shoulders for the rest of her days. There were the brown marks on the tortoise-shell to prove it – while the reptilian head darting out beneath certainly reminded one of some wrinkled old crone. Rather like my sister Mart, I recall thinking.

Then it was I felt a hand stroke my hair, and I sprang up, rubbing my wet cheeks. It was Jo. "Miri," he said, "I followed you down here. Please stop crying."

I wouldn't look at him. "Why should I?" I said. "You've been stuck up all week and you've treated me like dirt. I hate – hate – hate you, Jo Barzabdiah!"

"D'you grudge me a bit of fun?"

"When do I get my own back? Girls don't have bar-mitzvahs."

"You're green with envy, aren't you?"

"Of what, may I ask?"

"Oh everything – all the kow-towing and the gifts I've had."

"I don't care about any of that – "

"Mind you, I'm still waiting for the best gift of all."

"Not another one, for Pete's sake."

"Well, I'm not sure whether it's receiving or giving. A bit of both perhaps."

"Stop dragging it out and tell me what you want."

"Won't you have a guess?"

"Hate guessing."

"I'll come out with it then, Miri." He took me by surprise, leaning forward with his hands on my shoulders and kissing my half-open mouth. I wasn't used to boys taking me that seriously but Mart had warned me often enough about their dirty minds.

"I'll tell on you to my sister!"

He laughed. His blue eyes under their arching brows sparkled without losing their habitual gravity. They held the inward radiance of the Lake itself, and I realized for the first time that I loved him – the kind of love that doesn't come twice in a lifetime, as I know now.

He said, "I'm not making a pass at you. I want us to make our vows to each other. No one else need know – it'll be our secret."

So his indifference had been a tease after all. I really was special to him. Naturally I said yes and we made our betrothal then and there as best we knew how. I'll never forget his solemn voice, half-child's, half-man's: "Be consecrated to me according to the law of Moishe and of Israel…" It was all so touching, so absurd, but I'll swear no two lovers ever performed the rite with more sincerity.

Our formal engagement three years later seemed an anti-climax. We didn't get that far without a struggle. Salome was set on Jo

7

studying for the priesthood, Zabdiah equally determined that he should give his whole mind to training for business – and marriage didn't enter into either plan. Mart was more than willing to get me off her hands yet grudged me a relationship which had passed her by, while Laz was too sickly to interfere. None of them objected to our eventual wedding but it was agreed that we must wait: a fatal delay, as it turned out.

Betrothal in front of witnesses and blessed by a priest isn't a light undertaking. It's a contract permitting sexual union but not cohabitation for the space of a year. One year – I could've taken that, not the indefinite lapse of time imposed. Cass, whose upbringing in a back-street tenement wasn't touched by romance, listens with impatience. "You say he'd reached his majority by sixteen, same as a Roman lad when he puts on his toga virilis for the first time and takes off his bulla, his lucky charm of childhood. Well, why didn't he insist on the wedding – or elope with you?"

"Jo's not the sort. For one thing he was in awe of his poppa. Zabdiah's an explosive personality, his friends call him the Thunderer. For another, I think he took pleasure in denying himself, forgetting that I was going through the same. People praised us for our model behaviour, holding us up to their own sons and daughters who were having the time of their lives while we strolled down the village street hand in hand like a couple of shmucks. He's a born show-off, Jo, and it suited the saintly image he'd fashioned for himself."

"He sounds a regular wimp."

"If that were so, I'd have shrugged him off. There were plenty of others trailing their coats at me by then. No, it wasn't prudishness or simple vanity on his part. He genuinely believed in Higher Things. Sometimes he'd let his imagination off the leash when we were alone and paint word-pictures of his private universe, a paradise in which angels and strange beasts worshipped before the throne of the Mashiah."

"The – mashiah?"

"God's Chosen One who's coming to earth to redeem Israel and destroy its enemies. So Scripture says. It's a nation-wide fantasy, dear Cass, which your bricks-and-mortar mind could never hope to grasp."

"Don't put me down, dear Miri." He gives me a playful pinch with his square, calloused fingers. "I may've been drug-up the hard way but I've got my belief same as you, though I won't suscribe to the Mithras-cult, like a lot of our squaddies."

"Mithras?"

"Kinky Persian Sun-God who offers his followers immortality in return for their worship."

"Big deal… No, your gods are made of marble and sit all day in huge, draughty mausoleums being fed by the superstitious."

"And you Yedidim bend the knee to an ass's head hidden behind the veil of your Holy Place. Everyone knows that."

"Rubbish. The Debir is empty."

"In which case you worship – nothing. You're doggone atheists." Cass likes scoring points, it makes him feel superior. "You're a cussed crowd, you know that? Whatever we do, like putting the Emperor's head on our coins or carrying our insignia into your Temple, you call profane – and whatever we think unclean, your priests and Set-aparts think pleasing to their god. They even mutilate little boys to gratify this invisible god. Which reminds me of the latest –"

"Spare me, Cass."

"It's a short 'un. Some Goy applies to join the Sons of Yacob. Priest tells him, 'If that's your wish, you will gain a little and lose a little,' 'What'll I gain?' asks the Goy. 'Salvation and interest-free loans, my son.' 'What'll I lose?' Priest smiles. 'Wait till the ceremony, my son, then you'll find out.'

He tells them so badly – never makes funnies about Rome or his fellow-townsmen, I've observed, he has no sense of humour on that score! He goes on more seriously, "No, but it gets my goat to see your religious snobs refuse to set foot in a Gentile house and wash themselves to the elbow after contacting unbelievers. Talk about whiter than white – yet they dish out the dirt readily enough among their own kind. No intercourse with Aliens but plenty with their own gals…"

"Cass, please don't get steamed up. You'll bring on my head again. Look, I'm on your side. I've long seen through their laws and prophecies and fake Mashiahs – besides which, you can hardly accuse me of cold-shouldering foreigners. If that's so, what am I doing in bed with you?"

He rewards me with a warm hug. "Ah, babes, you're in a different league. I'd jack in the whole pack of toffee-nosed Set-aparts for one of you, any day. My, but you smell good!"

"And you've got the sass to call us lecherous… Well, it was hands-off for Jo, anyway. His paradise didn't exclude a hell for those who wallowed in the flesh – I must be prime candidate by now. He contented himself with spouting verse to me from Solomon's Canticle, lines about my breasts being like date-clusters on a palm-tree and him climbing up to reach me and our kisses sliding over lips and teeth like the choicest wine. We learnt most of it at shul and I was able to answer: Come, *let us go into the fields, the vineyards where the grape-blossoms have opened and the pomegranates are in bloom and there I will give you my love*. Pure corn, of course. I can see that now, but if ever there was a come-on… Trouble was he wouldn't rise to it – his bloody sense of honour!"

Cass levers himself out of our bed. "I wanted you to get the guy out of your head, honey, but you're making things worse brooding over him like a wet afternoon. Time I got into my kit; I'm almost due on parade." He climbs into his gear, the steel-plated leather jerkin, leg-guards and bobnailed boots, not forgetting his phalerai and the metal torques awarded for bravery in the field. My life, but he's proud of those! Looks like an ironmonger's stall in his full rig – and sounds like one, clank, clank. "When I come off duty, babes, I'll take you out to a bistro in town and stand you a decent meal. Then it's off to the stadium for the races and the gladiatorial combats."

"Don't feel like eating – and blood on the sand isn't my scene."

"How's about lust in the dust, then? Try and get with it, Miri, this is the last day we'll be spending together for some time. I'm off to the wars, remember."

That's a fact. The Tetrarch has got rid of his Arabian wife for a classier bit of goods to whom he's no right whatever. Herodias is his niece and sister-in-law at the same time! Aretas, the father of the Arab princess, doesn't approve of his daughter being jilted and has declared war on Antipas. Cass and the lads have to march south tomorrow and defend his stronghold of El Mashnaka by the Sea of Salt. These Jordanians fight nasty; God knows if I'll ever see him again – and what happens to me in the meantime?

"Sorry again, my sweet," I say penitently. "What say we do it right now, standing, as you suggested? That'll put me on my feet in more ways than one."

It's the least I can do in return for the security I owe him. I get up, still a trifle shaky, and he fastens on me like a leech. Never averse to it, good old Cass. Always on the go, these bold legionaries, they take where they can get – in transit. His valour-rings (for a different kind of struggle) bite into my boobs. Ever made love to a Roman in full battle-kit? Don't try it, sister!

"You're a miracle, Miri, know that? Hang around and I'll be back for more when this little shindig's over. That's a goddamn promise."

Yes, but fighting's in his blood. It turns men like him on more surely than sex and I know he'll risk his life, even against a load of wogs (to use his own jargon). Well, I can't afford to get broody over him too. A girl's got to look after number one in my line of work. He blows me a last kiss, buckles on his sword-belt, adjusts his scarlet-crested helmet and looks – magnificent.

His going leaves me free to pursue my interrupted train of thought. The events that led to my estrangement from Jo – or rather, his from me – throb like an aching tooth for all Cass's efforts to head me off. Recalling them once again is a sort of bitter therapy.

Will I ever forget my last attempt to drag Jo down from his celestial cloud-cuckoo-land into the realm of earthly love? Moment, mood and sensuality overcame discretion one empty Shabbat afternoon. We were seated side by side on yielding sand that fringed the Lake, hidden beneath the shadow of his beached boat. I'd heard his heady daydreams retailed, with mounting impatience, while my eyes dwelt on the fine hairs furring an eloquent forearm as it traced his fanciful inner images. Springtide scents, the feel of growing things, a quickening in the air about us: all heightened expectation – made our long waiting-ordeal seem an offence against nature. My hands, as if of their own accord, reached out and sought those secret places below his loose garment, hungry for him, for some responsive passion.

His reaction told me all. He thrust me away abruptly, scrambled to his feet, shaking with shock (was it my violation of the Holy Day or the impetus from an answering urge, repressed?), and turned on his heel. Tears of mortification burned my cheeks; thwarted desire smouldered in my loins; an enormous rage possessed me, hardening slowly into iron resolve. I adored him – and the Law allowed engaged couples to exchange intimacies. How could it be wrong? Already an inkling of our future stirred in my mind; if he chose to play the prude, I would get my back on him by playing the prostitute...

It wasn't just this fiasco but his enforced apprenticeship at Zabdiah's office immediately after that it set a gulf between us. If I'd been on the spot, occupying the time he spent away from ledgers and bills of lading, I might have saved him from harmful influences, but Laz's health required the purer air up north. I was miserable without Jo's company and the places we'd explored together, the Lake in whose snow-fed waters we'd so often bathed, gave me little comfort. I imagined him working diligently at his desk; had I known that tedium was driving his thoughts back to childish dreams of a transfigured world and his feet along a stonier path to the wilderness east of the City, I might've seen the danger in time and forced its issue into the open. Once I did find out, the damage was done.

The wilderness – that barren waste of sand and rock has bred prophets from the day Moishe looked down on the Promised Land. Israel thirsts for their message as the desert creatures thirst for refreshment, yet stones them for their scolding with equal urgency. No wonder none has declared himself since the days of Ezechiel and Jeremiah! None, that's to say, except the weirdo whose revivalist preaching reached Jo's ears, full of city dust. The fellow's his namesake, as it happens: Johanan, named the Baptist because he dunks his penitents in the River Jordan by way of purifying their souls. That kind of carry-on has an irresistible appeal for Jo (my Jo), exciting his spiritual fervour to its highest pitch. It comes from his momma, you know, the way my pale face and flaming hair came from mine; there's not a trace of his hard-nosed poppa in him, except for a quick temper like summer lightning. It's said that Galil spawns fanatics. Religious reformers are two a penny up north, not to mention cut-price mashiahs whose careers usually end in a bloodbath! Barjoseph, to take a sample of the latter, has lived in total obscurity as a carpenter in Nazrat for thirty years. They're all the same: the humbler their origin, the higher their determination to make the big time. The Baptist and he are cousins, by the way, though reared in different regions. It was in the hope of seeing Jo again that I met the pair of them for the first time.

We'd returned to Bethaniah at the end of one summer for Laz to consult his specialist, and any expectation that my fiancé would be waiting on our doorstep, regretting his involuntary brush-off, was quickly dashed. His parents were on it instead, bemoaning the fact that he'd freaked out and become the Baptist's disciple. Zabdiah's jowls were purple with displeasure, and Salome, who took her cue from him, flapped her hands in distress though I suspect she was secretly delighted, being herself a convert to Johanan's cause. Beside them stood Reuben Benesdra, the Job's Comforter, ever ready with his malicious tongue and roving paws. He expatiated on Jo's absence, deploring his behaviour yet planning to benefit from it. I could read the message in his shifty little oyster-eyes and wet lips: with Jo out of the running, I was virgin meat for his jaded palate.

"Johanan may be a priest's son," he told us in his high-pitched pedantic voice, "but there's something dubious about his origin. The mother, Elizabeth, was long past her menopause when he was born – and one might question whether Zechariah, his father, had not taken some younger woman to bed. Naturally the matter would have been hushed up. They were both elderly and soon died, leaving the child an orphan. He was adopted, alas, by that exceedingly sinister kibbutz on the western shore of the Salt Sea, who have cut themselves off from orthodox Jewry and Temple-worship on the grounds that we have compromised our faith – such insolence – and who claim to be practising religion according to its most rigorous laws as a preparation for the Mashiah's imminent arrival. In my humble opinion that is a cover-up for licentiousness; I'm told they drug themselves on opium and agaric, then indulge in hideous orgies. It's true that Johanan abandoned them, but he took with him their habit of total immersion and their spirit of intolerance. The man's a dangerous revolutionary, a demagogue who is trying to subvert the people from their leaders by a campaign of vilification. He'll be silenced before long, either by Rome or by Antipas in whose territory he operates, and I very much fear that his followers will go down with him."

I shuddered. " Can't something be done to save Jo from his delusions?"

He shook his head, enjoying my unease. "Young men are so impetuous and idealistic. Argument will only make him more obstinate. However, my dear, we could journey out together and judge the situation for ourselves."

The proposal suited Benesdra's book very well. Zabdiah refused to have any truck with the Baptist or with his son until he saw reason and begged his poppa's pardon, Salome was too scared of her husband to go with us, so he'd have me on his own. I had to take him up on it if only to catch a glimpse of Jo though the prospect wasn't inviting. Reuben's a fat, complacent cat, middle-aged and disgusting, the sort who never looks you in the eye. He's forever washing himself, like all his Set-apart cronies, and continues to chafe his hands even when they're dry – but he'll never rid them of their natural grease. He's the humbug of all time: lives like a lord while claiming to lavish alms on the poor, pretends affection for Laz his late friend's son, and for Zabdiah in whose firm he has shares, protests his holiness in between murmuring improper suggestions to yours truly. Ugh! What's more, he's a married man with teen-age children. There's worse, a lot worse, but I'd rather not think about that right now…

Anyway, we set off on mule-back. (I'm no rider but coping with the animal proved easier than fending off Benesdra's advances.) The summer's drought hadn't yet given way to milder autumn with its healing rains and the desert was a burning cauldron. To descend the eastern slope of Olivet is like a journey into hell. It's not just the heat but the desolate landscape that shrivels one's soul; mile upon mile of bare, featureless rock rolling to the horizon on either side, smooth-surfaced as if worn away by the relentless climate, or tortured into strange, terrifying shapes like clinkers moulded in some primeval furnace. No wonder travellers talk about demon dwellers haunting its vastness and whispering evil thoughts. Yet at its lowest point, the Jordan valley, parched browns and greys are relieved by lush greens. The grass grows tall and date-palms rear their canopies to cast welcome shade over the river-path. When each wadi is an arid rift seaming the terrain of a dead planet, the Jordan still flows, deep and beneficent, in its winding bed.

Here it was that we set eyes on a figure whose appearance aped his surroundings. Skeletal and ascetic, robed in a camel's skin with the uncut hair of a Nazirite dedicated to God's service, Johanan dominated the group of his followers and a fascinated audience. We heard his hoarse voice from off, carried on the still desert air, shouting, "Repent, you vipers, while you still have time. The Lord's flail is lifted to winnow his harvest and scatter the useless chaff…" As we approached; the bloodshot, deep-socketed eyes fixed themselves on us as if in accusation and roused my resentment. I'd hated the trip and felt confused at the thought of encountering Jo in this improbable setting. We might've been empty-headed tourists visiting a zoo to watch some savage animal prowling behind bars.

He was kneeling with his back to us a few feet from the Baptist, rapt and motionless. As I gazed at him, the world of Solomon's song came to my mind: Whither has your beloved gone, O fairest among women? The shock and the shame of his repudiation on thet fateful Shabbat by the Lake quickened my nerves as if they had hit me one moment before.

We were near to each other, as near as we'd been throughout our childhood, yet divided in spirit. He'd surrendered to the summons of a dope-crazed lunatic and I was consumed with self-pitying anger. Momentarily I'd forgotten the creature beside me; now I realised that it was Benesdra, not myself, whom Johanan's eyes were challenging. He started up again, lashing out at the hard-heartedness of Israel's religious elite whose black-fringed garments masked a multitude of sins (you'd have thought he was reading Reuben inside-out!) and I felt my escort's ringed fingers bite deep into my arm as they tightened in fury.

"Why don't you dish it out to him in return?" I goaded him.

"I don't care for the look of his bodyguard," he snarled. "Some of them are pretty rough-hewn characters who'd be only too ready to deal with opposition. Didn't I say at your brother's house that the man's an incendiary? He means to overturn the established order. Vipers, indeed! In next to no time, he'll have every underdog in Judaea snapping at the heels of the rich and demanding with menaces under a cloak of pious zeal."

I must say the Baptist's fan-club didn't seem particularly formidable. The two I recognised apart from Jo, were fisherman from Galil like himself, the Barjonah brothers, Simon and Andy. They were rough-hewn all right but hardly aggressive. How on earth, I wondered, had they got caught up in this charade?

Johanan addressed Reuben directly: "You Hasidim are forever rinsing your hands to wash away the defilement of the am-haretz, the unhallowed masses, yet your corruption goes deeper than theirs. Strip yourselves of those meretricious robes and plunge into the water, acknowledging your unworthiness and asking forgiveness for your crimes."

A watcher sneered, "It's his belly he doesn't want to acknowledge! What's another bath to a Set-apart – they're so bloody clean you could eat off them."

"It's a gesture of contrition acceptable to the Lord, the sign of a changed heart. True baptism that transforms a man's soul and makes him whole isn't mine to give. I can only foretell the advent of a power which will overturn the government of Israel and put its enemies to flight."

"There you are, " muttered Benesdra." Plain, unadulterated sedition." Conquering his fear of reprisal, he shouted, "The enemy in our midst is not the power of Rome. It's the likes of you, militant trouble-makers who stir up discontent and envy among the people."

The other studied him before replying and suddenly I had the impression of a sane, reflective person beneath his superficial oddity. "I wasn't referring to those who rule our country from afar," he said more quietly, "but to the forces of darkness, Belial and his cursed tribe, who seek a lodging in man's innermost self. It's their stranglehold which the Son of Man has come to break."

"By what right do you dare to proclaim the Mashiah? Are you Elijah himself returning to announce his millennium? When the Anointed One descends in all his glory, he won't be heralded by such as you – a flea- bitten anchorite who insults God's friends and inflames the poor against their betters."

"And how dare you presume to search the ways of the Almighty?" The Baptist's voice outpitched Reuben's nasal falsetto. "Were I to tell you that the Mashiah is among us at this moment, your blinkered self-righteousness would reject him."

The joker at the back of the crowd called out, "If he's here, why not point him out to us and we'll pay homage?"

The heckling had caused heads to turn, including Jo's. Deliberately I pulled off my headscarf and allowed the sun to blaze down on my red-gold auriole so that he couldn't avoid identifying me. I hoped to awaken his conscience but I was mistaken. His features have always been expressive and all I read in them was embarrassment overlaid with stubbornness. I could have stamped with vexation! Meanwhile, Johanan's hint had roused a fresh interest in the crowd, avid for sensation. He'd paused in his diatribe and gone back to the task of dunking his converts. They stood on the river's edge, half-stripped, awaiting their turn and I envied them, not their desire to be cleansed of sin but the coolness of the turgid waters. Noonday light burned downwards with its fierce glare and temporarily affected my vision because it seemed to me that the haze above the river gathered shape and substance while a thunder muttered overhead. Heat storms aren't infrequent in the desert but this was different; it was as if for an endless moment normality had been jolted into a new and awesome dimension – and I knew it wasn't so for me alone because those around were also staring upwards, dumbfounded. Was it mass hallucination? I lowered my eyes and saw a man emerging from the Jordan, his long hair and beard dripping. He was tall, wide- shouldered and strongly built but otherwise unremarkable in appearance yet Johanan had fallen to his knees before him, his baptismal cup discarded on the ground. His neophytes followed his example, Jo the last to do so. Had I but known it then, he was lost to me from that second.

He came after us when we'd wheeled our mules round for the homeward trek, Benesdra still growling into his beard about tub-thumpers fermenting rebellion and myself in a fit of black depression. I heard the slap of bare feet over the scorching rocks and glanced over my shoulder as he caught up with us. Slowing down, he tramped beside the beast, his head lowered as though meditating what to say. I gave him no help, looking straight ahead of me. After all, I was the injured party and it was up to him to justify himself. At last he raised his eyes and said pleadingly, "Try to understand, Miri. This is the biggest thing that's happened to me. The Baptist's a prophet through whose lips God is promising redemption to our nation. Money, worldly success - even our love for each other - mean nothing compared with that."

"Nor the fact that you consecrated yourself to me, once in secret then before witnesses, I suppose?" I laid the whip to my mule because Benesdra was snickering on my further side.

Jo quickened his pace to keep up. "Miri, I do love you, believe me, but a man may be called to some special way of life – and a woman, too. Won't you be one of us?"

I reined in, confronting him savagely. "Look, Sunshine, don't drag me into your spiritual hang-up. I'm just an ordinary girl who fell for a crazy shmuck. I don't intend to sit at your guru's horny feet and live on empty promises. I want to love and be loved, make a home and a family, grow old in your arms. If you can't give me those things, then for God's sake leave me be."

He looked all injured innocence. "Of course I renounce all claim on you, Miri. Another guy will offer you what I'm resigning."

"Very magnanimous," I sneered. "You know damn well it's not that easy. We're man and wife in all but name and a solemn ritual can't be retracted by a few casual words."

"If I release you in front of the Council, you'll be free to wed again."

"I'm not market produce to be sold and re-sold at anybody's bidding. You're the one I love, God help me. I'd sooner stay an old maid like Mart, with a shrinking womb, a cold belly and nothing to look forward to but death than get hitched to someone I don't care for."

"But don't you see?" his voice was shrill with the need to convince me. "Love and marriage are trivial matters compared with his coming."

"Who's coming? The Baptist's?"

"Not him."

"If you mean the Mashiah, you're as touched as Johanan and that bunch of loonies who egg him on. Where are the big drums, the hosts of Midian, the fiery chariots? You've been conned by a two-bit swindler and you'd better face up to it. Stop sublimating, come down to earth and keep the vows you made me when I was a kid and you were – just – a man."

"I – I'm sorry. I know how much I've hurt you. You always rave and storm like this to hide your true feelings. You hit out at anyone – the Baptist, me, even a Saviour you don't believe in though you've seen Him with your own eyes."

"Seen him?"

"The last in line to be baptised by Johanan, though – heaven knows – it should have been the other way round. Didn't you see the Spirit of God above him and hear the Voice confirming his Sonship?"

Reuben had levelled with us again, anxious not to miss out on any titbits for future scandal-mongering. Tact has never been his strong point and Jo's words were bait he couldn't resist. "What piffle, dear boy! Haven't you heard of a mirage? The sun plays strange tricks on one's eyesight." I registered the fact that even he had witnessed the phenomenon.

Jo all but ignored the interruption. He said tersely, "A died-in-the-wool materialist will deny the evidence of his own senses rather than admit the supernatural."

"How dare you imply that I am a materialist, a disbeliever, you young whipper-snapper? I and my fellow-Hasidim look forward to the coming of God's Servant predicted by Isaiah and others. But Miriam is correct." He had me by the arm once more, ghoulishly possessive, though unseen by Jo. "He will arise in splendour and his origin will not be that of human flesh. It was sheer blasphemy to ascribe Mashianic status to some nonentity shivering on a river-bank."

"Hasn't it occurred to you, sir, that the Son of Man must be human by definition and that He may have been born among the poor in order to give them hope?"

"Pish-tish, boy! We're talking of princes, not paupers. He will invite only his most distinguished subjects to the heavenly banquet which will mark his eternal reign."

"Yet if by any chance He chose to champion the oppressed, you might find yourselves down-graded, mightn't you? All your psalms and posturings would count for nothing."

"You see, Miriam? The ugly head of social discontent rears itself again... You at least are too sensible to be taken in by this pernicious rubbish – and you are fortunate to be rid of a misalliance. You're young and very lovely, my dear; there are many who would be more than willing to offer you protection, a mentor's guiding hand."

I hesitated to imagine where his guiding hand was likely to lead me. Couldn't Jo see what his desertion was letting me in for? I improved on the implication of Reuben's final words by adding, "If I'm to be deprived of my marital rights, Jo Barzabdiah, I'll take what I want out of life without reckoning the consequences. I'll have myself a ball..."

Then I spurred the mule and left him standing. It was a childish exit-line – yet I've fulfilled it to the letter.

TWO

I'm still in bed reliving the past when Cass gets back. He takes one look at me then pours another slug into my tumbler and hands it me. I swig it down, he strips.

"Feelin' better, Miri?"

"A bit, thanks, Cass."

"How's about a little foreplay to bring the colour to your cheeks?"

His muscular frame looks inviting as he towers above me, but the odour of sweat turns me off. I shake my head. "They shouldn't make you wear all that shmutter on parade."

"Can you see me drilling the lads in my underwear? Don't worry, babes. I'll sweeten myself up in no time and be the well-groomed escort for a beautiful lady."

He fills the basin and slaps water under his armpits, then wraps himself in his toga. It's the badge of Roman citizenship and he's mighty proud to be seen around in it. I like watching men go through their morning routine, the blade scraping rough chins and the dab of after-shave applied. Truly, they're vainer than we are. Now he smells good. There are no inhibitions between us and he watches me at my toilet as well. Dressing used to be a drag in my 'respectable' days: the kolbur followed by the baldinajja followed by the pirzomata wound about my middle and finally a veil to cover my head. Gentility demanded this elaboration – but I felt like an Egyptian mummy! These days a single garment's sufficient, loosely draped and low-necked to show the springing of my breasts. (That's permissible for a hooker, and I won't pretend I'm anything else.) A sprig of myrrh tucked into my cleavage – and Miri's ready for the fray. No make-up except a touch of carmine on my full lips to echo my crimson hair and no veil to hide my chief attraction. A girl in my trade has to make the most of herself.

Arm in arm we stroll out of barracks, Cass's subordinates grinning behind their hands at the sight of his girl, and one or two are not afraid to wink openly at me. They're Syrian recruits and I get on with 'em because I don't give myself airs. Abenadar, Cass's second in command, definitely fancies me. He's a decent sort for all his gruff, sergeant-major manner but absolutely loyal to Cass – so there's no risk of his taking advantage. More's the pity! No, I'm joking; I shan't two-time the only guy who's ever taken me seriously. Dear Cass – did he really mean it about shipping me back home as his mistress?

Tiberias is the brainchild of Herod Antipas, a fawning tribute to the Emperor who confirmed his rule over Galil and Transjordan. It's laid out on the pattern of every Roman township: two straight avenues intersecting at a forum and cutting the ground plan into symmetrical squares. That's the Alien mind all over, neatly compartmented and totally unimaginative. No orthodox Jew will set foot in the place partly because it's bung-full of Pagan temples, partly because it's raised over some prehistoric cemetery and contact with the dead is proscribed by Moishe. So the townsfolk are mainly confined to foreigners or drop-outs like myself. (Another black mark for Miri, whore and renegade.) Yet its streets are never empty. The sulphur springs outside its walls bring a regular host of neurasthenics throughout the year though rumour has it that many have been diverted further north to the lakeside villages where Barjoseph is performing his instant cures. People are so credulous when they're desperate for healing! Jo's idol dishes it out gratis whereas the spa makes money to enrich Herod's palace on the hill above Tiberias. That's a sight for sore eyes with its Grecian portico and forward-sweeping colonnades, its terraces and fountains. Cass tells me it's equally spectacular inside – all marble walls and mosaic floors with silk and satin drapes and the latest mod cons imported from abroad. Hopelessly vulgar, I answer to put him down, but I wouldn't say no to a chance of gaining an entry.

We dine at his favourite tavern, The Vine. As its name implies, they serve good vintages, Chian and Falernian – none of your Palestinian brew! The food isn't kosher but that no longer bothers me. Cass has a saying: 'when you go to Rome, do as the Romans do.' Suits me. He seems concerned for my immediate future but I find his attitude unreasonable.

"I don't want you drifting back to the streets, honey," he says with his mouth full. "I'll be thinking of you while we knock hell out of the A-rabs, and looking forward to more good times together. You've really got under my skin..."

"How am I to survive in your absence, lover-boy?"

"Um. Wish I weren't so short o' funds at the moment or I'd pay you to sit on your luscious butt. What you need is a retainer – some temporary employment."

"I could char, do laundry-work till you get back, I suppose."

"And ruin your lily-white hands? No way."

Abenadar would be glad to take me over while you're away. Only teasing!"

His eyebrows meet in a frown. "Don't rile me. He's a grand soldier and pretty straight, but I'll not have anyone messing you about. Besides, he'll be marching with us – thank Jupiter." He's thinking hard, an unaccustomed exercise. "Have you any qualifications other than your obvious ones?"

"Well, I can dance, though I've had no training."

"I believe it, Miri. You make love like a contortionist. Cool cat."

"Slick prick." This is a line of chat that usually leads to love-play but now is not the moment.

"Given your looks plus the ability to wriggle your bare midriff to music, you should be able to land a cabaret-job at the palace. Antipas never says no to an eye-catching floosie."

"And a floosie daren't say no to Antipas. D'you want me to end up in his harem?"

He laughs. "The guy's impotent, everyone knows that. Lived it up too much in his youth and ran outa juice. Anyway, the queen's got him under her thumb. She's a real tartar! Lets him drool and have an occasional grope – but nothing more."

There's food for thought in his suggestion. The Tetrarch will be presiding at the stadium this afternoon. Given half a chance, I just might be able to attract his interest – and then, who knows? I've no ambition to hit the high spots but at least I'd get board and lodging in luxury. When we make our leisurely way to the sports-arena, it's already milling with spectators. Today's show is a send-off for Herod's troops and Cass's rank gets me through the turnstyle without payment though we can't sit together. He must fraternize with his buddies on the far side while I mingle with the plebs. Luckily there's a spare seat close to the president's box that still awaits its royal occupant. How these Aliens love display! The programme starts with a procession: banners and drums, statues of their gods hauled along on tumbrels, the gaudily painted racing-chariots and last, the wretched gladiators who'll shortly mutilate each other for the crowd's enjoyment. Herod, wearing a laurel wreath on his grizzled hair and a purple-striped toga to conceal his beer-gut, appears to polite but lukewarm applause. Feeble son of an infamous father, he's no more popular with the Aliens than with us; we despise him as an Edomite, no true-born Jew, they look down on him as a client-ruler, the Emperor's arse-licker. He's self-indulgent, decadent, and he surrounds himself with mincing sycophants – yet at least he's no murdering tyrant who decimated his own family and massacred innocent babies.

I look up at him as he takes his place, scanning the audience below with a lazy, complacent smirk. The sun stands tall in a cloudless sky; its rays shaft down on my exposed hair but fail to penetrate the canopy shadowing him. I think his gaze paused on me for a second before passing on, but I can't be sure. Give him time, Miri, and keep trying. The show gets under way. Race-cards flutter like confetti and tick-tack men make their frantic signals as the charioteers line up at the starting-grid beneath Herod's praesidium. A cheer erupts as he drops the white cloth, and the Libyan horses bound forward on the first of their seven laps. Shouts of "Come on, the Reds!" and "Step on it, the Greens!" resound from rival factions – and I yawn. I'm not at my best, while kids' games really do nothing for me. Cass has described his experiences at the Circus Maximus in Rome; this is a provincial, down-market version by comparison and only the betting gives it an edge of interest. Not all the stakes are cash: perks, extra rations, even the right to sleep with another bloke's girlfriend (or boyfriend, if it comes to that) play their part. There's a lot of buggery among the legionaries stationed here; what can one expect from men whose profession throws them together and encourages macho relationships?

The thought prompts a return of my morning's preoccupation. Didn't Cass hint that Jo might be gay? He's certainly a pretty boy and as sensitive as a girl in some ways, at the mercy of his emotions. One minute he seems on a high, full of his exalted visions, the next he seems sunk in despair. I'm a bit like that myself but it never crossed my mind that he was too like me, too feminine in temperament. No, I'm sure he's all right in that department – Cass always goes for the obvious, oversimplifies. But this Barjoseph: what about him, thronged by moonstruck males? He's thirtyish, in his prime yet still unwed. A Nazirite opts for the celibate life through self-denial; on the other hand, it's a good camouflage for sodomy, isn't it? Makes you wonder what exactly goes on in the privacy of that travelling circus of his. Poor Jo, I hate having to entertain such suspicions.

The final race has ended in a tie, nobody wins, nobody loses. There's general relief or disappointment as they return their wagers to their pockets. I remember to give Antipas the glad eye without seeming too obvious. This time he responds, stares down at me with frank attention, then turns to say something to an attendant standing beside his chair – a dignified personage with the closed features of the perfect servant. What I'd give to hear their exchange! It's as well Herodias isn't gracing the scene with her dour presence; no doubt she feels herself above such meretricious amusements. Am I being over-optimistic? I don't think so. Antipas is notorious for picking up stray ravers though he usually sends out talent scouts to do the job for him. His family are all the same. His brother, Archelaus, who was deposed from the throne of Judaea before I saw the light of day, started on his downward path by grabbing some betrothed maiden of sixteen as he passed by in his own wedding-coach, and when that went down badly with the populace, slaughtered them right and left. Like father, like son. Grab everything you want, Antipas, but don't expect to have it all your own way! I've got my price – plus a tiny shred of remaining self-respect despite my disgrace.

Now comes the part I can't stand, the combat of gladiators. Why does the rabble get such a kick from watching unlucky wretches hack each other to bits? Thanks heaven there are no animals to be tormented on this occasion… Fighting-teams are led in at either end: on the left, a well-armed ludus of professionals marching forward in disciplined ranks, on the right, a gaggle of down-and-outers – convicts, slaves and prisoners of war whose chance of reprieve rests

21

on their survival in this unequal contest. They plod to their fate with heavy feet and lowered heads like the oxen being dragged to the Altar of Holocaust in the Temple, and I reflect that our cruelty, in the service of an inhuman God, is no less than that of the Romans.

I put my hands over my eyes as the killing starts but they can't blot out the swish of swords, the agonised grunts and screams, the baying crowd. There's nothing like a spectacle of carnage to get the juices flowing! It's all over disappointingly soon for the majority and the corpses dragged away leaving their crimson spoor on the sand. These splashes remind me of Jo and Jim, Andy and his brother Simon gutting their catch on the Lake shore: dead men to satisfy a bloodthirsty public, and dead fish to fill the stomachs of slobs like Benesdra... They condemn me for promiscuity but surely making love for a trade is better than making war on those who can't hit back?

The finale is to be a duel between equals: a retiarius, armed with net and trident, versus a myrmillo with sword and shield. Each is a veteran, I hear my neighbours say, owned by a lanista or fight-promoter. (Cass has explained all this to me in wearisome detail.) In spite of my nobler instincts, I feel compelled to watch. Expertise in any skill has a certain fascination and the show should be comparatively bloodless since its adversaries know how to defend themselves. They crouch, taking the other's measure, change positions and crouch again. The net sweeps out (hindsight of Jo casting over the dawn-grey lake-surface) failing to trap an opponent in its toils. Eventually the retiarius flings back his arm in frustration and hurls his metal fork. It's taken on the shield, falls uselessly and leaves him open to attack. The myrmillo doesn't hesitate for the crowd's decision; he rushes in and dispatches the retiarius with a single thrust.

Someone beside me says knowledgeably, "As I thought. There was needle between those two – some quarrel over a woman back in Rome," as I try not to be sick.

Is it over at last? I'm sure I've blown my chances with Antipas. I feel too tense and disgusted to cash in on the impression I made earlier. No, the myrmillo, having made his victory circuit, is standing firm. His lanista is offering a challenge to any taker. This is a nightmare. For two pins I'd jump into the ring myself and put the oaf to shame. There's a lot of jostling among the troops opposite and one of them leaps over the barrier. He's not armed but a sword is thrown down to him that he picks up. I recognize him as he straightens because he gazes up at me with a crooked grin, his jaw champing rhythmically on its eternal wad. Oh no, not my bold centurion yet! It has to be, of course. All his swanking and his valour-rings – they must be lived up to if he's not to lose face with his pals. Or can he be doing this to impress me? The idiot. As if I'd want my meal ticket to risk his stupid life, already endangered by the campaign ahead!

I was engrossed against my will by the previous match. Now I'm completely insulated from the folk around me, my whole being at Cass's side as he feints for an opening. Was I right after all when I told Jo I could never love another man? My dread is surely greater than I'd feel for a mere companion or a convenient stud... The pro. bides his time, playing his fish almost with contempt – but Cass is no tyro, he's a fine swordsman who's fought his way through many countries and hostile armies. His toga has the advantage of muffling the other's lethal blows in its thick folds, and the blood that stains its whiteness comes from a slash across the sinew of Cass's sword-arm. He shakes it impatiently as he circles the myrmillo; it must be stiffening up, paralysing his grip on the weapon. The gladiator guesses as much and delivers a mighty swipe. Cass parries but the blade is struck out of his hand to lie not far from his predecessor's trident.

Once again I cover my eyes, praying that his recklessness won't be rewarded with death. The whole stadium has gone silent. Then there's a full-throated cheer and I look up to see the myrmillo handing back Cass's sword and taking a fresh guard. If ever I happen across that guy, believe me I'll give him everything I've got, for free. Not all the bestial savagery pumped into a prizefighter by his trainer can drown that spark of decent feeling which makes a man a man. Cass could acknowledge defeat, I suppose, and retire gracefully, but that's like hoping for the moon to fall out of the sky. He's as eager as before to win the contest, weaving and ducking to avoid hurt. It's just not his lucky day. He retains his sword this time but the ten square yards of cloth that encase him catch at his legs and bring him to the ground. Once again a rapier-point quivers at his throat. I can hardly breathe, The myrmillo glances up at Herod who has the casting-vote. The stillness is deathly.

A quiet voice from behind makes me jump. "His Lordship wishes you to arbitrate on the vanquished man, young lady."

I shift round and find myself staring numbly at the retainer to whom Antipas had previously spoken. His hooded eyes and thin lips betray nothing. Discretion personified!

"Me? You've got to be joking."

If he is, he's playing it remarkably dead-pan. As Herod's confidant, he must think it unseemly to be carrying messages to a blatant prostitute but not even my plunging neckline affects his composure. "You. It's your privilege to pass sentence on the defeated one. His Lordship will abide by your decision."

Distractedly I look down at my soldier-boy spreadeagled at the myrmillo's feet. Then up at the president's box from which Antipas sketches a smiling nod of affirmation at me. The sun, now westering and low, lights up the underside of his features, giving him a strange Satanic look. Grinning Mephisto...

"There's a condition, of course," goes on the Ideal Servant. "His life for your own, should you choose to save him".

Is the haughty Antipas aware of my liaison with Cass?

" My – life?"

"Figuratively speaking. He will require your presence at his court, and your allegiance, from now on." For a moment the smooth mask drops and he adds in a different tone, "The old goat likes the look of you, my girl. He's grown tired of nut-brown, jet-haired Jewesses who submit to his desires yet despise him as a half-breed."

The spectators are getting restive, not understanding the delay. Some yobbo shouts, "Finish 'im off and we'll go 'ome for our supper!" Hastily I lower my thumb in Herod's direction, and at once his own is turned down. The myrmillo, gentlemanly as ever, bends and helps Cass to his feet. More cheering, spontaneous and heartfelt. The loser's reputation has gone up several notches, despite defeat, while this chivalrous ending to the day's sport makes up for its earlier blood-letting.

As Cass returns ruefully to his place with plenty of back-slapping from his mates, I say to the dispatch-carrier, "When do I show up?"

"Tomorrow morning will be soon enough."

"I've no belongings – nothing except what I'm wearing."

"Clothes go with the job – and a handsome wage if My Lord continues to favour you. He will expect you to perform for him."

Is there a double meaning in these words? Oh well, a girl has to earn her keep.

"My name is Chusa. I'm His Majesty's steward. You may request to be brought to me." He pauses and again the pomposity gives way to a murmured confidence. "Keep a weather-eye open for the Queen and you might last the course. Good luck!"

He turns on his heel, relieved at an irksome duty fulfilled. It's good to know that this Chusa has a human side – like the myrmillo. Once the President has departed to the same fanfare that greeted his arrival, we commoners are free to follow him. Cass, chaired by his fellow-officers, is disarmingly bashful and quite unaware that he was rescued from a premature grave by my intervention.

"No sweat, babes," he remarks once I get him to myself. "I never turn down a challenge and I felt certain the Boss wouldn't sign me off. I'm far too valuable to him and he needs my services badly right now with Aretas breathing fire down south. Why, if I'd had a shield, the other guy would've lost our fight."

"And you'd have given him the death-stroke?

"Yup, daresay I would. A fight's a fight – you've got to do things by the book."

"Then I'm glad it was the other way round." For all his kind heart, Cass accepts the conventions of soldiering. He'd never risk losing face or disobey an order, much as he dislikes his current employer

"I'll bet you were scared for me, doll?"

"Of course I was – and bloody furious with you for putting me on the rack. Now I s'pose you'll expect me to dress that injured arm of yours."

Mart's a dab hand at first aid. I'm not in her league but I do my best, wondering who'll patch him up if he sustains graver wounds in Transjordan. I think the general excitement plus loss of blood have taken it out of him.

"Cass love, shall we make an early night of it?"

"Suits me, sweetheart. There's always a thrash in the mess before we go into battle but for once I'll give it a miss. I've a more pressing engagement!"

Although this is our last night together for the duration, neither of us is in the mood for passion. The stored-up heat of summer is enervating and by mutual consent we take our mattress up to the barrack-roof. A night under the stars will be a pleasant alternative to sleeping in a stuffy, cramped cell partitioned off from other officers with other bits of fluff in their arms. When we've settled down, I tell him about my good fortune, omitting the decisive detail. He's delighted for me – and for himself, knowing that I'll be within reach for him to reclaim. But he has reservations.

"Miri, you won't get a swelled head, will you? Once you've got to be the toast of Herod's court, you mayn't be so willing to shack up with a humble square-basher like me."

I run my finger along his craggy profile. "Don't be silly. I bet you return with the honours of war hanging from you like a clutch of saucepans. Every girl in the district will be competing for your favours."

He's vastly flattered. "You're mighty good for a guy, Miri. I really don't want to lose you. What say we get wed?"

"You can't mean it, Cass. You're stringing me along, aren't you?"

"No, straight up. An army career doesn't leave much leeway for a settled relationship, it's true, but I'm not as young as I was and I don't fancy staying a bachelor the rest of my life."

"You'd consider making an honest woman of me – a Yiddish girl who's gone to the bad and earns her living on the game?"

"You mustn't put yourself down, Miri. I'd be marrying a glamour-puss who made the odd mistake or two but who's got a whole lot of loving to give the right kinda guy…"

Yes, maybe, but is he the right man? I feel mean and ungrateful, yet the truth is, I'm still hooked on Jo That was what made me so angry when he calmly gave me my marching-orders in the desert and calmly wished me well. All the same, this is an invitation difficult to resist.

"Tell me about the marriage-rites in Rome," I say to gain time.

"Well, there's co-emptio. That's when a guy buys his wife from her pater – but I've no spare cash and you've no pater. Then there's a stylish affair called confarrateo where they put on a slap-up ceremony and the couple share a cake to represent their union. It's strictly religious and confined to the upper crust. I was thinking of usus, common law. Nothing to it: if we lived together for three years in a row, we'd be considered legally man and wife. It's not binding. The bride is free of obligation at any time so long as she stays away from her husband for a number of days – or nights."

"There's no such let-out for an Israeli woman. The groom can divorce at will but she's stuck with him even if he proves unfaithful. It's a man's world."

"You're dodging the issue, Miri. Will you or won't you?"

I take a deep breath. "You've sprung this on me, Cass, and I'm not prepared for it. I'm damn fond of you and in your debt for dragging me out of the gutter. Don't worry. I shan't let you down. If we go on as we are without committing ourselves, won't that fulfil your requirements?"

"I s'pose so…" His restless movement tells me he's not happy with my answer. "Seems a mite unromantic somehow, and leaves too many loop-holes for my liking. Let's be honest: you're still hedging your bets – waiting for your fisher-lad to beckon you back."

For a mutton-headed Alien, Cass can be quite perceptive. I say, "Perhaps. Strangely enough, it was after a friend's wedding-feast that I made up my mind to cut my losses and make for the bright lights."

"You're back on track one," he sighs. "I'm always strung up before going on campaign so maybe another stroll down memory lane'll put me to sleep. Pick up where you left off this morning. When you hear me starting" to snore, you can call it a day."

I gaze up at the velvet sky studded with its necklace of stars and try to picture the village of Kana, twenty miles west of Tiberias. A wedding is quite an event in the provinces, entailing a general holiday, feasting and merry-making on a grand scale. Abigail, a girl of my own age from Migdal, was the lucky bride. We were betrothed on the same day and a double wedding had been scheduled for us – so the occasion was a bitter-sweet one to me. It was springtime, the season for marriages, and we'd returned north. Laz was too sick to attend but Mart was determined to organise things for everyone else, as usual. They'd both got the Barjoseph bug in a big way, like many others, since Judaea had been alive with the report of Johanan's witnessing. The man of the moment was reputed to be coming to the do as an acquaintance of the bridegroom's family, and Mart wanted to meet him in person for the first time. She has a fixation on religious celebrities, being pietistic in a narrow, puritanical way, and she's a sucker for ham-acting. Barjoseph has become the centre of her universe, along with Laz, from that day forward, and I hear that she entertains him at Bethaniah or Migdal whenever he cares to drop in.

I'd have avoided the whole shebang if Abi hadn't been one of my closest friends. The prospect of seeing Jo with the guy who'd cut me out on what should've been our happiest day, was a painful one – and I knew they were inseparable by now. Mart and I set out to prepare the messima. I had to put up with sidelong glances and whispered words of malice or pity, but my sister was in her element ordering the rest of us around. Naturally she found something to criticize: "The food's adequate but they haven't laid on nearly enough wine. It's sure to run out once the toasting starts..." As it happened she was right.

"Not so good," interrupts Cass. "A bad omen. It won't happen at our send-off, believe you me."

I ignore him, recalling the sourness of an occasion which I should have been sharing as Abi's equal, the congratulations which should've been mine as well as hers. She looked so adorable as we led her in procession to the bridegroom's door with the village-band striking up and spring flowers scattered in her path, so radiantly happy as she and Caleb stood beneath the chuppa to receive our good wishes for their future. It was brought inside and set up above their stools at the table's centre: stools, not modish triclinia, and plain fare rather than the delicacies of the rich, for this was a country wedding where high spirits won over gracious etiquette. The flow of home-brewed wine ensured that. It might just have lasted out but for the invasion of Barjoseph and his associates. They came unpardonably late, having set out from the south and mistimed their journey, so it appeared.

Mind you, the conversation had anticipated their arrival; his name was on everybody's lips, whether for praise or derision. His critics dwelt on the circumstances of his origin, well known in Galil. 'A wood-cutter and the son of a wood-cutter' is a term of abuse in Palestine yet they called in question the second part of that phrase, where Barjoseph was concerned. As with the Baptist, his cousin, a cloud hung over his birth though it was the mother who came under general suspicion. (There are quite as many Benesdras up north as down south.) The child had come into the world a lot too soon after her nuptials, it seemed, and they said that the poppa, Joseph, had wed his young bride in a hurry to save her from abuse and shame.

He was a mature relative of hers, now dead, leaving her to live down the scandal in solitude. She too was invited – though the knowledge of her sin, in their opinion, should have kept her away. Memories are long in Galil and charity in short supply. I was no better: my sole thought was that Barjoseph rated as a bastard in more senses than one!

When he and his gaggle came on the scene at last, I recognized him by his height and breadth of shoulder, remembering the figure on Jordan's bank. From close up, I saw nothing to admire about his jet-black hair, parted in the middle and framing a tall forehead, aquiline features, tanned by his outdoor existence and a beard half-concealing his mouth – but I glanced twice at the grey, eloquent eyes with an odd light shimmering in their depths. On the whole I wasn't impressed and wondered what others saw in this quiet, unassuming guy who scarcely opened his lips throughout the meal while his mother sat as silently beside him. She looked more like her son than most mommas do. She was tall for a woman with grey, well-spaced eyes that resembled his and a face that, despite her age, seemed younger than that of Mart who was busy plying them with food and drink. My attention was chiefly directed at – you know Who. He paled a little at the sight of me, no doubt reminding himself of his broken promises. Was he visualizing how we might have looked under that striped canopy instead of Caleb and Abi? Or was he still absorbed in another vision of himself, seated at the right hand of the Mashiah above the clouds of heaven? Poor fool, I thought, he's never grown up.

"I'm waiting for the big scene, honey," prompts Cass sleepily, "the moment when the booze ran out."

It happened midway through the messima. Horribly embarrassing for Caleb and his parents: even in rustic Galil there are proprieties to be observed and hospitality mustn't be stinted, however many of those present are gatecrashers. The feast would have been a subject for satire years after if it had ended dry! But it didn't. In fact the crisis went unnoticed except by me, and Barjoseph's hangers-on. Most of the guests were pissed already but I'd stayed sober out of chagrin, nursing my resentment. Whatever it was that actually happened passed so unobtrusively that I couldn't be sure of it myself. I saw the steward lean over to have an anxious word with Caleb's poppa, upturning an empty flagon to illustrate his point. Barjoseph's mother had also seen and she said something to her son, He shook his head – rather abruptly, I thought – yet she persisted with a hand on his sleeve, and he gave the steward a sign indicating the water-jars ranged along the back-wall for ritual ablution. Bewildered, the steward put his nose to the first jar and sniffed. I've never seen such a comical look of surprise overspread a face as he straightened up. Then he dipped his flagon into the contents, took it over to the host and filled his cup – with sparkling deep-red wine! Soon every cup had been replenished and one of the guests bawled out a compliment about the best being left till last.

"Did you taste it yourself?" Renewed interest has chased the drowsiness from Cass's voice.

"No I didn't. I refused to be taken in. It was obvious that some mistake had been made, the drink-supply mixed up with the water – though I admit this was unlikely to have escaped Mart's beady eye. What was so unnerving, though, was the sensation I'd felt inside me when Barjoseph gave in to his momma's pleading and raised his right hand towards the jars. It was like some unearthly force had invaded the room and halted time in its tracks, both frightening and marvellous. I can't really describe the effect but it certainly shook me up..."

"Miri, snap out of it. You've gone into one of your trances." Cass's voice comes to me from a distance and I pull myself together.

"Silly of me. It must be all these memories racing through my head. I'm so muddled, Cass, I wish I could sleep."

"You were kidding of course – but you had me bothered for a moment there. I don't want to be lumbered with some sort of spaced-out freak."

No, that's not at all your style, dear Cass. What you want is a cutie whom you can show off on your arm, a first-rate cook and a perfect momma to your future children. I qualify for the first but I'm not so sure of the others. As for going all fey and mystical, I wouldn't have given it a second thought if it hadn't been for Jo's insistence after the feast. He collared me outside Abi's new home and demanded what I made of the 'happening' his master had just performed.

"Happening?" I asked sullenly.

"That's what we call his miracles – when he defies the laws of nature – or improves on them."

"Pure accident, you idiot! The wine must have been in those pots all along. Makes you wonder if he hadn't got Caleb or his poppa to set it up for him in advance."

Jo looked quite injured as though my cynicism was a personal attack on him. I suppose it was, in a way. The messima had brought my anger to a head and I was seething with rage. "D'you imagine for one moment," I went on, "that the Lord's Anointed would waste his time doing conjuring-tricks to save his host from appearing foolish or improvident?

"The Master never sets out to impress. His happenings always contain a lesson for those who are able to learn from them. This is the first time he's used his powers in public; I think he was demonstrating that his own authority overrules the rituals of the Set-aparts. They purify themselves with water – but he can change the same water into wine. He tells us you can't put new wine into old skins because the fermentation will burst them, and that his vintage will be the one we'll drink with him in his kingdom..."

Well, I ask you –what a load of bull! Probably, the effect of Superman's free booze. I wasn't about to give Jo the chance to improve my soul or renew his proposal that I should join the squad. I could see he was angling to introduce me to his master for a long, cosy chat which would end with Miri bathed in tears of penitence, grovelling at Barjoseph's feet. I was near enough tears as it was: tears of hatred and exasperation.

"You realize we should have been man and wife on this very day?" I stormed at Jo. "I'm through with you and your holier-than-thou parade of virtue, It's come between us and wrecked my life. I'm going to walk out on the lot of you and grab myself a piece of the action wherever I can lay hands on it. You may get a kick out of chastity but I'm flesh and blood. I'll make my name – and yours – stink to high heaven and I'll wallow in the shit with every drab who's been shoved deeper in it by so-called friends only concerned to save their own grotty little souls."

I'm ashamed of that speech right now; there are moments when a voice I'd barely recognize as mine seems to speak through me, uttering obscenities. Anyway, I daresay he put it down to temper and expected me to think better of what I'd threatened to do. He was wrong and knows it: my fall from grace has become a talking point in Galil (where there's little to discuss except last year's blight and the price of fish), almost as much so as Barjoseph's rise to fame. The bad and the good – we make a perfect contrast, and gossip veers between our twin extremes.

THREE

Cass is sound asleep. My bedtime story's done the trick and he's snoring through his boxer's flattened nose like a grampus. I feel as wide-awake as ever, keyed up by my fears for him and tomorrow's ordeal for myself. This looks like being a kind of watershed in my life, so I suppose that it makes sense to think through the chapter of disasters that has led to my present situation.

I didn't return to the villa with Mart, knowing that delays and explanations might shake my purpose. I set out then and there for the highroad south, on a wave of fury, which carried me several miles before I was aware of my blistered feet and aching limbs. Dead tired from the day's traumas, I made a nest for myself off the beaten track and fell soundly asleep – an art I appear to have lost. Next morning I woke refreshed and much calmer but with a more realistic attitude of mind. I'd no intention of returning home like some naughty child, yet the great Unknown was daunting. All I had were my natural endowments – no cash, no protection and the prospect of a ninety-mile journey through the badlands of Samaria, a region hostile to strangers and beset with bandits. My best hope was to meet up with some well-disposed traveller by horse or coach on the same route and to hitch a lift, though this too has its obvious perils. Still, I was young and high-spirited; the April sunshine poured down on me, newborn lambs were sucking at their mommas' dugs in the green meadows while, to my left, the Lake's serene countenance reassured me like an old friend. The chalk-white ribbon of road, built by legionaries for their own use, was leading me across the lush plain of Jezreel. Twice a year since infancy I'd travelled the length of Palestine with my family but like most Jews we'd taken the longer route via the Jordan's east bank in order to avoid contact with Samaritans, those descendants of Assyrian interbreeding and profaners of the Law. Such a scruple scarcely worried me now and the sooner I reached the City with all its fancied glamour, the better pleased I'd be. I don't think I had the slightest idea how I was to fulfil my vow of depravity but assumed that the road to ruin would be well sign-posted. In that I wasn't mistaken.

My luck was in. Before I'd gone a mile on my sore feet I heard the clash of hooves on gravel, the creaking of wheels behind me, and, looking back, saw a dust-cloud approaching. It proved to be a covered wagon drawn by a pair of jaded hacks. I paused gratefully, thumbing a lift. The wagoner, a burly granite-faced type, reined in

31

and surveyed me insolently. For the first time I began to feel truly vulnerable – a young girl, alone, at the mercy of fate. His stare had a measured, sinister quality as if he were weighing up the possibilities of a defenceless female on an empty road. Then his face split into a grin that did nothing to quiet my dread, and he gestured with his whip to the place beside him. I was tempted to refuse the offer until desperation won over alarm.

We travelled in silence for some time before he spoke, in a guttural Syrian dialect. "A girl like you shouldn't be on her own in these parts. Have you no family – friends?"

I hesitated to admit my isolation. "I'm on my way to Bethaniah, west of the City, where my parents are expecting me. They're well off and if I don't turn up within a day or two, they'll have search-parties scouring the country for me."

"Sez you. I'll stake my life you're one of these youngsters running away from home for a bit of a thrill. You're all the same. You hope to find easy employment – or maybe a Prince Charming who'll sweep you off your feet and into his magic palace. There's just one way you'll make out in the City, my gal, and that's by selling your skin on its streets."

Little did he guess that his words expressed my precise intention! He chewed a straw for some minutes as if he'd forgotten my presence, then continued with a sidelong glance: "You're a real dish, I'll say that for you: freak colouring and a ripe figure for your age. I reckon you've not turned sixteen?"

"I had my eighteenth birthday last week."

"Pity. The greybeards fancy their fillies tender. Any sexual experience?"

I didn't care for his line of interrogation. I said, "What's that to you? Please stop and let me down."

"There's no need to take on like that. It's not in my interests to deliver shop-soiled goods, get it?"

"Deliver? What d'you mean?"

"I travel the land in search of bints like yourself. That's how I earn a crust."

A woman-snatcher... I'd heard of men who kidnapped unsuspecting girls and sold them to unscrupulous villains as fodder for their nefarious practices. What on earth was I getting into? Instinctively, I edged away from him as if to escape, but he laid his whip across my body, pinning me against the backboard.

"Not so fast, my wench. You asked for a lift and you can make do with the consequences."

"If I'd known – "

"Wouldn't have made no odds. I don't pass up a sitting duck. Like it or not, you'd've had to climb aboard." His chuckle grated on my ears. "From the second I laid eyes on you, I says to myself, 'Here's a gift from the gods. Eleazar, the old skinflint, will be chuffed to bits with this one – and I'll come in for a bonus."

"Who – who's Eleazar?"

"My boss, a pimp, with sticky fingers, and a hole where his heart should be. My luck was clean out till you showed up; I'd bagged a brace o' miserable sluts who had to be quietened down." He lifted the flap behind us and I made out two motionless bundles lying in the covered interior. "Hardly worth the effort. They'll serve for Eleazar's knocking-shops but not for his rent-a-girl business. Same difference, of course: one for scruffs and the other for the well-heeled but it all comes down to a bit of cunt in the end. I'd say you're due for the second."

"Let me down! You can keep your boss and his trading in innocent girls. I'll go my own way."

"Likely. If you 're going to get stroppy, I'll force what I gave them scarecrows down your pretty throat. But why not be sensible? You've got to make a living in the City. You've a straight choice of my boss's set-up, all for the necessities provided, or some street-corner scrapping with the other hell-cats for custom. Meeting me, I'd say you'd fallen on your feet."

He had a point, I saw that. If this Eleazar was a heartless procurer, as he admitted, at least his organisation would give me a start. I'd told Jo I meant to hit rock bottom – and this was a sure way to do it. From that moment I sat firmly on my doubts, made no effort to get away from my unlovely captor and after two more days of his company, I glimpsed the City's ramparts rising against the sky with less terror in my bowels than I'd anticipated. We drove through the Damascus gate and a maze of streets skirting the Temple until the wagon halted in front of an insalubrious-looking building. My fellow-prisoners had long since come round through still dopy from the poison they'd been fed, and we were thrust inside like so many market heifers. Other girls lounged in a dingy hall-way, glancing at us indifferently, but my eyes were on the bent shuffling form that emerged from an inner room to examine his merchandise.

Eleazar was a caricature of the miserly yid who plays a role in so many of Cass's quips. Garbed in a stained and ragged tunic, he inspected the three of us with a calculating shrewdness in his eye; his wizened head swaying forward like the tortoise on the Lakeshore. My companions received barely a glance.

"They'll do for my brothels in Bethesda," he remarked. "There are gaps to be filled – natural wastage, you know." His last phrase held menacing overtones. He turned to me. "This one is another matter, Naaman. Such tresses, like a sunset on autumn leaves, and those slanting emerald eyes... How do they call you, young woman?"

"Miriam."

"A commonplace name though a melodious one. I think we may select something more – exotic. Esmeralda perhaps? When you've been equipped with garments to match your colouring and flatter that nubile figure, you'll be the prize of my collection. Did she come willingly, Naaman?"

"Not at first, Sir, but I made her see sense. She'll take to the life as well as the best of 'em. Don't she rate extra?"

"Indubitably, yet the others are almost worthless. You shall be paid accordingly."

Muttering "Old tight-arse" under his breath, the Syrian shovelled his two also-rans out of the door, presumably to drop them off at some downbeat bordello. I hope they survived but saw neither them nor their captor again. Meanwhile, Eleazar spelled out my duties to me. He called the set-up a dating agency, which gave it an almost respectable sound, and painted my future with him in glowing colours. I should be 'hired' by appointment to his carefully vetted clients for the evening – or possibly the night. Was I untouched, without knowledge of men? I judged it best to admit the truth though at my age it was humiliating to do so. So comely a girl a stranger to love? That was hard to believe but no matter; I should soon be blooded, as he put it, and he would teach me how to guard against an unwanted pregnancy. (This, at least, has proved a valuable lesson to learn!)

As Naaman had implied, I'd fallen on my feet. The establishment provided my lodging and the clothes in which I flaunted myself. I was fed, sparsely by Eleazar but exquisitely by his gushing customers, and my daylight hours were free, though I frequently slept through them after a night's exertion. Yet the Syrian was also right in his assessment of his boss. He paid us nothing and even confiscated the trinkets a satisfied lover might lavish on us. He must have been as rich as Croesus, what with the agency and his chain of whore-houses, yet he played the part of a humble back-street Jew in order to dupe the rich. They expected him to haggle and drive a hard bargain – and he certainly did! That wasn't the only act he put on, as I was later to discover.

He catered for the wealthy without discrimination: Romans, Greeks and Arabs as well as Israelites. Our busiest times coincided with the major feasts when the Ashkenasim poured into town from Egypt and all points west. Their piety didn't deter them from indulging in illicit sex once out of range of their sharp-eyed womenfolk but I noticed with relief that no Set-apart from the circle my Poppa had known figured on Eleazar's list. To go to bed with one of my former 'uncles' would have shaken my bold front. You'll be wondering how I took to this changed existence? Well, I enjoyed the dressing-up and the adulation, which came my way. What girl wouldn't? Soon I became the brightest star of Eleazar's firmament and a cynosure for eyes at the smart nightclubs and restaurants where I met my dates. As for the favours they exacted from me in the privacy of their love-nests, apprehension swiftly dissipated to be replaced by pleasure in acquiring the necessary skills to meet a client's need. My sexual continence had built an internal pressure demanding release, and I gave them a lot more than their money's-worth. I recall one guy saying to me the morning after, "You're smashing to look at but even if you were as ugly as sin, I'd date you a second time – because you make love so generously." I treasured that remark. You'll think I'm over-sexed, and maybe I am, but the physical side isn't everything. I cared for those I slept with, even on a one-night stand, and tried to make up to them for their frigid, nagging wives, their disappointments in love or their dread of impotence. I like to think that I brought a transitory solace into their lives. There were bad scenes now and again: perverts and psychotics who acted normal till they got you alone then tried to bludgeon or strangle the love-object into submission. I got wise to this danger, however, and learned to fight my way out of trouble. A word to Eleazar and they'd be struck off his roster. I was far too precious a commodity to be put at risk!

Yet despite my success I wasn't contented. For all the glitter and variety of a call girl's career, I couldn't get the memory of Jo out of my system. Shall I ever? Left to myself by day, I'd continue to brood over my loss and, in the darkness of some rented apartment, my desire was stimulated by the fantasy that I was in his arms rather than those of a stranger. This plush existence was too comfortable, too sleek and streamlined for my liking. It blunted the raw edge of my revenge for his neglect. I still longed to spit on the self-centred virtue, which had betrayed me and warped my future. I wanted to eat dirt, roll in it, and crush every atom of decency, which remained to me. If I couldn't possess him, I'd make sure that his precious conscience stung him for the rest of his days. Yet I was shortly to find out that there was a depth of degradation even I couldn't stomach.

It was one of Eleazar's principles that business shouldn't be transacted on the day of rest. From Friday evening we were free for twenty-four hours and permitted to wander the City at will so long as we'd merited his trust. I presumed that screwing must be one of the thirty-nine Shabbat prohibitions. So on a Saturday morning I felt relaxed for a change and looked forward to my leisurely stroll through the daylight I rarely saw. Spring had given way to summer and the sun blazed on buildings, accentuating the warmth of tawny stone, the sparkle of gilt spikes set into the Temple's walls in order to prevent its desecration by birds. That vast white and gold wedding-cake raised by the father of Antipas and still unfinished after forty years would be housing the majority of the City's populace on the Holy Day, leaving its streets blissfully empty, clear of human dross; even when Shabuoth, the Feast of Weeks, had brought many pilgrims flooding to this shrine, they too were at worship within. So Miri, the sinner and apostate, had the township to herself.

On that occasion I made my way northwards, climbing the stepped and cobbled streets towards Fish Gate through which

Zabdiah's carts would trundle, carrying their produce to the tables of the affluent. Beyond lay the grim, square fortress of Antonia, symbol of the oppressor's power, casting its shadow over my path. From the bastions, I knew, soldiers would be keeping watch in case of some disturbance in the Temple precincts. A few years back, the procurator Pilatus had launched his career ingloriously by setting troops on a crowd of worshippers demonstrating against violation of Jewish Law. Not only had he allowed banners to be paraded on consecrated ground where images are forbidden but he'd confiscated money from the Corban, the priests' treasury, to finance his brave new aqueduct south of the city-walls. Unfortunately his legionaries slaughtered a number of harmless pilgrims from Galil, thus offending their ruler Antipas, as well as the whole of orthodox Jewry. Pilatus is a born bungler with two left feet. No wonder, I reflected, he kept armed guards on every parapet of Antonia and in front of the massive doorway while he was in residence. As today.

I watched them strutting to and fro on sentry duty: Syrian conscripts harnessed and helmeted in Rome's colonial service. Their officer seemed a genuine Latin to judge by his features; he wore his regalia with a certain panache that won my unwilling admiration, his scarlet crest as vivid as my own auburn mane gleaming in the sunshine. He gave me a long, appreciative stare before wheeling back to his duties, and I wondered idly whether we'd ever make closer acquaintance. I liked his warm brown eyes and cleft chin, the way he carried himself. He looked a real guy – and I was growing tired of elderly businessmen on the razzle, chinless misfits with too much dough and too little blood in their veins. Most well-reared Jewish girls wouldn't have given the time of day to a Roman legionary, a member of the occupying forces, but I felt no such inhibition.

I wandered on with no particular objective and found myself in Bethesda, a sleazy district of slum dwellings and jerry-built shacks which housed a population of down-and-outers, the 'great unwashed' to use a favourite term of Benesdra's. By now the prayerful were streaming out of the Temple's Tadi Gate and we converged at the wide pool with its five-arched portico and tiered paving. I used to stand here as a kid, intrigued by the legend of its miraculous powers and by the human wrecks who strewed its steps like flotsam on a beach. It's said that once in a blue moon an angel comes down to stir the surface and at that precise moment it can cure any infirmity. Many of the cripples have taken up permanent residence in the hope of a lucky break and there ain't a lot of good will in the way they jockey for first dip! I'd longed to witness a healing, full of pity for those who must have waited years to win the jackpot. Even now I recognized one invalid from the past – a paralytic who lay on his mattress along the lowest stair. So near and yet so far; he couldn't shift the few necessary inches without a helping hand, and which of the rest was likely to give that? No, nothing had altered. The pool still gave off its dank odour while the arches repeated themselves in its smooth, impassive mirror.

As I watched, a figure emerged from the passing throng and strode over to my old friend on his pallet. Barjoseph. I drew back into shadow, guessing that Jo must be somewhere in the vicinity. I was wearing a scanty little number, which left little to the imagination, and a sudden access of shame came over me despite my resolve to cheapen myself in his eyes. Yes, there he was with his associates from Galil plus a couple I'd not seen before: a man who resembled Barjoseph on a slighter, less imposing scale, and another who looked hardly better than a thug. So the circus was expanding in quantity – if not in quality.

Their leader leaned forward towards the paralytic as if to add a coin to those contributed by kind souls for his upkeep. It struck me that he was onto a good thing financially: could it be that he was hamming it up in expectation of charity? Then Barjoseph, having exchanged a word with him, took his hand and gently drew him to his feet. The cripple tested his newfound legs as though incredulous of so quick and complete a cure, his face a study in astonishment. As for me, I swayed and had to lean against a pillar, momentarily knocked out by that strange sensation which had overwhelmed me at Kana and previously by the Jordan. Thinking back, it must've been the stench of gangrenous limbs and the dinning of the crowd that made me come over faint...

"Miri, you're unwell." It was Jo's voice. He'd seen me and approached to offer his support.

I pulled myself together. "I don't want your sympathy," I snapped. "I'm perfectly all right."

In his state of exaltation he ignored my snub. "Did you see what happened? The Master healed that poor bloke – simply told him to take up his bed and give thanks for God's mercy!"

"I doubt if he'll do that," I retorted. "He was stashing it in just now but your hero has queered his pitch. He's been rumbled."

Jo's quick temper, a gift from his poppa, erupted. "You're determined to discredit him, to reject the evidence of your own senses. I tell you, Miri, he's the Chosen One for whom our nation has waited so long, the Star that shall rise from Yacob. Won't you turn your back on the past and throw in your lot with him before it's too late?"

As he pleaded with me, I became aware that Barjoseph was watching us from the far side of the pool. There was something hypnotic about his steady gaze and I had to wrench my own from him before spewing out the bitter cud of my grievances. "He's got you where he wants you, Jo – a brain-washed zombie! That's no reason why I should be conned by him, too. Besides which," I added, twisting the knife, "he'd hardly welcome a female tagging on, would he? Male company's more to his taste."

"What on earth are you getting at? You can't mean – "

"Oh but I do. Isn't it obvious? He's watching us at this very minute in case his pansy-boy is lured into sin by a slag, a painted harlot. That's what I am, Jo, you can see for yourself, a woman who sells her assets for cash... And it's all your doing, his as well, because you left me to chase after your dream of perfection. They say good can come out of evil. Well, the opposite's true in this case. You've fallen for a smart-Alec with the gift of the gab, a street-corner conjuror that wins his audience by fraud then feeds them his leftist propaganda. Meanwhile, your wife's sleeping around with all comers and heading straight for the gutter."

To underline my point, I pulled my silk bodice further down, giving both of them an eyeful, and Jo blushed like a schoolboy before returning to his beloved master. No doubt an apology was in order on my account for sullying his idol's eyes, not to mention a quick prayer to offset the influence of evil...

I should have left it there. I don't know what made me go after them through the Temple-gate – sheer curiosity perhaps, or a reluctance to lose touch with the guy who meant everything to me in spite of my angry outburst. I kept my distance, feeling thoroughly out of place in this sacred enclosure teeming with Levites and pilgrims, its giant façade of snow-white marble ornamented with a golden cluster of grapes and the smell of incense wafting from its hidden altar to perfume the whole City with its sweetness.

Barjoseph was leading his followers to a knot of sharp-voiced Hasidim who surrounded the wretched ex-cripple. Some sort of indignation meeting seemed in progress. They were slanging him for daring to carry his bed on the Shabbat. You're not allowed to pick anything heavier than a dried fig on the day of rest according to their rules. One of Cass's better jokes is about the Greek, the Egyptian and the Yid who were trying to prove the supremacy of their own gods. The Greek said he'd prayed to Hera for his wife's fertility and she'd given birth to twins. The Gyppo had prayed to Ra who saved his land from a plague of locusts, and the Jew had to think hard if he hoped to cap their stories. He said he'd once found a purse full of coins lying in the street. He couldn't pick it up because it was the Shabbat but he prayed to Moishe's God – and all of a sudden it became Friday! Even a fiction can't outdo their humbug, though. When a Set-apart wants to grab hold of something on the Holy Day, he tells a Goy servant how nice it'd be if the object was put into his hand – and all's well. It's easy when you know how.

What had riled these Holy Joes was the man's claim to have been cured on the Shabbat, of course, and this was their way of getting at the healer. I heard his whine: "But he told me to roll up my mattress and give thanks in the Temple..."

"Who told you?" The voice was Reuben's, reedy and supercilious; but what caught my attention was the figure that stood beside him.

Eleazar! My employer was all but unrecognisable, garbed in the fringed tunic of a Set-apart and looking too good to be true with combed beard and a sanctimonious expression on his shifty old face. So this was his other self – a joke far funnier than any Cass had ever told, so long as disgust didn't turn one's laughter sour. I guessed my job-security would be at risk if he glimpsed me gazing at him but it proved harder to avoid Benesdra's roving eye.

The answer to his question came from a different source. Barjoseph spoke quietly yet his tones reached me on the perimeter of the Great Court.

"I did."

"By what right did you violate Moishe's Law, might I ask?"

The reply was indirect. Barjoseph looked about him. Then he said, "If an animal fell into some gully, which of you would hesitate to pull it out on the Shabbat rather than sustain financial loss? The Law was made to serve men, not to exact their slavery."

"The saving of life is permissible but this man has been diseased for thirty-eight years on his own admission. His life was not in danger and he could well have waited another day."

"I was concerned for the life of his soul. My corporal cure was secondary to that." Barjoseph turned to his beneficiary. "D'you feel better – inside?"

"Dunno, Sir. Yeah, s'pose I do, come to think of it."

"Good. The healing is complete. Be off with you, friend, and earn an honest living in future."

The other went away, still getting the feel of his restored limbs while I pondered Barjoseph's last words. He'd sussed out the guy, as I had, and his 'cure' was a fake. Just as I'd reckoned. The analogy he'd drawn did nothing to placate Reuben.

"You dare to forgive sin – a privilege that belongs to Yahweh alone?"

"My Father works without ceasing and I must do so, too. Our activity is shared."

Bloody fool, I thought dispassionately. He's chancing his arm against scum like Benesdra by pretending a special relationship with the God of the Torah. They'd make short work of him for blasphemy – and of his pitiable stooges. I was anxious for Jo, not his misguided master.

"Do you, a nobody, claim to be God's son?"

"Those are your words, not mine. It is, after all, a claim we're all entitled to make,"

The titter of appreciation annoyed Reuben. "Don't quibble with me, carpenter. Isn't it a fact that your cousin, the so-called Baptist, named you as Mashiah?"

"I don't need the testimony of a man, however inspired he may be. Those who receive my Father into their souls know me for what I am."

"Yet you break the laws which He imposed on Israel."

"We are above the law, he and I. You Sephorim and Hasidim imagine that God can be found in the pages of Scripture which you pore over day and night, but He hasn't a place in your hearts – or you'd welcome my message."

"You would have us neglect the teaching of Moishe in favour of your own?"

"No, it's Moishe himself who testifies against you when he tells us, 'I will raise a prophet , I will put words into his mouth, and those who do not hear I will have vengeance on.' That prophet is Johanan and you are questioning his pronouncement."

It was touch and go. Honestly, I didn't think he'd get out of it alive. Some of his opponents were bending down for stones left lying in heaps by the Temple workmen; death by stoning is prescribed for blasphemy. Nevertheless he escaped – Lord knows how. One moment he was there, the next gone, while his merry men had already beaten a circumspect retreat. As I made my way back to the agency. I was shaking with unrelieved tension. I realized that Reuben had spotted me in my street-girl attire and that he'd be sure to make capital out of the sight.

How right I was! As often as not, a client who wished to preserve his incognito would arrange for one of Eleazar's girls to be sent to a private address; so I wasn't surprised, a day or two later, to be given such an assignation. A male attendant accompanied me to the rendezvous (no woman can afford to cross the City on her own by night unless she's after game) and left me at the gate of a courtyard fronting an expensive apartment block. The gatekeeper, a po-faced individual, led me to the door indicated and I tapped on it discreetly. After an interval it was opened and the occupant stood back in the shadow of a hallway till I was safely inside, then led me, his head turned away, to an inner room. Cats look alike in the dark – so do elderly rakes. I suspected nothing till he spoke.

"For shame, Miriam."

Benesdra confronted me with a glare of moral outrage, which sat ill on his self-indulgent features. "To think that a girl of good family, one whom I have dandled on my knee, should lower herself to such a calling! Thank heaven your dear parents are not alive to see it."

I kept my head. "How did you know I worked for your pal Eleazar?"

His eyes, never candid, became shiftier than ever. "I – I am in his confidence. I happen to be aware of his – interests, and seeing you arrayed so blatantly, it occurred to me that you might be employed by my colleague."

"Did you ask for my services by name?"

"Of course not. I'd hardly have wished him to assume our former acquaintance. He described his most – promising 'escorts' at my request and I identified you without the slightest difficulty. Your beauty is being sadly misused, my child."

"So you rented me on the spot." The conviction that his motives were dishonourable reassured me. I felt I could cope with a dirty old man better than with a lecture on morality! "D'you intend to tear me off a strip or take advantage of me?"

"You are insolent, Miriam. I judged this the wisest procedure to get you away from your bawdy-house and have a serious talk with you about your disgraceful conduct."

Sez you, I thought. I'll bet you've been a customer of Eleazar from way back, if not a partner in his trade, raking it in from the exploitation of kidnapped girls. Aloud I said, "I don't have to stay here and listen to your sermons."

"Leaving would be a serious error of judgement on your part. You are legally betrothed to the son of the worthy Zabdiah and your present way of life lays you open to the full rigour of the Law as an adulteress…"

Threats had replaced his paternalism. For all my contempt, I shivered inwardly. Like sacrilege, adultery can earn a sentence of death in Palestine. The sharp stones that I'd imagined caving in Jo's defenceless skull might well be rained on mine if Benesdra acted upon his knowledge. He'd heard my betrothed renounce all claim on me yet chose to ignore the fact. What mercy could I expect from such a shyster? All the same, I felt certain his menaces were a lever to extract some personal benefit for himself – and this I was prepared to contest.

"Come clean, Reuben. What d'you want from me?"

"An acknowledgement of your wickedness, Miriam, and submission to the penance which I shall impose on you." He swept aside a curtain to disclose his love-nest complete with canopied double bed, its sheets invitingly turned down. The purpose was sickeningly apparent. "A Set-apart is not as other men. His affections are blessed by the Almighty and have the power to absolve sin rather than to condone it. This is not a rented flat but my own property. From now on I want you to consider it yours so long as you continue to attend my needs."

Nothing in the world could have struck me with greater repulsion. To trade my services for a whoremaster's upkeep was one thing, to be coerced into doing so by a prick who considered himself above the sanctions he imposed on others was quite another. "It's you who's the wicked one," I said. "You disgust me, and even if you'd treated me as a casual lay instead of trying to blackmail me with fear of punishment for a wrong I hadn't done, I'd spit in your face!"

Baffled by my ferocity, he lost control, pawing at my frock and slobbering over me. "I've watched you grow from an enchanting child to an incomparable ripeness - watched and waited…My desire for you can no longer be mastered. If you won't surrender to me, I must force you to comply."

I fought my way out of his embrace and panted, "If you lay another finger on me, I swear I'll dig out every detail of your collusion with Eleazar and show you up for the twister you really are!"

My hunch proved correct. He drew back like a scorpion ringed by fire and, seizing my opportunity, I got out of that tainted room. The gate-keeper held up his lantern as I sped past him and its light revealed a sly grin. Evidently Benesdra was no pal of his, either, while his habits were well known.

This episode, combined with my former doubts, decided me to quit. I tackled Eleazar the next day, telling him that I wanted out. He listened with a forbearing smile: a patriarch indulging his wayward daughter.

"Here you are given fine shmutter, excellent food and lodging in return for the esteem of my distinguished clientele. What more do you want, my dear?"

"I – I prefer to be independent." It was useless attempting to explain my true reasons.

"You're a very foolish young lady. Have you the slightest idea what prostitution entails – for that will be your sole alternative?"

"Haven't I already prostituted myself for your benefit?"

He threw up his hands in stage-horror. "This is not some sordid house of ill fame, Esmeralda. It is dedicated to providing civilized strangers to our City with the most refined of feminine company, such as yourself. You are far too precious to be let go."

"I was hauled over a barrel by the last client you set up for me, Eleazar, and I'm tempted to give you a taste of his medicine. You see I saw you with Reuben Benesdra in the Temple. How you lapped up the reverence of your lowly admirers, an Abraham born out of his time... If I let on what you really get up to when you're not playing a man of irreproachable virtue, you'd be a laughing-stock condemned by your own kind."

It was a bluff but, as with Reuben, it came off. He glanced at me without dissimulation and I saw him at last for what he was. "If I release you from your contract, you won't put the finger on me?"

"I swear. Your conscience is your own affair and I owe you something for saving me from starvation."

"You will leave in the clothes you wore on your arrival?"

"Yes, you old scrimshanks, though I've never received a shekel for hiring out my body to your customers, civilized or otherwise."

At the end he reverted to his ham-acting. "I would say 'Come back to me' once you've sampled the life ahead of you, but I fear you would have lost your allurement. Beauty does not often survive the squalor of the streets."

Foresight isn't my forte, as you'll have gathered by now. I'm a creature of impulse driven by my urges - possessed by one demon or several, some might say. Here I was by my own will, skint, without accommodation and ignorant of what lay in store for me. I suppose I was banking on my natural talents to hook night-prowlers who would spirit me off to some cosy little pad and actually pay me for my services! How naïve can you get? As I reached the City's red-lamp district that evening, it came to me that I should've wangled a slot in one of Eleazar's low-rate brothels and traded freedom for a roof over my head. However, I was too proud to acknowledge my mistake. The first hour of a new career robbed me of all my confidence. Rival slags were actively hostile to an unknown contender, darting dirty looks at me and even hustling me off their chosen patch. This was an introduction to the foul language and wildcat jungle of the underworld; if you've raised your eyebrows over my crudity of speech, I can tell you it's down to the time I spent as a common whore in the city-stews.

Only one of those plying for the same custom showed compassion for a newcomer. She sidled towards me tentatively and said, ""I've been watching you between jobs, trying it on and getting the brush-off. You're fresh to the game, aren't you?"

That was a blow to my conceit after a jet-setting debut! Yet her friendliness was consoling and I admitted my total failure.

"It's your technique that's wrong," she said. "You're hanging it out, making yourself far too obvious. They call this the Holy City, don't they? There's plenty wanting what we offer but they're scared of being seen with a tart because of the vigilantes – the 'Keep Zion clean' brigade. The way to get round them is by giving your address as if you were no worse than some hotel tout. They meet you on the doorstep. After that its straightforward."

"Thanks for the tip. Trouble is I haven't a place of my own nor the cash to rent one."

"Then you won't get your man till kingdom come." She hesitated. "Look, why not have a shufty at my pad? If it suits you, we might go halves on the cost, once you're earning."

"That's decent of you – but won't it cramp your style?"

"Not if we take turns. I'd be glad to lay off the game if it's only once or twice per night - and glad of your company."

A few minutes later, I was resting my weary legs in the broom-cupboard she called her room. It contained little more than the basic requirement of her calling, and that we sat on side by side, sharing a bowl of vegetable broth. By the light of an oil-lamp I studied her soft, rather pudgy face with doe-like eyes and a gentle mouth – the sort who'd rouse the bully in a certain kind of guy. Indeed, a yellowing bruise on her left cheek indicated as much. There was something else about her, a lack of focus in her gaze and a lassitude of manner, which later I learned were due to taking drugs. I think this resort (which, thank God, I've never contracted) contributed to her fate.

She returned my appraisal with interest and a shy smile. "My, but you've got what it takes. That gorgeous hair and smooth skin. Wish I had half your looks…"

"I think you're pretty, as well – pretty enough to make a decent living."

She shook her head dolefully. "The men I hook screw a lot more out of me than I do out of them. And they don't pay for the damage, either." She rolled up her sleeve and displayed more bruises, some of them recent.

I said fiercely, "If they try it on with me, they'll get as good as they give."

"They won't. You're not the type to take things lying down, I can see that. You've got class." She was gazing at me so wistfully that I felt almost uncomfortable. She went on, "I'm so glad you said yes to my invitation. I've always wanted a girl-friend but they used to avoid me because of my – trouble. They thought I was unclean."

I didn't like to ask why, but it was obvious she meant to tell me, being the sort who longs to confide every detail of her most intimate ills.

"Ever since I reached puberty," she began, "I was cursed with a continuous discharge. You can't imagine what it's like – the discomfort and the feeling that you're – dirty, different from others. Folk got to know because I couldn't hide my shame. They despised me for it. The Set-aparts treated me as a source of contamination and expelled me from the society I'd been brought up to. That's why I became a scrubber, up north where I was born. You're from Galil too, aren't you?"

"Yes and no. I used to holiday there."

"I thought so. You've a trace of the accent. Well, I'd given up hope of recovery when the guy they all talk about – Yeshua Barjoseph – came to teach in our neck of the woods. You know who I mean, of course?"

"Of course."

"You don't sound impressed. Believe me, he's a wonder… He told us how his father's kingdom was open to the downtrodden like ourselves, not to the rich and mighty. His words made me glow inside – me, a good-time girl who'd never dare stick my nose into shul for fear of being hounded out by the rulers. Yet it was to us, not them, he was promising salvation! 'Those who weep now shall be comforted,' he said."

"He knows how to get the masses on his side, I'll say that for him."

She missed my sarcasm. "He went down big in Galil, that's for sure. It wasn't just his preaching but still more his healing-powers. The cripples and lepers – they didn't want uplift or long-term promises. They wanted to be made well and get on with their sinning." She lowered her head." Like me, I suppose. I thought if only he'd take away my curse, the blokes would flock to me instead of turning away in disgust. But I was too mortified to ask him outright. If I touch him, I thought, that might do the trick and no one need ever know. Wherever he went, the mob pressed round him, clamouring for cures, so it was easy to get close without being noticed. I managed to grab his tunic-hem before I was shoved aside."

"Were you hoping for magic – like touching a lucky charm?"

She shook her head. "That kind doesn't work. This did. I knew at once that my bleeding had stopped. Twelve years of the curse, then release, like a dripping tap being turned off. I felt clean, inside as well as out… I was sure I'd got away with it but he stood stock still, looked about him and said, 'Who was it touched my robe?' In spite of that milling crowd, he knew power had gone out of him, you see – he told me that afterwards. He was looking directly at me and I fell to my knees, confessing what I'd done and why. The bystanders edged away from me, afraid of being defiled, but he scolded them. He said, 'It's not physical disease that corrupts but the impurity which festers within.' Then he asked my name. 'Susannah,' I told him. 'Well, Susannah, you must give up a way of life that degrades you.'"

"Did he fancy that the healing would restore you in the eyes of the world – that you'd be able to mend your ways and earn a respectable living? If so, he must be simple-minded."

"He proposed that I should join up with him and look after his needs as only a woman can. You may smile but you're wrong; he didn't mean what you're thinking."

She'd misread my expression. I knew he hadn't meant that – we all know his tastes where sex is concerned. I was smiling to myself at the realization that his words virtually rehearsed those of Reuben, yet with such different meaning!

"Did you sign on obediently, Susannah?"

"Yes, for a time. Being with him did me good and I was so grateful, but I couldn't live down my reputation and I felt it was harming his cause. The Set-aparts kept attacking him for associating with a strumpet, He called them 'whited sepulchres' in return, like those tombs they paint which look so bright and pure on the outside yet are full of dead men's bones. He told me not to mind them but I did – for his sake. A few weeks back I left him, on the quiet, and came south to pick up the one trade I know."

Whited sepulchres. He had a good line in repartee, at any rate. I thought of Benesdra and Eleazar in their dazzling robes, and had to giggle. One up to Barjoseph… Mind you, once I'd got to know Sue properly, I was able to see through her imagined cure. She was a hypochondriac who'd no doubt induced her own menstruation by constant worry, and her trust in Barjoseph's magic had brought her back to health. She was somebody who 'enjoyed' sickness just as I believe she half-enjoyed being mauled by psychos and having the marks to show for it, A born victim. I was never quite at ease with her, suspecting that she wanted more than friendship from me, yet I felt responsible for her and anxious to save her from herself. I did my best and failed (which is small comfort).

I don't want to think about that period. Apart from our hand-to-mouth existence, it was fraught with potential violence that never touched me though it did for Sue in the end. She started to go steady, if that was the right word for it, with a swine who seemed to get more fun out of roughing her up than lying with her, to judge by the bruises she'd show me next day. I'd no desire to mix it with the brute – a hulking Anatolian labourer with tattooed forearms and the look of a gorilla – so I stayed out of their way while giving her fair warning. "Lose him," I told Sue. "Tell him to go jump. If you encourage him, he'll only get more slap-happy and one night he may go all the way." But she wouldn't. Perhaps she felt that his blows were a kind of reparation for her abandonment to sin – or was it the downers she took which lowered her resistance? One evening when I got back from a fruitless trawling for custom, things sounded real bad, banging and thumping, drunken oaths followed by screams that dwindled into piteous whimpering. The door was bolted from inside – just as well since, had I obeyed my first instinct and rushed to her rescue, there'd have been the pair of us laid out for the City-morgue. Yet something had to be done and done fast,

I ran into the street again, praying for help. By blessed chance a patrol was rounding the corner a hundred yards away: legionaries act as city-fuzz when they're not being soldiers, and they impose a pretty strict curfew while turning a blind eye on us whores because we have to earn a crust. For once I needed to attract their attention even if it meant a spell in the cooler. I waved down the officer in charge and gasped out my fears for Sue. He got the message with commendable speed and spat out a wad of gum.

"Right, lady. Lead me to it."

The sounds had given way to a still more sinister hush. My knight in armour kicked the door open with a splintering crash. The next moment he was grappling with a monster: trained tactics versus undisciplined muscle. It was short and sweet. Almost before I'd caught my breath he had the bloke pinioned in a Roman arrest, twisting his right arm behind his back and jamming his own heel down on the other's instep. Then he turned Sue's assaulter over to his four men. I went in, dreading the worst. She lay sprawled across the bed, her thin garment ripped apart to display multiple injuries over breast and stomach, no longer bleeding. Her head lolled at an unnatural angle, its eyes open but sightless.

"Oh God…"

"Too darn late, I'm afraid. Bastard's broken her neck."

I felt tears welling to blur my vision. "What am I to do? She had no relatives in Judaea, nobody who cared whether she lived or died

– except me."

"Take it easy, Miss. We'll see to that side o' things. Sex-killings are part of our routine." The officer gestured to a couple of his subordinates who raised Sue's body between them and followed her murderer, well guarded by their mates, into the street. The legionary held the oil-lamp closer to my face. He grinned.

"Seen you somewhere before, ain't I? Will I ever forget that head of hair? . So you're on the game?"

"I nodded miserably, recalling his scarlet crest outside Antonia.

"Do yourself a favour," he said with no hint of reproof in his husky voice. "Lay off it. I'd hate to come on a dish like you stretched out in some sewer with your throat slashed. Happens all the time. Whadda they call you?"

"Miriam – Miri to my friends."

"Then it's Miri for me. I'm Cass. Caius Cassius Longinus, Centurion of the Twelfth – if you want the full rubric."

I'd recognized him by now as the Latin type I'd set eyes on the day Barjoseph did his stunt. From near he looked older, but I go for lived-in faces and I couldn't help liking his.

"Thanks, Cass. If I'd latched on sooner, you might've saved poor Sue. She was a gentle, harmless creature and I'll miss her." Her story came back to me, bringing out the pathos of her death. She'd got so little out of life apart from that one moment of blinding joy in Galil. If Barjoseph was truly the Mashiah, he should be tackling the deep-rooted ills of society, which put defenceless girls at risk instead of telling them to accept their lot and promising pie in the sky.

"You're crying," Cass remarked, putting an arm round me in a brotherly fashion. "Sorry if I sounded cold-blooded. Soldiering doesn't leave room for the finer feelings. When you get to know me a whole lot better, you'll find there's a heart somewhere beneath all this tin-plating."

"Am I to know you better?"

"Depends on you, honey. I'm an Alien and a Goy – persona definitely non gratis with your fellow-countrymen."

"I'm not choosy. Can't afford to be. I thought you might draw the line at a Yiddish hooker…"

"I'd guess you're a cut above the average, certainly in looks. I'd like to pull you out of it and and give you a little tender loving care."

At base, it was much the same offer as Reuben's. Most girls would've welcomed the patronage of a prosperous Set-apart yet scorned to be a legionary's mistress. I didn't hesitate – and I haven't regretted it since. It was shortly after Cass and I shacked up together that he got transferred to Herod's service, which explains my being here, outstretched on a barrack-roof beside his sleeping form, as dawn creeps over the Decapolis.

This is the miracle hour, which used to entrance me as a child, with its mystery and its sense of a return to innocence, but it affects me no longer. Caught up in the rat race and immersed in its corruption, I've said good-bye to my inner peace forever.

FOUR

Cass, my friend and lover, is a totally different person from Cassius Longinus, faceless unit of a fighting-machine that has crushed the known world under its remorseless tread. Our leave-taking is hurried, almost perfunctory – for private feelings must give way to the call of arms. This is a side to his character more foreign to me than his racial extraction: an unswerving loyalty to the legion, based on his sense of duty. We Jews are individualists. We refuse to conform and our hatred of war is so deep-laid that our men will not be conscripted by Rome. This is why Antipas has had to cadge military support from his natural enemy Pilatus – and why I'm standing here disconsolate, watching my man march away to do battle with an Arabian emir.

Is he lost to me? I don't doubt his good faith, but a guy so rash as to take on a trained gladiator is unlikely to play the coward in war. I must learn to stand on my own two feet once again and face the future with my own brand of courage. I depend on my ability to impress a fickle, self-regarding monarch whose interest in me may already have waned. Keep your fingers crossed, Miri, and don't let your nervousness show in your eyes.

I leave Cass's billet with a last look back at its cramped quarters which have been a home to me, then make my way up the slope leading to Herod's palace. Its wings curve forward on either side of the central block like marble arms outstretched to fold me in, yet I feel rebuffed by the remote grandeur of its Roman style, the sculptured architrave and elaborate portico. I long for the humble, ramshackle dwellings of the fisher-folk huddled by the lakeshore. Herod's creation seems a trespasser on our countryside, as Rome itself has trespassed on our liberties. The paved esplanade under my feet is less welcoming than the dry warmth of summer grasses and I sense that I'm crossing a divide between the familiar and an unknown continent.

Several minor functionaries are lounging on the semicircular stairway leading up to the main doorway, and I ask one of them to take me to Antipas's steward. He eyes me with an appreciative grin, and then says, "Ah, the glamorous redhead. Yes, we were instructed to look out for you. Follow me."

He leads me through a side-entrance and along vaulted passages skirting a magnificent atrium whose central basin of rainwater reflects the morning sky. We climb marble steps to the upper floor where His Majesty's private apartments are situated, my guide informs me. It appears that Chusa's suite neighbours them – as befits a confidential servant. The major-domo receives me with a glance of condescension, his carved features as inscrutable as before. Behind him through the doorway I see a plump woman seated and a fragile-looking boy leaning on her chair. They both smile at me and I feel myself to be among friends. So Chusa's a husband and father; can he be as formal towards his wife and son as he is in his professional capacity?

He remarks, "You're prompt, young lady, a good beginning. The Tetrarch insists on punctuality. He has not forgotten his agreement with you and looks forward to watching you show your paces. But first you must be made presentable." Then he lapses as he did yesterday into a colloquial turn of phrase and becomes a human being: "He likes his dancing-girls tarted up. Don't be fooled by his spiel about artistic expression – give him your full routine, as though you were performing in a strip-joint, and you'll be in for keeps."

He leaves me in a theatrical dressing room strewn with props and smelling of grease paint, where court entertainers are rehearsing their acts. A juggler catches silver plates, a conjuror extracts eggs from improbable parts of his anatomy and musicians practise their scales. They look at me with a hostility reminiscent of my rivals on the street-corner but display grudging admiration when I emerge from an overhaul by expert attendants, adorned in layers of diaphanous gauze and with my hair burnished to a crimson glow. One of the girls holds up a copper mirror and I gaze at myself in its polished surface. Not bad… I prefer my beauty reflected in the eyes of those about me.

Chusa's is waiting outside the door. Graciously he lends me an arm and conducts me to the audience-chamber where my fate will be decided. My heart sinks at the sight of its sumptuous furnishings; the courtiers lolling beside a gilded throne whose occupant leans back at his supercilious ease. How am I to perform at a royal audition after a sleepless night and the departure of a lover I may never see again? I feel Chusa's arm impel me forward in spite of my stage-fright, and I glide over the mosaic floor to curtsey in front of Antipas. He honours me with a lingering inspection beneath drooping lids, and then turns to his lickspittles.

"What did I tell you?" he inquires. "A superb creature – a positive jewel in Solomon's crown. Let's see whether her dancing matches her appearance." He snaps his fingers and the quavering note of a flute invites me to commence. Its melody evokes the landscape in which I used to dance alone as a youngster and I return in spirit to the mood and rhythm of that private ecstasy, forgetting these artificial surroundings as the music sets my limbs in motion. Cymbals and tambourines add their percussion, quickening the tempo, and I sway, discarding my veils one by one until only the last remains. The flute continues to weave its insidious spell but I cease, rejecting Chusa's advice. Some instinct warns me to preserve my dignity as a woman before these shallow spectators.

Applause rattles round the chamber. Herod bends forward, smiling a gold-toothed smile. "A most creditable performance, young lady, refreshing to my somewhat jaded palate. I congratulate you on tempering the erotic with a maidenly discretion. Your hidden treasure isn't for public scrutiny, eh?"

His suggestive emphasis is greeted with a sly amusement. I keep my cool, wondering whether Cass has under-estimated his master's proclivities.

"Your name?"

"Miriam, my Lord."

"Very well, Miriam. I shall expect you to minister to my aesthetic enjoyment from now on. You may kiss my hand."

He extends his arm and I approach to obey him. Suddenly his fingers grasp my shoulder and he pulls me to him, stroking my hair with his other hand. "You gorgeous piece of goods, "he mutters thickly. "I shall call you Circe, seductress and daughter of the Sun who alone can have created those flaming tresses…"

Appreciation of his manoeuvre is replaced by a pregnant hush and he lets me go, staring blankly over my head. I turn and see Herodias surveying us coldly from the doorway. The chiselled features of a Hasmonean princess betray no reaction to the scene but her obsidian eyes and thin-lipped mouth are hard and unforgiving as I slip past her on my way out. I've made an enemy through no fault of my own.

As I settle into the routine of court life, I have the feeling that I'm walking a tightrope between Herod's lusts and his wife's disapproval. If I give him encouragement (not that I've the slightest desire to do so) she'll seek to get rid of me; if I keep my distance, he'll dispense with my services. There's no love lost on either side, that's for sure. He took her on for the prestige of her regal ancestry and she got her talons into him because he ranks higher than his brother, her former husband. For all her haughtiness she's a hooker just like me, selling her body for the sake of power rather than for the self-contempt which is my motivation. What on earth am I doing in this stagey set-up? I'm well fed and pampered like some prize specimen simply because my looks have won an old rake's favour. If I were cynical, I'd say that the wages of sin are – excellent! But I never set out to prove that evil pays dividends; I wanted to rub Jo's nose in the filth of my own depravity. They tell me Barjoseph's cause is flourishing among the villages not ten miles from here while I spend tedious days and weeks in this gilded cage. Is it likely that Jo, labouring at his side, knows I'm the rising star of a degenerate court and, if he does, what's that to him compared with his selfish resolve to save his own soul at the cost of mine?

Luckily I'm not left to brood through the daylight hours over my discontent. Chusa's wife Joanna has made friends with me. She's a motherly, affectionate being and my aloneness has gained her compassion. I'm always welcome to their suite and it relieves my boredom to help her with the supervision of the palace household, for that's her job. Mart would be amazed to see me checking laundry-lists and examining surfaces for dust! In many ways Joanna makes up for the Momma I lost so young and I share her with her teen-age son Joab. He too recalls my family to me because he suffers from the same wasting sickness as Poppa and Laz. I can tell it by his hectic flush, the constant dry cough and bloodstains on his hanky. Poor kid, he tires so quickly for all his animation and needs to take long rests to ease his breathing. Joanna coddles him of course and even Chusa softens in his presence and becomes a devoted father.

My other pal is Salome, Herodias's daughter by her previous marriage. She's a cute little morsel about Joab's age and the plain fact is she's got a schoolgirl crush on me. Despite Momma's annoyance, she dances attendance on yours truly, insists on brushing and combing my hair and pleads with me to teach her my cabaret-act. Some might consider her a drag yet I'm flattered by her adoration and glad of a confidante through whom I can relive my own childhood. Herod, her doting stepfather, frequently surprises us together, accidentally on purpose. The word goes that he wed Herodias but fell for Salome and I wouldn't put it past him. As men grow more elderly their sexual tastes seems to get younger – Benesdra being a case in point. He puts his grizzled head on one side, calls us his lovebirds and treats us like a sugar daddy. It makes me shrivel up with embarrassment, plus the suspicion that he'd prefer either of us on our own, so I cling to the child's company for both our sakes.

It's just as well he has other things on his mind at present. News from the south is good. Aretas, his indignant ex-father-in-law, has been driven out of El Mashnaka, the stronghold that Herod calls Machaerus in the Roman tongue, and his Arab troops are being contained at Petra, his capital city. Antipas means to show the flag, by moving in and taking possession of the liberated fortress, with its neighbouring township built by his poppa. Nobody dares to say it, but the latter would have led his army in person rather than skulk a hundred miles away wallowing in the fleshpots while better men (like Cass) risked their lives to rescue his dynastic pride. Anyway, he's rustled up sufficient nerve to visit the scene of action now that it's comparatively safe. Not alone, however: his entire retinue must travel with him, dancing-girls and all, so that his pleasures may continue unabated. I'm not sorry, mind you. Anything will relieve the monotony of this existence, even a spell in that parched, inhospitable region of the damned! The thought of it brings back a vivid recollection of the Baptist, a figure as austere and uncompromising as the desert itself. His name is a forbidden one at court; it's rumoured that he's been vilifying the royal pair as twin bigamists and denouncing their union as immoral and incestuous, which it undoubtedly is. Herod pretends to treat Johanan as an outrageous joke but the queen is predictably furious and would love to stop his mouth. So far it appears he's had the horse sense to stay out of the royal territory, where he's safe from arrest.

He has one ally at court – Joanna. She's a pious body, not in the superficial, self-congratulatory way of the Set-aparts but genuinely so. When Herod resided at the Hasmonean Palace, his favourite residence in Judaea, she went out to hear the Baptist preach and has, I believe, subscribed to his cousin's cause. Another dupe – though a sincere one! For obvious reasons she's had to keep her religious foibles a secret: if Johanan has an implacable foe in Herodias, Barjoseph has another in her husband. His mission in Galil has aroused the Tetrarch's alarm since he's reported by spies to be preaching sedition. Having stirred up a nest of hornets in Judaea, he's now making the north too hot to hold him – yet Joanna insists to me that his words are those of universal peace.

When our exodus gets under way and Herod's retinue hits the road, I travel in Chusa's well-sprung conveyance. From its window one can see forward to the royal litter carried by Nubian slaves and backward to the tail of our procession stretching almost to the horizon: teams of baggage-camels carrying provisions for the journey, courtiers and retainers on horseback and carts containing heirlooms and new-fangled accessories which His Majesty refuses to leave behind. The torrid summer is fading into autumn, the season of the first rains, and a refreshing dampness is in the air. Peasants sowing the furrowed fields stare at our passing with no friendliness in their gaze; one has the temerity to shake his fist. In the towns where we requisition lodging overnight there's a sullen submission to royal prerogative and an atmosphere heavy with censure. Chusa remarks in the privacy of our carriage, "The Baptist's strictures have evidently not gone unheeded. These people resent the public display of an illicit union."

"I hope and pray he stays out of the Queen's way," says Joanna. "She's a vengeful woman."

"It was unwise of you to show interest in that firebrand's teaching, wife, still more so to subsidise his cousin. You might be compromising my position."

"Yet you didn't forbid me, Chusa dear."

"No. You have a generous heart and your instincts are sound. I daresay there's some truth in what both of them claim – even a touch of the divine if Barjoseph's powers are to be believed. All the same, one must remember one's place and keep one's opinions to oneself. If Herodias is a bitch, the King has the makings of a tyrant. Never forget his ancestry! A smooth passage to the throne has made him lazy and complacent but once he identifies some threat to his supremacy he'll act with all his father's ruthlessness."

His words, which renew my dread on Jo's behalf, prove only too well founded. Our convoy, crossing the frontier between the Decapolis and Perea, Herod's domain, halts abruptly. Above the grinding of braked wheels and stamping of hooves I hear a familiar voice rise in strident condemnation.

"Unholy wedlock stinks in the Lord's nostrils. Scripture lays down that no man, be he king or commoner, shall take to bed his own niece or his living brother's spouse. Hear this, Herod Antipas, and your sinful consort."

We crane out of our window, Joanna tense with anxiety, myself merely curious. Herod's mounted bodyguard whose officer is binding his wrists with a rope, which he tethers to his own horse, already rings the Baptist's haggard form. What possessed the man to wait for our cortege on royal territory and challenge the Tetrarch to his face? Herodias must be delighted! Those about Johanan are making a circumspect withdrawal; they've the look of Set-aparts rather than disciples and I suspect he may have been decoyed into danger. He submits calmly to his arrest, showing no resistance as if content at having delivered his mind directly to the king and queen. We draw in our heads, ashamed to watch his humiliation as he stumbles at the horse's crupper, yet his presence reduces Herod to insignificance and his wife to a railing strumpet. He alone is used to the wilderness through which we travel on the last lap of our journey. His leather-soled feet have covered every inch of it and its sparse yield has sustained him throughout his mission. We skirt the eastern shore of the Salt Sea, lying like a grey shield beneath the cloud-wracked sky. They say this is the lowest area of the earth's crust and even late-year gales blowing across the mountains of Moab can't lighten its sultriness. Somewhere beyond those foothills, Cass must be leading his lads against the ranks of Araby or on the lookout for a deadly ambush round the juts and sallies of tortured rock. My fears run parallel with Joanna's – but it's a different man I'm praying for!

Eventually the naked heights of El Mashnaka loom ahead, shadowing the salt-caked waters below them. The vision sends a prickle down my spine for I heard legends in my childhood of the King who first fortified the mound, Alexander Jannaeus of grim renown. He's survived as a bogeyman to scare naughty kids with, a monster that waded through blood and filled his cave-dungeons with his enemies. Those legends seem horribly real as I gaze at the great cliff honeycombed with cavern-mouths at its base. Is Johanan destined to follow Alexander's victims into their rat-infested depths? This is hardly a setting suited to Herod's epicene tastes; as we climb the last slope I can see why he finds it tolerable, however, for his father's city is spread before us, a reproduction in miniature of

Tiberias or Caesarea and strangely incongruous in its savage environment. My Lord will want for nothing here; he'll be able to resume his velvet-padded existence, to enjoy his jugglers and jesters and dancing-girls in undisturbed serenity while jackals and hyenas prowl outside the battlemented walls and white-winged desert eagles hover above the carnage wreaked by his feud with Aretas.

We file between splintered precipices of granite and draw up at the ghost town's gateway, exhausted by our long haul from the north. The Baptist's rope is detached from the harness and he's frogmarched towards the towering rock. Joanna gazes after him, stricken and speechless. Does she know of the labyrinth where a man can live and die forgotten by his kind? Little as I regard him, my own pleasure in the luxury of court-life is soured by the thought of his ordeal. Not that his confinement is altogether solitary – for once we've settled in, Herod conceives the bright idea of making him a figure of fun to vary court entertainment.

Every so often Johanan is dragged over to his palace in chains and exhibited like some circus monstrosity in front of his tittering sycophants. The ignominy is all on their side as they snatch at his rags and deride him, while he stands, impassive and dignified, unresponsive to their baiting.

"Make us a prophecy," Herod teases him. "Tell us how the bastard from Nazrat will be taken up to heaven in a chariot of fire and descend to judge mankind at the world's ending. I love fairy stories. Better still, take a leaf out his book and perform a miracle for me."

The Baptist deigns to reply. "God utters his truth even through the lips of the profane. What you say of the Mashiah is no lie – but only he has the power to suspend nature's laws and he does so, not to provide a thrill for seekers after sensation but to enforce his claim to kingship."

"Kingship?" Herod's brow darkens. "He dares to usurp my title and you, wild man, to support him? You may kiss my toe as penance for your audacity."

He puts out his foot as once he offered me his hand. Willing participants in this charade force Johanan to his knees and thrust down his head. When they wrench it back by the long, lank hair, a gob of spit glistens on the satin instep. This insult is the pretext for physical abuse. Once their victim has been hustled out of the chamber, a trail of his blood stains the rich Persian carpet in front of the king's throne.

"It ought to have been rolled up before we had the swine in," is Herod's parting comment. "Such commodities are too precious to be trodden by a yokel's feet. Come, sweet Circe, pick up your tambour and dance for me. Your charms will dispel the aftertaste of that disagreeable scene. How I hate violence even when it is necessary…"

Taking courage from the Baptist's defiance, I decline to oblige him. Instead of blows, I receive a gracious acquiescence for I'm no longer treated as a mere entertainer – yet I sense that Antipas stores up the memory of slights against the day he'll demand his royal dues from me. I'm only grateful his wife wasn't present to add her vitriol. She rarely presides when I attend on His Majesty, hating to watch his eyes feast on me, though I know she harbours thoughts of a more extreme revenge for the man who proclaimed her guilt. She wants him done to death. Her husband refuses to gratify her whim, partly because it pleases him to cross her and partly because he fears adverse publicity. Johanan is venerated by the common folk whose loyalties can make or break a king, whatever Rome may decree.

Joanna is determined to visit him in his isolation. She feels he needs a woman's care, but I'm not so sure he'd welcome it. I agree to accompany her all the same since a spice of adventure might relieve my unbearable boredom. We must keep our scheme from Chusa's ears, let alone those of the queen. Its success will depend on the complicity of his guards, and it's lucky that they're friendly to us both. Joanna has nursed them in sickness from time to time and I have the advantage of being Cass's steady. We wait for a moonless night in order to avoid being seen making our way between palace and citadel. Then we set out, Joanna laden with a wineskin and titbits from the larders to tempt Johanan. Even so short a journey in the dark has its terrors as we recall the devil-haunted tales about this benighted region. The massive cone of El Mashnaka reared against the sky seems still more formidable than by daylight and, while I'm far from superstitious, I share some of my companion's timidity, approaching the guardhouse. We're blessed with good fortune; Abenadar who's returned from the front for a minor wound is in charge of the detail. He holds up his lantern to identify us, and then grins. We whisper our purpose to him.

"Strictly against orders," he says gruffly. "If it got out, I'd be in deep shtuck. Then again, if I let you down, young lady, I'll catch it from Longinus soon as he gets back – and you, Ma'am, have been tending me a treat. I'll turn a blind eye but for Gawd's sake don't push your luck. And mind the rats!"

No idle warning: the flickering gleam of sconces set in metal brackets above our heads reveals furry bodies darting across the floor of beaten earth as we pick our cautious way forward through a winding passage deep into the rock face. On either side of us yawn cavities, some natural and others excavated, presumably to house the long-dead captives of Jannaeus. Johanan inhabits the last of these, sitting cross-legged with his shaggy head bowed in meditation. He doesn't look up as we reach him, seems to have distanced himself from an awareness of his surroundings. We place our frugal offering at his side. After a few moments his hand gropes out to finger the flask, the cooked meats.

"I thank you, whoever you are." His voice, though subdued, echoes hollowly off the dank walls. "My vows forbid me such delicacies. They give me spring-water and stale crusts which suffice for my needs."

Joanna murmurs, "Master, you must take more nourishment if you're to survive imprisonment."

"Wine has never passed my lips and never will. Don't be concerned on my behalf – I've known greater deprivation than this."

He raises his eyes at last and studies us quizzically. "You call me Master... Yes, your features are familiar to me, good woman, as one who came to listen, not to mock. And this child who ornaments Herod's court yet hangs back when his toadies persecute me with their cheap jibes and their fists has also, I believe, made her pilgrimage to Jordan's banks – though not to receive its purifying waters."

"You remember my visit, Sir?" I ask, astonished.

"Your auburn hair stood out vividly against a drab background as it does now even in this gloom. You kept questionable company on that day, child, and keep no better at the present. I fear nature's gift of beauty has led you astray." He pauses. "I've another reason for recollecting every detail of that afternoon. It was then that I had the supreme honour to baptise the Lord's Anointed."

"Your cousin Barjoseph?"

"My cousin Yeshua. I knew when he came to me that my mission was drawing to its close; the bearer of good news must make way for the Prince whose reign he has heralded. That was why I stood in Herod's path and invited my arrest – though his agents imagined they'd tricked me by their cunning. Yes, I'm content to end my life as a captive, safe in the knowledge that those who followed me are now the disciples of the Mashiah himself."

"Such as Jo Barzabdiah?" I still can't say his name without a tremor.

"My namesake? A fine young man whose soul burns with a pure flame. You know him as well?"

"I knew him – as well as I knew myself. We were childhood sweethearts, you might say."

"Then I promise you'll be so again, though fate has separated you for a time."

"Is that the prophet speaking or the sentimentalist?" My laugh grates on the silence. I'm tempted to accuse the man who first caused our estrangement but the words die on my lips. He has enemies enough as it is.

The shadowed face breaks into a smile, which transforms its gaunt features. "Let's say I'm speaking as one who reads hearts rather than surface appearances."

"You mean that all this has been a bad dream and that we'll be lovers again?"

"Not according to the flesh. The love you share will be dedicated to Another in whose being all human affection is sanctified."

Before I've time to ponder his meaning, a hiss from Abenadar warns us that we mustn't prolong our visit any further. We take our leave of the Baptist and hand over the untouched provisions to his guards on our way out. They're delighted to swig the wine – Herod's best vintage – and our gift will ensure their co-operation for the future, I hope. Joanna takes my arm with more than her usual tenderness on our homeward trip and I realize that, like Johanan, she's understood what lay beneath my admission.

"I'm so glad we visited him although we could do nothing to relieve his wretchedness," she whispers. "I'm sure it was meant to be – for your sake rather than his, my dear. I guessed that you'd experienced some tragedy and needed comforting which, in my ignorance, I was unable to give. For all his resignation, the Baptist remains a true prophet!"

Later that night she comes to my bedroom and I tell her everything: our secret betrothal, my rage at Jo's desertion and the horrors I've wished upon myself ever since. No judgement or reproof – she lets me unburden my troubled spirit and soothes me with her tender compassion. When she's gone, I feel a sense of inner peace that I've not known for many months.

We continue visiting the lonely prisoner. Gracious speech doesn't come easily to him, but I think he's thankful for our companionship. He likes to reminisce, telling us of his earlier life, an orphaned childhood and adoption by the Essenes dwelling on the far shore of the Salt Sea.

"They are stern, holy men," he says, "and they live in expectation of God's Servant. The prophet Enoch, whom they call the Teacher of Righteousness, is the light by which they foresee his coming, a light that was mirrored in my soul because I'd recognized his advent while still in my mother's womb. Yet I came to reject their doctrine. It was based on hatred rather than love. They didn't want to convert others, merely to earn redemption for themselves. Like the Zealots and the Siccarioth, they looked forward to his arrival as a signal to take up arms – his adversaries must be mown down in the ripeness of their sins, consigned to eternal damnation… Oh yes, they had their battle-plans drawn up like military generals. I knew in my bones how wrong they were for all their piety and self-denial. The Mashiah's war is a spiritual one and its weapons are patience, pardon, and love. So, on reaching maturity, I left them and went where God's grace led me, calling others to a new covenant with the Lord."

In this colony of depraved, pleasure-seeking wastrels, his sincerity strikes a heroic note. It's not easy to empathize with him as an ordinary mortal but I've come to treasure our snatched minutes together and share Joanna's concern for his safety. Herodias never relaxes her efforts to get him killed, and I'm afraid her persistence will wear down Herod's resistance in the end. If only I could get him on his own and plead for Johanan's release... No, for all his partiality towards me, I'd be snubbed roundly for meddling in political matters, affairs of state, which don't concern a mindless bimbo. Why should he repeal a sentence - unless there was something in it for him? I've given no positive encouragement since the morning I refused to drop that last veil and, without my collaboration, he can't hope to evade his wife's all-seeing eye; but now's the time to show willing. I'll trade my body for the Baptist's freedom!

A woman can say so much with a meaningful glance or a suggestive sway of the hips. I daren't put my invitation too explicitly but he's not slow to catch on – probably thinks I can no longer fight against his sophisticated charms. Actually I'm as little attracted to him as I was to Reuben though his defects are better disguised. When I'm good and sure he's snared, I slide a note into his palm one evening while kissing the hand he always extends to me. "I am lonely at night, My Lord." A veiled message which betrays urgency but nothing more; if he takes it amiss, I can protest that I only wished to speak to him in confidence about some personal grievance. On the other hand, my rendezvous gives us the best chance of outwitting the queen who'd never condescend to visit a slut like myself. In case things go wrong, however, I've arranged for Salome to be on tap and to dance for her stepfather as I've taught her. She's only too eager, the precocious little show-off, and her presence should disarm suspicion.

While she flutters her drapes and rehearses her steps, I listen for his approach with bated breath. He's light-footed for a man of his bulk and his knock takes me by surprise. I open the door cautiously, and Salome runs forward to greet him with a flirtatious curtsey. His plucked eyebrows go up at seeing her, and then he smiles his commendation of my artfulness as he raises her to her feet.

"My paired love-birds," he croons. "What pleasanter prospect could a man ask for after a tiresome day of administration – particularly when beyond the range of prurient eyes or wagging tongues?"

His stepdaughter pipes up: "May I dance for you, Sir? Miriam has shown me how to do it – just like she does!"

"Then she must have been patient with my little nuisance-box." He winks at me over her head like a stable-lad. "Your novice-steps will be an agreeable prelude to our more serious – ah – assignation, my sweet."

The child writhes and pirouettes and wriggles her narrow hips in a parody of adult enticement while I tap out the rhythm for her. Herod has settled himself on my couch, his casual manner not quite concealing a lascivious delight in her exhibition, and when she's finished, he leans forward to trap her in his arms, withdrawing her final drape.

"A father may look on his own daughter in a state of nature," he remarks to me as though justifying the gesture, "and permit himself a good-night kiss." He does so at some length then packs her off with a smack on her dainty rump. She gives me a grateful glance before leaving the room, ecstatic at Herod's response. I watch her depart with mixed feelings; she scarcely realizes as yet what lies behind his paternal fondness but should she lose her innocence, he'll be like putty in her hands. One day she may wield a power over this middle-aged hedonist, which could outstrip the dominance of her mother and be used for dubious ends...

I've laid on wine and pastries for Herod's enjoyment. He sips and nibbles unhurriedly, certain of a more appetizing dish to follow. We talk idly of this and that for some time and I'm glad to postpone an undesired climax to our meeting. But inevitably he begins to nudge our dialogue into a more intimate channel, paying flowery tributes to my looks.

"I've wanted this for so long, my dear, an opportunity to have you to myself – but my wife is unbelievably jealous of her conjugal rights and I couldn't be sure you were ready to risk her displeasure or satisfy my deepest wish."

"My Lord, you're entitled to the obedience of your subjects in regard to their terms of service, yet what I think you have in mind is something else, a gift which any woman may grant or withhold. I'm prepared to surrender it on one condition."

He sits bolt upright and appraises me through narrowed eyes. "What's this – you mean to barter your favours? Have you forgotten that you're speaking to a king? I could command you under pain of a whipping."

"You once said that violence distressed you."

He laughs ruefully. "Why, so I did – and so it does. You're resourceful as well as enchanting, Circe. I seem to recall that this isn't the first time we've bargained. The last saved a man's life, didn't it? I'm an Arab by extraction, as my critics keep pointing out, and I confess to a partiality for haggling. What's your condition?"

I draw a deep breath. "The Baptist's liberty in exchange for my compliance."

His smile switches to a frown. "You go too far, young lady. The man has spoken publicly against my character and my marriage. He's attempted to stir up rebellion among those who already resent my rule. My position in this nation of fanatics is a precarious one at best. I owe my tetrarchy to the whim of an emperor whom I daren't offend and to the tolerance of those I govern. If self-styled prophets are allowed to get away with slandering me, I risk the possibility of a religious uprising while at war with Aretas. Not only should I have to fight on two fronts but also Tiberius would no doubt relieve me of my throne for incompetence. I can't let that happen."

"Whether you set him free or not, his followers will spread his condemnation of you through the land."

"Then they'll be rounded up and punished. I've agents

everywhere who sniff out my enemies, you know. D'you suppose the Baptist's arrest was coincidental? He was delivered into my hands by a subterfuge."

"No, My Lord, he submitted to a ruse with his eyes wide open. He knew his task was done and that the cause he'd preached lay now with another."

"His cousin? My spies keep me well posted on that one. He's a slippery customer, forever skipping between Galil and Judaea – but I'll take him out when the moment's ripe. His birthplace makes him a subject of mine so he can't escape me – nor can his peasant troop. These demagogues camouflaged as holy men – wolves in sheep's' clothing – must learn that their populist teaching doesn't pay."

Thank God he's betrayed his intentions. Somehow I have to get away from here and warn Jo, or at least his poppa, about the danger. No father, however fed up with his son's foolishness, would refuse him protection from the king's wrath.

"So you see, my dear Circe," Herod continues smoothly, "I've good reason not to oblige you, much as your request intrigues me. Why should a girl like yourself be concerned for such a freak as Johanan?"

"Purposeless cruelty offends me. He's a spent force and his release would do you no harm."

"Yet if, as you admit, he gave himself up to imprisonment, why should he not accept my hospitality?"

"I think he's resigned to it. My real fear is for his life. The Queen's resolved on that."

"Herodias has no authority to act. Her will is subject to my consent."

"She's well aware that your family has a ruthless past, My Lord, and she's banking on the hope that you'll follow your father's example."

"If my father was a tyrant, he took his cue from his ancestors. The Hasmoneans were steeped in blood before ever he was born. Jannaeus was legendary in his own lifetime for his savage reprisals. He had hundreds executed merely for throwing bad fruit at him during some religious ceremony where he'd muffed his role – and watched them die on crosses from his palace while making love to his concubines. Alexandra, his wife, murdered two of her husband's brothers to ensure the throne for her son Hyrcanus, whose ear was bitten off by his own nephew since a mutilated man could not be priest-king of Israel. Juicy little detail that, eh?" He shivers in refined disgust. "In the next generation his rivals sent the handsome princeling Aristobulus to Mark Antony in Egypt who'd a weakness for pretty boys, hoping he'd gain support against my father's faction. Aristobulus was the favourite brother of his second wife Mariamne, so no wonder he came to suspect her of treachery and had her killed."

"He didn't stop there, did he, My Lord? He murdered her two sons and ordered another child of his to be executed, from his own deathbed. Didn't Augustus Caeasar remark that it was safer to be Herod's pig than his progeny? Not only that, they say he had a whole batch of boy-children slaughtered in some village south of the City because of some prediction that one of them would succeed to his kingdom…"

Mart used to scare me rigid when I was young, telling me that black King Herod crept into folks' houses at night and cut the throats of naughty kids.

"Dynastic assassination is a habit of self-made monarchs. If he hadn't cleared the decks, I and my brother Philip might never have reached our thrones. I'm duly grateful to him – and perfectly willing to follow in his footsteps if the need arises. However, killing's a nasty expedient, its crudity repels me, and I assure you that your evil-smelling friend has nothing to fear apart from his enforced seclusion."

I've small trust in his words after those cloudy threats about Barjoseph and his travelling circus. Despite his confidence of my eventual amenability, I'll stick to my terms. Why should one who lets a far better man rot in his filthy underground jail have his pleasure handed him on a plate?

"Come, daughter of the Sun," he presses me. "We've dallied long enough. My consort and I sleep apart as you may have suspected but she has means of interrogating every servant except for my faithful steward and if she finds out my whereabouts, you might very well be keeping company with your precious prophet by morning."

He advances on me and I back away. "Oh no, My Lord, you haven't honoured my condition."

He feigns injured innocence. "Why, my love, I was only going to help you divest yourself of those clinging garments. Did you imagine that I meant to – assault you? Copulation is so animal, so grotesque. My sole desire is to gaze on the fullness of your exquisite flesh without tasting its forbidden fruit."

Cass was right after all. Herod's requirements aren't those of a normal man, yet I remain stubborn. True lovemaking, even when adulterous, has a rightness of its own; it's an embodiment of the need to be united with one's partner. The thought of exposing myself to his clinical eye and watching him dribble with impotent lust nauseates me – as does the insult to my womanhood. He sees the resolution in my face and makes a grab at my robe. I sidestep and he clasps me clumsily, pulls me to him with unexpected strength. For a second we're in close encounter and I glimpse a pale reflection of his father's ferocity in the petulant, spoilt-child expression. Instinctively my hands reach upward to tear and claw at that slavering mask. Cursing, he lets me go and without hesitation I make for the door. Then I'm out of the room to which I lured him so unwisely, and running to the one place I can call sanctuary, Chusa's suite. I've no wish to involve him or Joanna in this fiasco yet I must seek her counsel.

She opens to my urgent knock and, recognizing the panic in my eyes, draws me gently inside. The room's mercifully empty but for her; Joab's sleeping in his chamber, she tells me, and his poppa is on evening rounds. Hastily I report what's just occurred. If my stratagem shocks her, she can at least approve my motive. "I have to get away," I conclude. "It's not so much that I'm scared of Herod's fury – he can't afford the bad publicity reaching his wife's ears – as my need to warn Jo of the risks he's running tagged on to Barjoseph."

"You can't cross the desert on your own, Miri. Besides, you'll be hunted down and brought back in disgrace."

"I'd thought of that. But if my going is inconspicuous enough, I doubt whether Herod will pursue. He'll have his work cut out explaining a badly scratched cheek!"

"Wait – you've given me an idea… You can't go to ground in the palace or within the town-walls come to that. Yet the caverns of El Mashnaka would be a secure hiding-place overnight. Tomorrow I set out with the wagoner to fetch fresh food-supplies from the City and maybe we can contrive to smuggle you aboard."

"If they raise the hue and cry, Abenadar will hand me over. He has his own security to consider."

For so ingenuous-seeming a person, Joanna proves herself a master-tactician. Inside an hour I set out alone, wrapped in her voluminous clothing, my giveaway hair tucked under a black veil. Nodding at Abenadar with a hand over my face as if stifling a yawn, I push a wineskin into his expectant hands – a muzzy head might save me from recognition if our plans go awry. Now I'm Johanan's co-tenant in a dungeon I know too well, where concealment is no problem whatsoever! The Baptist, more alert than usual as though some inner voice had warned him of my crisis, listens to the summary of recent events. Do I detect a gleam of mischief in his red-rimmed eyes as I outline our plan of escape?

"You should never have offered yourself as a counter for my release," he says. "The Almighty charts the course each of us must pursue; to obstruct his providence is like kicking against the goad. However, your present purpose is a sound one. The Mashiah's time hasn't yet come…"

I dismiss the ambiguity of his last words. "We – we thought there might be a chance of getting you away as well."

"No, I shan't flee the wrath to come. The worst Antipas can do is give me deliverance from this ill-used body of mine. A martyr's death is the seed-corn of a faith, which will change the world. I shall pray for your safe passage, my child, and not from his puny vengeance alone. You have a greater enemy whose strength lies in his access to your soul."

The crucial stage of our scheme occurs when Abenadar summons me to leave. Discipline is lax; mounting guard on a man of peace chained to an iron staple seems so superfluous that his sentries don't hesitate to desert their post for a call of nature or some minor commission. We're relying on that fact. When the call comes in a voice already slurred by drink, I sit tight and Johanan answers for me: "The steward's wife went away when my guard was absent. She's been gone these ten minutes, my good man."

"Then she should've waited as per usual," Abenadar grumbles. But he accepts the fiction and we hug ourselves in glee. Can anyone bar me have seen the Baptist in this schoolboy mood? It's hardly a restful night: my dread of monster-rats is greater than that of discovery while swaying lanterns beyond the prison-barrier and the shouts of a search-party keep us both on vigil. Herod is at least going through the motions of apprehending an absconder... It's many hours till exhaustion lulls me to sleep.

Daylight makes scant inroad on the cavern's gloom; ears rather than eyes must pick up the vital clues – wagon-wheels creaking in the distance and the guard's footsteps as he crosses the drawbridge over the fort's surrounding ditch for reasons that are private. The first hasn't yet impinged on my hearing but the second I must take advantage of. I mayn't get a second chance. I give my fellow-prisoner the one and only embrace he'll have enjoyed from a woman's lips since his old momma's passing, then slip out, sensing his gaze watch after me. He gave his life to God; let God help him in his extremity! The coast seems clear and I scamper across the causeway behind the mound to crouch in a sheltering gully. These are the tensest moments for there may be pickets posted at any point in the bleak landscape.

At last I hear the welcome ring of hooves and peep out to see a cart, hooded like Naaman's, lumber and jolt through the town-gate. Joanna, stolid-featured, is perched beside the driver, holding him in conversation. She persuades him to pull up his horses where the spur of El Mashnakar's rock hides his conveyance from general view. Round to its rear she goes, as if to check the hood's fastenings – but instead unties them for me. Within seconds I'm inside, snug as a bug, the awning's tied down again and we're rolling.

"Yes," I hear Joanna reassure the wagoner. "All's well."

FIVE

Our journey across the desert is arduous enough to require at least one night on the road. The wagon makes an adequate sleeping-place for Joanna and me, while our driver keeps watch over his tethered beasts. He's scarcely reacted to the appearance of a stowaway apart from scratching his head in bewilderment. Joanna has chosen her escort well: he not only looks vacant but has some congenital speech-defect, which will prevent him from reporting my presence and getting her into shtook when she returns.

By mid-morning of the second day we clatter through Bethaniah and I ask myself whether Laz and Mart are installed in our southern home or still up north. To see my brother again would be a joy – but this would mean braving the she-dragon's outraged fury. It's no use: the existence I've led since leaving them will always come between us, an unbridgeable gulf. By the same token I'll do my best to avoid Jo and his mates if they happen to be in Judaea. Once I've passed on my message to his poppa, I suppose there'll be nothing for it except to go back to my street-corner career and trust Cass will come to my rescue a second time. Yet now that I've broken with his boss, it's hard to see how we can resume our relationship, unless he gets a transfer to rejoin the City brigade.

Once we're through its gateway, the bustle and animation recall me to the present. Here we must part: Joanna to make her purchases in the seven great markets of Zion so that Antipas and his bloated chums can fill their bellies till they gag and start again, Roman-style, while I beard the formidable Zabdiah in his den – as much king of his mercantile domain as is Herod of his territories. We say little to each other but embrace warmly. It's unlikely we'll meet again, unless by chance, and the loss of one who's been a momma to me drains my pleasure at the sights and sounds of Judaea's capital. I barely glance at the bazaars with their gaily-striped canopies and colourful wares or listen to the cries of street-vendors; the busy hum which should quicken my pulse after the desert's frightening stillness. Yet my heart does race as I thread my way towards Fish Street. Is it for fear of confronting an irate father-in-law or my urgency to deliver crucial news?

The counting house of Zabdiah's premises is open to the street. I enter diffidently. Oza, the head-clerk, fails to recognize me – though once the old man held me on his knee. I'm still swathed in Joanna's garb and I've drawn her black veil across my mouth like a yashmak, not wanting my features to be identified by those who must know of my shame. No doubt Oza would hesitate to admit me to Zabdiah's inner sanctum, but my air of respectability gains me an entrance.

The proprietor is seated behind his massive desk. My first sight of him for some time shocks me; his burly frame seems to have shrunk and the bluff, ruddy cheeks have fallen in. He used to radiate prosperity and health yet now he looks downcast and defeated, a shadow of his former self. Jo's freaking-out must have been as big a blow to him as it was to me. For a minute I ignore the man beside him who's peering intently at me. Benesdra, Zabdiah's devoted friend – and my ill wisher.

He says slowly, "Those alluring jade-green eyes, I'd know them anywhere in spite of all that camouflage. This, Zabdiah, is the girl who has plunged your good name into disgrace."

Jo's poppa, who has risen stiffly to greet me with a formal bow, pauses then studies me more closely. Angry at Reubven's suggestion that I've masked myself deliberately, I tear off the veil and let my hair fall free. A high colour floods his pasty jowls, his thick brows bristle above congested eyes, and the famous spasm of ungovernable rage shakes him with its thunder.

"Miriam! How dare you show yourself here, on my property – a brazen tart, a violatress of Israel's Law, a reproach to your own family, as well as mine…" Following this outburst, he sinks back into his chair, exhausted and breathing hard. His hand goes to his heart as if to muffle its pain.

I say quietly, "I came only to tell you, Sir, that Herod's spies are on Barjoseph's trail and your son is in imminent danger of arrest as one of his accomplices."

"That clown. I offered him the finest start a lad could ask for, the chance to take over the firm, which I've built up by the sweat of my brow – and he chucks it away for some crack-brained farrago about a fake mashiah. Not that his idiocy excuses your deplorable conduct as my daughter-in-law."

"Aren't you concerned for his predicament or mine? I was the one let down and my 'deplorable conduct' as you call it was the result of his betrayal."

"I fail to see the connection. He behaved badly towards you, I admit, but it doesn't follow that you had to sink to your present level."

Benesdra stokes the flames. "The whole City talks of the well-nurtured Jewess who has whored with Aliens and belly-danced before a mongrel king. I am disgusted to find myself in the same room as a Jezebel."

"You weren't so particular when we last met."

His oyster eyes squirm under the fleshy lids and he moves to safer ground. "My sentiments must give place to Zabdiah's greater cause of offence. You'll have to answer to him, my girl!"

"And answer you shall," the other storms, his anger on the upsurge. "You're an adulteress according to law and you must pay for your crime."

"This shmuck knows very well that I'm not. He heard Jo release me from my vow."

"I heard a lovers' tiff which ended on an ugly note through your ill temper. You wrung the concession out of him." Reuben flings wide his arms in a practised barrister's gesture. "A legal union cannot be dissolved by word of mouth alone. My friend is correct; you must be taken before the Knesset and charged in due form."

How he's hugging himself at this opportunity to carry out his threat! I've spurned him, struck a mortal blow to his pride and his integrity; now he'll exact the full price. I could walk out of this dusty hole and lose myself in the rabbit warren of backstreets as I did before, but I scorn to do so. I'm innocent of the sin imputed to me and ready to face my accusers.

The Council sits throughout the day in the Court of Hewn Stone at the Temple's southwestern corner, an assembly of priests and elders twiddling their thumbs as they wait in idleness for some miscreant to be arraigned in front of them. Benesdra is of their number. He and Zabdiah frogmarch me to my doom, each holding one of my arms – two uncles escorting a fractious niece, some passer-by might think, if he failed to read our features. We cross the paved terrace of the forecourt and they hand me over to the Temple police. I'm led like a felon to trial and made to stand alone in the chamber's centre, flanked on either side by a three-tiered semicircle of stone benches from which my judges scrutinize me gravely. Reuben is my prosecutor.

"No sin is more heinous, more execrated by our nation than adultery," he commences grandiloquently. "No being is more odious to us than an adulterer or adulteress. She is an abomination whose evil doing desecrates all that we hold sacred. Does not Scripture tell us that a loose woman's lips drip honey and her speech is smoother than oil but that within she is bitter as wormwood, sharp as a two-edged sword? Her ways wander and she does not know it."

My ways have wandered all right, I reflect. They've brought me to this public exposure and the likelihood of a swift ending but no nearer the one who was to shape my destiny. I could cap the quotation with another, from the poem Jo and I used to recite during our courtship: 'upon my bed by night I sought him whom my soul loves but found him not. I called him but he did not answer. I rose and went about the city, in the streets and in the squares. The watchmen found me as I went about the city, they beat and wounded me, they took away my mantle…' The last has yet to happen.

Reuben's fat finger points at me. "This shameless wench is daughter by betrothal to our highly esteemed citizen, Zabdiah, here beside me. However, she has prostituted herself with those who are our oppressors, the hated Kittim – profane and ungodly." He pauses for effect. "The Law proclaims that adultery by a betrothed maiden merits its full rigour. It is written in the fifth book of Moishe that you shall bring such a one to the gate of the city and stone her with sharp stones. This injured father and I, his representative, demand that justice shall be done!"

I feel the strength which holds me upright melt away. For all his hatred of me, I'd not anticipated so extreme a reprisal. His case is deadly in both senses of the word. I've no recourse, no right to testify on my own behalf – nothing bar the mercy of these strict, unbending men on whom I must rely. Already there's an atmosphere of finality among their ranks. If only Jo were here to defend me... As they debate my guilt, a group of Set-aparts enter the hall and approach the president. I overhear one of them say, "The Nazrene is teaching in the Outer Court. We need reinforcements to oppose him." Not surprisingly, Barjoseph – it must be he – takes precedence over a common trollop. For once I'm glad he's in the vicinity; it means that Jo, my one remaining hope, is at hand.

The Nasi, a wily-looking priest, strokes his grey beard thoughtfully. "Why shouldn't we invite his opinion on the case we are trying?" he proposes. "Whatever the Carpenter decides, it can be used against him. If he condemns this girl, he'll be contradicting his claim to forgive sinners; if he pardons her, he'll be condoning her defiance of the Law. We shall have him trapped at last."

There's a chorus of assent. The members file out and my captors push me roughly after them. Reuben looks aggrieved. He'd have preferred the issue resolved without further appeal and been ready to fling the first stone himself – out in that fatal quarry beyond the west wall where so many have died in anguish. As for Zabdiah, he walks with bowed head and dragging feet as though regretting the tide of self-righteous indignation on which he's acted. The man's sick. Like me in all my youth and vigour, he has a stench of death about him. Our eyes go to the tall figure that stands ringed by spectators, not the elite but ordinary folk, the ebionim despised by their betters who have always listened to his words and applauded his healing powers. He glances towards me and I feel his gaze rest on me as if fully aware of my dire quandary.

The Nasi outlines a seemingly watertight case against me, and Barjoseph passes no comment. Finally the trap is baited and set: "You call yourself a master of the Law, privy to the wisdom of Yahweh. How then do you pronounce upon this proven adulteress?"

Barjoseph bends and traces characters in the dust as though dissociating himself from the affair. The priest attends, determined to have an answer. At last his addressee straightens and looks at my judges for the first time, his eyes burning with contempt.

"You hypocrites!" The voice is low-pitched, as I recall it, yet echoes back from the Temple-walls. "You find fault with others when your own offence cries out to my Father for punishment. If you'd remove the speck from another's eye, take the beam out of your own." Now he's glaring at Benesdra, the same withering look his cousin once directed at him. "Whoever is free from sin, let him cast the first stone."

Silence ensues. Then, one by one, my judges turn and go from the court, leaving my twin accusers and me. Even the guards have freed me, uncertain of their duty. Zabdiah, whose anger has blown over like a summer storm, clears his throat. "I – I'm sorry it's come to this, Miriam. You've done wrong but I was partly to blame for postponing your marriage to Jo – and he, too, must take some share for abandoning you." His glazed eyes search for a sign of his son as mine have already done, but for once the faithful few aren't in evidence. Maybe they've grown timid at their leader's constant challenge to the Establishment and are skulking in some less conspicuous spot. Zabdiah turns wearily to Barjoseph; I nerve myself for a fresh paroxysm, but the fight's gone out of him and he speaks quite humbly.

"If you, Sir, would remind my boy of his obligations..."

"Jo has responded to a higher obligation," answers Barjoseph. "He's volunteered to attach himself to my cause. Would you deny him the right to choose what seems best to him?"

"He owes obedience to his father."

"Exactly. His Father in heaven has sent him to me. No earthly parents' will outrank his."

Zabdiah's shoulders sag, he sketches a resigned gesture and takes himself off with the air of a defeated man. Benesdra, made of sterner stuff, stands his ground and snarls, "You are no qualified exponent of our Law, carpenter. You have frustrated justice by your intervention but believe me, it will take its full course on the day you yourself are submitted to the Knesset's verdict – and mine will be the loudest voice to denounce you!"

Barjoseph doesn't stir himself to reply. Instead, he points downwards to his previous writing in the dust. The letters are reversed from where I'm placed and I can't make them out, but Reuben, reading them, starts then flushes unbecomingly to the roots of his scanty hair. Without another word he departs, and I'm alone with the man to whom I owe my misfortune – and my life. He smiles at me, a frank, almost roguish smiles which lights up his serious face. For a fleeting second, the man I've judged, who's refused to judge me, becomes a real person.

He says, "It appears there's no one who condemns you. Neither do I. Go your way and try to resist temptation."

"Without the support of my husband, I have to earn a crust by any means I can."

"I didn't mean the tempting of illicit sex but that of despair. A body that's served base needs can rise above them for a nobler purpose..."

I bite back a retort. This fellow seems able to deflect my bitter spite, the aftermath of nervous tension. Yet I won't thank him for what he's done. He may have saved me – but for what? He holds the one person who makes life worthwhile in his leading strings and while he refuses to judge or sentence me, I'll be hounded to a living death by torment and proscription. The quarry would've been a quicker, more merciful release.

Eventually he, also, leaves in search of his menagerie. I want to go after him, make one last appeal to his decency – but my pride, despite the battering it's taken, is too strong. Still dazed by a danger so narrowly escaped, my nerves strained to breaking point. I walk over to where he was standing and stare at what he wrote before trampling feet obliterate it: a street-name and a number. What on earth can they have meant to Reuben? Then I latch on – and inward laughter lightens my hopelessness. It's the address of his love-nest, the apartment to which I was once directed! So I'd not misread the twinkle in my advocate's grey eyes... However he acquired this little item, Barjoseph clearly has a sense of humour.

With the release of an unbearable tension, hysteria bubbles up. I fling back my head and peal after peal rings hollowly against the stone walls in an empty room.

It's only later, while I'm pondering my future such as it is, that the cause of this near-disaster returns to me: Herod's threat. If I'd known that Barjoseph was in the vicinity, I might've been spared all its beastliness by telling him directly yet, given the chance, my personal crisis drove it from my mind. Shall I go after him? I decide against it. My few encounters with Jo's master have been ill-starred: the wedding at Kana when I started on my downward course, the Shabbat incident which led to Benesdra's evil designs on me and now the scene of my public humiliation. I must turn my back on him and on Jo. Cut both out of my life for good and all. Things look bad enough without my clinging to the torture of an unrequited passion.

What am I to do? I've no shelter, no cash to rent one. The salary I should've earned from court has been sacrificed through necessity and the thought of competing once more with those hellcats of the streets depresses me beyond bearing. I'm back to square one. With the sun's setting. The City cowers and wraps itself against a winter chill. I do the same, thinking this is no season for a hooker. My steps have led me to the sleazy quarter where trade can be found but I'm on my own. The other night birds haven't braved the cold or else they cornered the available market earlier and are now tucked up in bed with some customer's arms to warm them. This isn't a reassuring circumstance; a solitary pro sticks out like a sore thumb and is liable to attract only the grim attention of vigilantes. That's all I need! I'm positive I'd kill myself rather than face the consequences of fresh arrest – doing time or being sold into slavery. Even now I suspect I'm being watched. There's a shadowy figure on the far side of the street who's been lurking for ages, loitering with intent, the law would call it – but with what intent? He may be some thief on the prowl for pickings, but if so, why does he show such an interest in yours truly?

I could move away, out of his line of vision – or pluck up my courage and solicit him. After all, that's what I'm here for. I choose the second resort. Some would-be punters are too diffident to approach a tart; one learns to pick out the waverers and help them make up their minds. Yet this bloke shows no sign of uncertainty. He waits for me: a stocky, motionless silhouette with one leg awkwardly bent as if lamed. From close he looks decidedly unprepossessing in the moonlight, his crooked-featured face thrust forward on a thickly muscled neck. A bad hat, I reckon, the sort who'd've battened on poor Sue. My second thoughts come too late. He anticipates my offer.

"What's your price?"

"Enough to keep me for a day or two – if I like your company, buster. If I don't, there's no deal." Act tough, Miri, let him know you're not the please-trample-on-me type.

"My place, mind."

"Done," I say promptly. "I'm between moves at the moment."

"Follow me."

Not a gracious sort of guy – nor an open-handed one since he clearly expects a reduction in charge. As he limps ahead of me through the shrouded alleys towards the unappetising area west of the fruit-market, I half regret my good luck. It's not unknown for the Keep Zion Clean brigade to try it on like he's done, then nick you at the other end, yet I'm fairly sure he's not in that racket. He looks too much of a villain himself! On the other hand, I feel I've set eyes on him somewhere before, without being able to pin him down. Perhaps he remembers seeing me as well and wants to 'improve our acquaintance' the way men most favour. Red hair and a curvaceous figure can be mixed blessings…

He halts abruptly at a doorway set into a blind wall, then muffles a fist in his cloak and thumps three times. Why so cautious – and who is on the other side? It's not the custom to share a scrubber with your mates.

"I – I think I'll be off," I stammer. "This is outside my usual beat."

"What's the hassle?"

"I didn't cater for two – or more."

"Doubles the cut for you." He grasps my arm in a pincer grip. "Don't make trouble, sister. You're due for a big surprise."

Here's a metal grill fixed to the door. A slat on the inside is withdrawn noiselessly and a pair of eyes peers out at us. Then bolts slide back and a shove from my escort bundles me into a darkened room. I trip over some obstacle and fetch up on my knees to the sound of unfriendly laughter. Dazed, I try to make out my surroundings by the dull glow of banked firelight. The room, stinking of stale food and unwashed clothing, contains three blokes: my lame snatcher (for that's what he must be), a nasty-looking specimen sprawled across an unmade bed against the far wall and the one who admitted us. He's lean, tallish, and his features remind me of Barjoseph's for some reason, though they're on a meaner scale. He's first to speak.

"Bring her nearer the fire, Jude."

I feel the same iron grasp as before haul me over rough boards. The flames give out little warmth.

"Yes, that's her all right. I'd know that head of hair anywhere... Was there any bother?"

"Not a scrap, Si. She fell for it like the cheap little scrubber she is."

The other laughs mirthlessly. "Not cheap, Jude; never that..."

This two-way conversation's getting on my wick. "Look, what gives round here? I'm a working-girl earning an honest shekel and I don't go for this strong-arm stuff."

"An honest shekel?" Barjoseph's double has a more urbane manner than his colleague. "Honest, maybe, but hardly honourable. I've a dossier on your activities, young woman. This morning you stood trial for promiscuity with enemy Aliens and were acquitted through intervention. We intend to set the record straight and drum you out of business once and for all."

"Who – who are you?"

"We are patriots. It is our task to eliminate collaborators like yourself in preparation for our Leader's triumph."

What price the vigilantes now? These resistance-fighters are infinitely worse – urban guerrillas operating outside the law.

"Are you Zealots?"

"The Party has no name other than what the Romans elect to call us, no entrance-fee or rites of initiation. Its members qualify by their deeds. Jude, who inveigled you here, is of the Siccarioth – you'll identify the trade he follows by his weapon. Show her, Jude."

The other, grinning unpleasantly, plunges a hand under his cloak and drags out a cut-throat razor, flicking its blade back with a dexterous thumb. A dagger-man! The breed, which makes a habit of stabbing its victims in crowded places then joining in the search for their murderers, like other honest citizens. Am I to be notched on its handle as next in line? Now that my sight is adjusted to the half-light, he appears still less savoury: a caricature of villainy, scarred like a fighting-dog, with blackened teeth and the vein-patched skin of a drunkard. Nevertheless he's an oil-painting compared to the third man, on the bed, whose semi-imbecile leer widens his mouth yet doesn't reach the pale, unblinking eyes. There's something of the wild beast about him...

"Ah, you'd like an introduction to Yeshua Barabbas?

Unfortunately he cannot speak for himself. The Romans saw fit to tear out his tongue for sedition. His whole existence is dedicated to taking vengeance upon the national enemy."

I play for time. "Is he the – leader you mentioned?"

"Far from it. The one we serve is not an undercover agent like ourselves."

His choice of words prompts a fresh fear. "You aren't working for Antipas, by any chance?"

He laughs grimly. "Of course not. We consider that degenerate as much a usurper as Pilatus. No, our leader is a trueborn Jew who preaches openly, winning converts to the cause. His methods are dissimilar to ours yet his goal is the same: to shake off foreign tyranny and redeem Israel. He is to be the nation's saviour."

"Harming a two-bit tart won't do much to redeem Israel."

"You sell yourself short. You're an educated, upper class Jewish girl who should know better than to prostitute her race and religion. You need to be taught a lesson. Jude is all for 'rubbing you out' as he puts it in his regrettable argot. Luckily for you, I exert some little influence over him and I feel it will be sufficient to – impair your very evident beauty."

I recoil like a creature at bay, my eyes on the open razor. Jude has been swigging from a greasy tumbler during our exchange and his hand is none too steady. Do they mean to cut me up? The man called Si smiles coldly at my reaction. "There'll be no pain – apart from injured vanity. Jude's going to play the barber. He'll divest you of those colourful locks, which have snared so many men. In future you'll have to earn your living by different means of enticement."

It's a cat and mouse game. Three cats to one mouse. Jude shows no hurry to begin his unaccustomed labours, bloodshot gaze relishing my helplessness. No doubt they imagine I'm paralysed by dread but this is a re-run of my sparring-match with Herod (though the odds against me are far greater) and past experience steadies my nerves. The door-bolts weren't shot home after our entry, a point I didn't fail to observe, and my fingers grope for the handle behind my back as I cringe in feigned terror of the blade.

"I'll shave you to the bone, Milady," Jude rasps. "A cropped head is the treatment prescribed for dirty little traitors…"

The latch gives, soundlessly. I yank open the door and dash out into the night, followed by a stream of oaths. This is a thieves' quarter to judge by its seclusion and secretive atmosphere – if they come after me, there'll be no questions asked, no Cass marching to my rescue. Don't fool yourself that you're clear, Miri. Just keep running! Already footsteps pound behind me and I register the dot-and-carry-one of the swine that lured me to his lair. Thank God the others aren't abetting him in the chase. I'm fast on my feet – was able to outstrip Jo and Jim in the old days – and I stand a good chance against crippled Jude. At least I'll give him a run for his money, the money he owes me and hasn't paid. Problem is – where do I go from here? I've no bolthole, no pal from whom to beg refuge. It's past curfew, the streets are empty of townsfolk and any watchman I might pass would probably assume I'm a wife running from her lawful husband. He'd raise no hand to help me in a world where man is master!

My initial luck deserts me. Rounding a blind corner, I trip over a loose cobble and stagger. He's on me like a starved wolf. Flashbacks to Herod's slavering grin and Sue's sadistic killer pass before my inner eye. My life, but his arms are strong - for all his legs' imbalance.

"I hired you for a whore," he hisses on a gust of foul breath, "and I'm going to have you for one – gratis."

I should have reckoned on this, once chance went his way. Hate and desire go hand in hand with such guys: sexual assault can satisfy both. Yet I wasn't bluffing when I told Sue I could fend off unwelcome passes. A vicious knee up the crotch doubles him, and his fertile repertoire of obscenities. The face raised once more to mine is a devil's-mask: fury goaded by frustrated lust. I know – who better? – That explosive mixture's potential, and I'm not hanging around to offer first aid!

. I maintain a steady distance between my pursuer and myself but I can't shake him off. His uneven tread has a sinister, relentless ring. The City's a giant snare, its outer walls hemming me in; I must get out of it into the open where I can hide up from Jude and his razor – for nothing short of slitting my throat will satisfy him now. Yet every gate will be shut and guarded. Clear your mind, Miri, stay cool… There is one-way out: you learned about it as a child, studying Scripture. Hezekiah's tunnel! Remember how the king commanded that the spring of Gihon beyond the eastern battlements be shut off from the Assyrian besiegers and its waters channelled underground to feed Siloam's reservoir inside the City? That's my escape-route, my sole hope. I veer southward, following the course of the Cheese makers' Valley, which separates the twin hills of Zion. Crossing one of its viaducts, I make for the terraced slope leading to Siloam at the southern tip of David's abandoned city. If I can cover the remaining distance before my wind gives out, I'll have a definite advantage. Not only will Jude find the pool's stepped descent a problem but also its high-water mark during this rainy season will favour me. I swim like a fish as any of my lakeside friends could tell you and I doubt whether he can swim at all with his gammy leg.

A waning moon gleams faintly on the water's surface and reveals the ragged opening through which spring-currents flow beneath the Kidron Valley and the City-wall. Midnight bathing has no dread for me; to breast the Lake's swell in darkness used to be a thrill. Wading through a subterranean passage is a different matter. I loathe feeling closed in and I've no means of guessing the clearance between its ceiling and the water-level. Drowning, however, might prove a welcome alternative to facing Jude... I stumble down the spiral staircase carved into the pool's side then lower myself into the drink. Moishe, but it's cold! I'm well out of my depth and already having to swim as I steer for the tunnel's aperture. High above, my would-be captor leans over the parapet and swears like a trooper. I shan't wait to find out whether he means to follow. I take a deep breath and plunge into the unknown. If I fail, my corpse will be discovered tomorrow floating in the reservoir – by no means the first – and those who witnessed my disgrace will assume suicide. Well, it's all but come to that.

My feet touch bottom, my head's clear of the vault so far. It's easier to swim against the current than to tread bottom: swifter, too. The tunnel curves in on itself, I reckon, winding northward, parallel to the eastern wall, before twisting out to Gihon. As I fight for energy, I think of Hezekiah's work force quarrying against time, one group starting from either end – and the dramatic moment when each heard the other's voices through the partition that divided them. Their digging once saved the City; tonight it's saving a single, useless life – so, long as I'm able to hold out... The journey seems endless; the tidal pressure a living enemy sapping my reserves. Yet at last I'm sobbing and panting my way towards a greyness, which heralds the end of this ordeal. I emerge under a star-strewn sky whose spacious canopy has never appeared so blessed to me, and then lie, inert, on a grassy bank.

I mustn't rest here, ripe for the taking like those quails that drop exhausted after long flight. I drag myself to my feet, my eyes on the tunnel's mouth. One minute, two – no sign of Jude. Has he abandoned the chase? Instant relief gives way to sober reflection as I review my options. This reprieve is temporary: by daylight he or his cronies will be on the lookout once more, searching the neighbourhood. I can't elude them forever unless I put sufficient distance between us. Yet to travel east or north would be to risk Herod's patrols, not to mention the random chance of highway bandits, while the south is aswarm with warring Arabs. I feel totally alone in an inimical world, banished from my own kind and the prey of those that wish me ill. Suddenly the spirit drains out of me; I throw myself down again on the turf and sob my heart out like a small, distressed child. I want to come in out of the cold, to forget and start over as if all this had never happened.

Bethaniah. I'm within two miles of home. I'd sworn never to go back and eat humble pie, yet no alternative lies open for me. I pull myself up, my drenched garments swathing numbed limbs, and climb Olivet's slope. I know this path well by day since it leads from the city to my village, winding through a plantation of olive-trees whose knotted boles and dusty leafage shelter an oil-press. This is a kind of pastoral oasis on the flank of an arid hill and, as a child; I'd stroll here to enjoy its gentle serenity. Lying beneath the boughs, I learned to escape from time into a private universe beyond the reach of the senses, a nothingness richer than my everyday experiences, and when I got home, Mart would rebuke me for long absence. By night, its enclosed garden has an altered look: the twisted branches seem to writhe in torment, the roots stretch out to trip me and a stored menace in the air oppresses one's soul. I feel an impulse to pray for deliverance from my inner devils – but I've lost the habit and words refuse to come.

I top the Mount of Olives and gaze down towards Bethphage and Bethaniah laid out before my eyes in a ghostly pallor. Here's a hint of dawn not far distant over the horizon, the sudden, fierce dawn of the south, which spreads like lava across Moab and strikes sparks from the Temple's golden minarets. The darkness, while it lasts, is better suited to my furtive, inglorious homecoming – a stray harried by wolves, seeking shelter in the fold. I'm trembling from exposure, my body one huge ache. As I approach our house set snugly into the hillside, its pale face and shuttered windows swim before my vision. Physical and mental stress has pushed me to breaking point and I just can't take any more. I feel myself falling – falling.

Consciousness creeps back on leaden feet. My eyes open to a setting that's ingrained on memory yet curiously remote: the four walls of my little bedroom, its roughcast ceiling with the stain shaped like a magnified spider in one corner, the table at which I toiled and dreamed as a child. An oil-lamp, perched on it, gives wan illumination via a flame dimmed by the morning light streaming between the slats of the closed shutters. I'm blissfully warm, wrapped in a dry tunic under the patchwork coverlet whose fringe I used to suck for comfort. I'm tempted to do so now!

At this merciful interlude my mind's vacant, a slate wiped clean, then the trauma of recent events begins to return, driving out lassitude. Past merges with present. Somehow I've recrossed the divide separating me from my early youth, yet a part of my brain clings obstinately to the pains and frustrations it's endured since then. Even the sameness of this room fails to reassure me; it's one made over to the dead, a memorial of the girl who once inhabited it yet is no more. Only my state of utter collapse gained me entry, I'm convinced of that. Had I announced myself boldly, Mart would've sent me packing. I won't have her grudged pity, the cold charity of an upright woman, nor wait for 'I told you so' on her tight lips. I'll get up, though my legs feel like water, unclose the shutters and slip away by the escape-route I so often took in former days to avoid her bullying. I'm all but gone when the door opens and she's standing in front of me, hands on hips.

"Unwilling to face the music, Miriam?" she says harshly. "Reluctant to listen to a few home-truths? You were always one for skiving out of trouble, weren't you? Yet now that you've brought it down on your silly head, you crawl back snivelling to big brother and sister. You abandoned us in Galil without a word, lived on immoral earnings and heaped disgrace on your family – yet you'd like us to pretend it never happened. Well, you've another think coming!"

In my heart of hearts I'd expected no less. I tell myself that she's a caring sister, her anger is justified and others will say the same – but if only she'd show one spark of sibling sympathy, I'd be thanking her for taking me in and saying sorry as best I can. Instead, I feel childhood's mutiny seethe inside me and wish I'd been more spry in my efforts to get away. Some sister!

"If you feel like that, why didn't you leave me to die of pneumonia on the doorstep?"

"Stop dramatizing yourself. I should've left you for my own part but I was overruled."

"By Laz, I suppose?"

"Yes, by your tender-hearted brother – and the rest."

"The rest?"

"The Master and his followers. They're downstairs preparing for their return to Galil. We make our home available to him when he's in Judaea. It's the least we can do…" The line of her eyebrows, almost meeting across her high-bridged nose, softens and a kind of pious rapture chases the anger from her face. My resentment swells. She slags me off for my misdeeds yet reveres the man who brought about my downfall. The walls and flooring of our house are solid stone, hacked out of the hollow in which it nestles, and sounds don't carry well – but I can register a distant hum of conversation. I'm determined not to stick around where I'm no longer welcome but a part of me longs to give Laz a hug and a whispered apology, another part can't face the future without one last sight of Jo, for all my resolution.

I push past her to the landing and shakily descend the stairs. Faces look up from below: dear Laz leaning beside the hearth, no better to judge by his unhealthy pallor, Jo's blue eyes wincing away from mine, Jim, Simon and his bro Andy, others less familiar – while Superstar sits like an uncrowned king in their midst. Confused by numbers, I hesitate for a second then jump the last three steps and run over to my brother. He's all I have left and he holds out his arms to me as I knew he would. I kiss his tremulous mouth, watch the blue veins throbbing at his temple with a catch at my heart.

"How are you, Laz?"

He strokes my hair with a hand through which daylight seems to shine. "Not so good, Miri. Better for seeing you again…"

"Your going nearly killed him." Mart's raised voice from the landing. "Each time we got news of your latest escapade it set him back. If he never recovers, it'll have been your fault."

Reluctantly I withdraw from his arms. Happiness is outside my scheme of things, a mirage. I thought I possessed it once, gazing across the Lake at early morning or folded in Jo's embrace, yet now I'm sure it can't be found, not in the brutal, teeming City, not in the courts of princes – nor here among strangers devoted to an ideal I can't share. Their eyes are still on me as I turn to leave. I read compassion in them. Give me Mart's strident condemnation any day! It scalds me, a surface irritant, but pity burns like acid deep into my soul. One gaze alone ignores me; Barjoseph looks away, expressionless. Some entity within fathers malignant bile and goads me with its many tongues. This is the guy who bust you wide open (they tell me), the slob who stole your chance of happiness. Look at him sitting there, so smug and self-possessed! He turns away because your plight means nothing to him. Now's your moment! Give it him hot and strong; you won't dent his armour of complacency but you'll do yourself – and us – a power of good.

The voices take over mine and I hear myself scream, "Give me back Jo, you son of an unwed bitch! If you can work wonders, undo the damage you've done and make us what we used to be to each other."

You could cut the silence with a knife. Not one of these zombies would address their 'Master' as I've just done. Mart, who's followed me downstairs, grates, "I said we should leave her outside, the foul-mouthed little whore. She's past redeeming." Grasping me by the shoulder, she steers me to the door.

"Lay off me," my demons shout. "I'll go of my own accord, D'you think I'll stick around with a crowd of pious freaks? I'd sooner take my chances against threats and knives in the big bad world... All right, so I'm a whore. I like sex, I like men with what it takes, Alien or otherwise, and I give 'em all I've got. I'd not swap that for your narrow, dried-up existence, Mart, pinning your hang-ups on this phoney mashiah. It's your body, not your soul, that aches for his healing touch – but there's nothing doing in that direction, sister mine, 'cos he's a raving queer."

The filth pours out of me. Deep down my real voice pleads, "It isn't me speaking. For God's sake believe that..." Yet it can't reach my throat.

"She's possessed – Miriam's possessed!" Mart hisses, scrambling over the floor and kneeling before Barjoseph. "Master, you have the power to drive out demons. Won't you free this wretched child as you freed the lunatic at Gerash?"

His eyes rest on me now, pensive yet not stern. How grey and still they are – like the Lake at first light. He says quietly, "Unless you will me to cure you, Miriam, I can't act."

The voices answer for me. "Spare us your party-tricks, if you're not a charlatan, then you must be in league with Beelzebub himself."

He smiles. "Would Beelzebub cast out his own kind? It's a contradiction in terms. You'll have to do better than that." Is he talking to me or the trespassers inside me?

"Think yourself bloody clever, don't you, Yeshua Barjoseph?" they chorus. "You don't fool us. Keep your witch doctoring for the simple-minded. Miriam knows another sort of magic – and it's stronger than yours." My hands go to the neck of my tunic as if impelled from within; they draw it down, baring my boobs in sensual invitation. "Well, Carpenter, how do these grab you? You call yourself God's son but stroke this warm, sweet flesh and confess you're no more than a man."

"Again you contradict yourselves. You accused me of perversion yet tempt me with a woman's beauty. Back off, you infernal tribe. I want to speak to the girl alone."

His tone of quiet command subdues the force inside me. My arms are freed from its control and hastily I pull up my collar, feeling blood rush to my cheeks. (It's long since I've known that kind of shame!) Not for a moment has his gaze wavered from my face. He says gently, "You're filled with bitter grievance towards me, Miri, because I've deprived you of your lover. A human and perfectly understandable reaction. By giving yourself over to evil, however, you've made room for my enemies within you. I can expel them if that's what you really want, yet it means that your whole life will be reversed. Your love for Jo won't vanish but it'll become selfless, no longer carnal, and merge with his in a yearning that's far deeper."

His echo of the Baptist's words reminds me of a promise made in that joyless dungeon cell. I'd dismissed it at the time as sentimental pap, a consolation-prize for a disappointed child, yet now its meaning bursts on me with an overwhelming impact. The sense of where I am deserts me, and I'm aware only of this man whose eyes caress with an infinite tenderness.

"Earthly attachment must surrender to my demands. You see, Miri, I want you also to be mine…"

The beast inside me struggles back to life, savage with hate – and fear. I must fight it on my own. By a supreme effort I retain mastery of my voice: "Heal me, Yeshua, please heal me. Drive out my devils and take me to yourself."

He lifts his right hand and his lips move in prayer. A sudden anguish stabs me like a mortal wound and I fall at his feet, my hair overspreading them in a crimson haze.

"Miriam, be cured."

Jo once proposed that I should join him and his fellows in the service of their idol. His wish has been granted. I'm in love through every fibre of my being with Yeshua, son of Joseph.

SIX

An hour later we set out for the north. I'm still groggy from the strain of my get-away and I'd have liked nothing better than to rest up, hugging this wonderful secret, yet I know Yeshua will be safer in Galil while Antipas stays south with his network of spies. I shall keep my thoughts to myself on the journey; avoid making this absurd infatuation too obvious until I've adjusted to what's happened. I'm confused, you see; apart from my fixation, I don't feel any different inside. I've not gone all-pure and holy as he probably supposes – nor do I regret the sins I've committed in the past. Worse, I can't make myself credit his claim to be the Chosen One of Israel. Oh, they all fancy he's worked one of his miracles and made a convert out of Miri (Jo is tremendously bucked) but the truth is I've simply fallen for Yeshua the man, well, love is a kind of miracle, isn't it?

Laz and Mart are staying in Bethaniah. He's too ill for travelling and she's simmering with rage at yours truly – imagines I'm playing up her precious Master and posing as a reformed character in order to ingratiate myself, even though she herself pleaded for my cure! How long will it be before she comes after us to check that I'm behaving myself? It's odd that I should feel the very lech I accused her of, yet I won't disguise it under a cloak of piety. That's one gain from hitting rock bottom; I'm no hypocrite. My acquaintance with Eleazar and Benesdra has taught me to mistrust the species. Mind you, they're only two out of a Pharisaic bunch. As we trudge the road to Yericho, the Holy Joes dog our footsteps, sniping at Yeshua and trying to score points off him.

Not all the Hasidim are two-faced, to be fair. They number the best as well as the basest in their ranks. They say the Master Hillel teaches an honest doctrine and Jo tells me there are those in the Knesset who support Yeshua, though not openly, preferring to keep a foot in both camps. It may be one of this sort who persuades him to pause then asks him the secret of eternal life. A leading question!

"Observe the rules my Poppa gave Moishe," replies Yeshua.

"I do so," says the other. "I don't tell lies or steal or kill. I honour my parents and I'm no adulterer."

"Forget the don'ts – they're all implicit in the do's. Love God with all your heart and soul. Love your neighbour as yourself. These are the whole of the Law."

"If I didn't love god, I'd hardly bother to respect his prohibitions. Yet who precisely is my neighbour?"

"I'll answer your question with a story." Yeshua glances round him as if seeking inspiration from the view. It's a pretty restricted one. On either side of us tower overhanging cliffs, which squeeze the sky above to a pale blue ribbon. This is a dangerous route to travel alone, a favourite haunt of muggers and fanatics who hide behind the rock-spurs at hairpin bends then ambush the unwary.

"There was once a guy who took this very road," he begins. "He was an Essene, one of those who pray and fast in expectation of the Mashiah's coming. Little did he know it, but a robber was skulking in a crevice ahead of him on the lookout for prey. The robber identified his victim by his costly robe of white linen and jumped him as he rounded a corner. He clubbed him down, snatched the garment and took off, leaving him unconscious."

We all nod wisely. It's a realistic scenario: 'robber' is a common term for Zealot and the latter are at constant war with Essenes, the brotherhood to which Johanan belonged. This reminder of my own treatment at the hands of Jude and Si isn't a pleasant one...

"Nobody passed for a while, then along came a Levite followed by a Sadducee, both stuffed to the gills with every axiom of the Torah, you may be sure. The man was bleeding and to touch another's blood would contaminate them – besides, he wasn't one of their lot and they had business-matters to attend to in Yericho, which couldn't be delayed. So they passed on, leaving him to the flies. Finally a Samaritan came by – one of your crossbreeds and heretics. There's less love lost between Jews and Samaritans than between robbers and Essenes, as you all know, yet he gave the guy first aid, then carried him over his saddle to the nearest khan where he paid for him to be nursed back to health." Yeshua pauses, "Have you grasped my moral, friend?"

The questioner looks thoughtful, then nods, thanks Yeshua and turns back to the City. Others, including Simon Barjonah, are less satisfied. He remarks, "I don't get it, Master. The first two were in the right, surely? As for the Samaritan bloke, he'd no respect for our customs. They're ignorant outlaws, as you said. So where's the pay-off?"

Yeshua sighs and shrugs his wide shoulders. His luminous eyes search the bewildered faces and fasten on mine. "Will you make my meaning clear to this thickhead, Miri?"

Taken by surprise, I venture, "Aren't you telling us that human love has no boundaries, Yeshua, and that it should outweigh sectarian prejudice? All men are our neighbours, Jew or Gentile, and all are equal in Yahweh's sight."

"Well said, my dear. Our newest recruit passes with flying colours."

A Set-apart peers at me malevolently. "Don't I know that face? I could've sworn..." He leans forward from his steed and twitches off my headscarf. "Ah, I thought as much. You're the bawd whose skin was saved yesterday by this fast-talking seditionary. He's taken you under his wing, has he? Come on, the rest of you; let's get back to the City and spread it round that the Nazrene consorts with an adulteress. We know now why he wanted her preserved from the stoning she merited!"

Susannah's reason for leaving Yeshua with all its tragic consequences comes back to me. Mud clings... As the dust of their hooves swirls in the distance, I've an impulse to pursue them – make the break while I still have strength of will, but his arm restrains me. "Will you be off just as we've made friends, Miri?" Already he's adopted the diminutive used by Jo and those who know me well. He goes on, "It's not my way to choose the company of saints. Take a look at this shower: Matt who used to line his own pockets by screwing money out of the poor, Nathaniel who was tempted to go in for drug-dealing on a big scale – and the rest who are far from redeemed characters."

His description doesn't go down too well. "We don't claim to be anything special," protests Simon, "but we've given up our livelihood to follow you, Master, I've got a missus who gives me hell for neglecting her, and the others 've jacked in their chance of marriage for your sake. This girl's a self-confessed hooker. We all know her career – the whole flamin' nation knows it – how she had it off with high and low. Swanned round in palaces, made eyes at Antipas, shacked up with his legionaries... I admit we're all sinners, like, but it ain't fair to put us on a level with her."

"So you think we ought to ditch her, Rock?"

Yeshua employs fun-names for his mates. He calls Jo and Jim the Sons of Thunder because of their explosive poppa. Why has Simon become Rock? P'raps because he's solid bone between the ears! He's certainly built like one, massive and broad in the beam with a wind-beaten face. Yet for all his bulk, he's an overgrown baby inside, soft at the centre – all mouth and no guts, I'd reckon.

He says, "Ditch 'er? I didn't say that Master. We know you've come to save sinners, you've told us often enough. It's just that her kind of sinning is worse than ours."

"Worse than stealing or making profits from the weakness of others – worse than all the petty selfishness that most of us practise every day of our lives? Worse than spiritual pride, which seems to be your chief defect at the minute, Rock? You and I have put our indulgences aside simply because our work requires us to be free of domestic ties – and other diversions. Physical passion is no crime in itself: on the contrary, it's the fullest and most normal expression of man's capacity to love. Jo will recall how much his sweetheart meant to him before he came on a love that went beyond theirs. As for Miri, she felt she'd been robbed of something, which was good – a perfect relationship. She set out, therefore, to destroy every trace of goodness that remained in her, as if it were a poison in the blood. She wanted to prove to herself that evil is the only reality. Yet there are grades of wickedness, as you say, Rock: the wronghood of those who proclaim their own virtue while exercising every vice under the sun is far greater than a childish perversity aiming to get its own back on the one who let it down. This was the real extent of Miri's fault, and the means she adopted were also childish. But the danger of playing with fire is that you're liable to get burnt. Those who learn to live by the flesh rarely succeed in rising above it. Luckily, she's never lost her faculty for love, giving more than just her body… She'll come to see that sex isn't the only way of reaching out to others, and that the love of the spirit can bring richer rewards."

He's answering Rock while addressing me, almost as though he'd known my mind's working from the start! It disconcerts, to say the least – but he's wrong about that last bit. Does he suppose I've turned into an angel overnight? I'm still a creature of this world, not the next – so help me, God – and I've got him well within my sights. His touching faith in my 'better self' only adds to his attraction. Idealists are so naïve! It's high time I took a part in this dialogue; while the rest squabble about which of them has given up most to follow Yeshua, I shnuk up to his side.

"Why did you pick on me to explain your story, Yeshua?"

"Because you yourself have experienced what it is to be rejected, Miri."

"Yet I know nothing of your teaching."

"You're closer to its essence than most of the scholars who strain their eyes over sacred texts. My Poppa reveals to children what he keeps hidden from the worldly-wise."

"I'm not a child. I may've acted like a spoilt brat in the past but I've grown up since." It's difficult even to hint at what I long to tell him. "I – I'm sorry about those ghastly things I said last night. It wasn't really me speaking."

"I know, Miri."

"But it's true I did believe you must be, well, kinky – unmarried and surrounded by men-friends. That's how stupid I've been! I see now that you're not a bit like that – you're one helluva of a guy whom any girl would go for…"

"Thanks." He turns his head to smile at me with that roguish afterglow in his grey eyes. Breathtaking. How could I ever have thought him sexless, unappealing? He's no Greek god, that's for sure, yet he has the kind of face, which grows on one. Especially when he smiles like this or when he's telling stories. Then it's like a lantern lighting up shadows, joy shining through sadness. Yes, I can sense sadness about him as though he sometimes doubts the success of his mission or maybe the role for which he's cast himself. Look at the way his tale of the Samaritan was misunderstood.

"When you spin yarns, Yeshua, do they just come to you out of the blue or are they thought out beforehand?" Anything to keep his attention on me…

"I decide on the point I want to make then let the details grow out of what I see around me or what happens to be floating through my mind."

"Why did you pick on the Zealots, in particular?"

"I was thinking of what brought you to Bethaniah, Miri. You know, that thieves' kitchen and the guy who meant to lop off your lovely hair."

I draw in my breath sharply. How in God's name can he…? Wait, maybe I gave away something while dead to the world: delirium, they call it. I mustn't allow myself to be fooled by his telepathic act the way Sue was. It's a man I'm going for – not some psychic mind reader.

"Speaking of which," he adds casually, "you've no need to replace your headscarf. It deprives us of the pleasure of admiring your chief adornment."

"Only loose women go bare-headed. I – I didn't want to show you up in front of strangers."

"Frankly I don't give a damn for social niceties. Life's too short. It cheers me to see those flame-red tresses, my Poppa's gift. Besides, you'll be a live advertisement for my campaign against discrimination."

Obediently I remove Joanna's veil and shake my head free to scatter the long strands becomingly - a gesture that used to irritate Mart. She'd have preferred it cut short or braided into plaits, but then she always envied me my 'crowning glory'. To my astonishment and delight, Yeshua puts out his hand and strokes its waved locks spontaneously, an action forbidden to one who's neither related nor affianced. His poppa's gift they may be – but they're mine and I'll most willingly make them over to him if he'll have me.

We reach Yericho by nightfall. Twenty miles on Shanks's pony: quite a haul, but I've stood up to it well, a fact the rest acknowledge as they begin to accept me. It's my new love that's kept me going, I'm certain of it, plus getting away from Judaea with its associations. This place, where all roads meet, is merely a stage on our longer journey but a nice one to rest up at. Fed by an underground spring which never runs dry, it's a lush green oasis the year round and its date-palms are out of this world – they make wine that has a kick like a stallion and even knocks Cass back. The town itself is the usual oh-so-boring imitation of Rome, built by Herod's poppa (I prefer the nearby ruins blasted by our ancestors' trumpets). Yericho is the lowest-lying town on God's earth and its heat is stifling, so we climb a fair way up the mini-mountain to its west in order to sleep cooler tonight. No putting up at roadside khans, you'll notice; we're a Romany lot and we camp out in the open under the stars. I'm glad. I hate being enclosed, as you know, and there's no risk with eleven hunks to shield me from prowlers on two feet or four. Mind you, I could do with just the one. Patience, Miri… We've bought grub with the cash subbed up by casual well-wishers and a fire is lit to broil the river-fish (we're no distance from Jordan which winds like a silver snake to our east and below). The mullet, with slabs of barley bread and date-wine to wash it down, tastes delicious after our long, hungry trek.

Food and drink, specially the last, loosen tongues as we relax our limbs. I get to know some of my comrades on a friendlier basis. Their turn of speech is as diverse as their backgrounds: from Jo and Jim's educated refinement to Rock and Andy's native roughness. Matt, the tax collector, seems the odd one out. He's older than the rest with the flabby look of a fat man who's thinned down. No doubt he lived like a lord in his affluent days, taking bribes from the rich to reduce their taxes while making up the shortfall by stinging the poor. It's a dirty trade. He tells me he went out one day to scoff at the wandering Nazirite and something Yeshua said about a camel and a needle's eye got to him. There and then he sold all his assets and, being a childless widower, obeyed the Master's call. Sounds a bit far-fetched to me; more probably he got fed up with being treated like dirt – publicans are detested as the agents of Rome – and decided to score off his critics by turning over a new leaf. Having spent half lifetime bookkeeping, he's a compulsive scribbler: jots down every word and act of Yeshua's with a view to becoming his chronicler. Hopes, maybe, to recoup his losses with the copyright, slight as that hope might be… This annoys Jo who claims that Matt is illiterate and one day he'll write the definitive account, from memory!

Nat Bartolmai tells a different tale. It seems that in his younger days he was all but roped into some drug-distribution racket (Sue's decline and death may've been partly down to it) and he spent a morning wrestling with his conscience in the shade of a fig tree. Along came Phil, whom he'd known in Galil, saying he'd found the Mashiah and that Nat should get in on the act. Nat was sceptical but he went with his pal and Yeshua behaved just as if he'd been expecting him. You don't know me, Nat said. Oh but I do, answered Jeshua, I saw you sitting under the fig tree. The way he said it made Nat realize he'd also sussed out what was in his mind at the time, hovering between right and wrongdoing; from that moment he'd no more doubts and chucked in his lot with Yeshua. Another case of falling for a rather obvious trick, I'd say, since his background could easily have been checked. The fact is these guys wanted to believe, they'd reached some crisis in their lives and needed a ready-made solution.

Then there's Tom, a dour, down to earth type who's very loyal to Yeshua yet doesn't rant about him the way his pals do. He's a man of few words altogether and his dialect's so broad that I've learnt little about him from his own lips. That goes for a couple more characters as well: Jude and James whose momma (same name as mine) is some relation of Yeshua's family. Which leaves the Sons of Thunder – one of whom I know only too well – plus Rock and Andy. The former has apologised for his rudeness to me, by the way, admitting that he tends to run off at the mouth. He's a decent sort at heart, I suspect, though very full of himself, as if he'd earned senior status among Yeshua's troop and had some right to speak for the others. Yet after all he's only a rough fisherman who latched on to Yeshua because of an unlikely 'happening', which he loves to repeat.

"Told us to let down our nets, he did," I hear for the third time in one day. "The night had been stormy, we'd caught bugger-all and by dawn we'd jacked it in. He made us row out to deeper water. We were using a dragnet, two blokes in each boat working the cables. Fish swim through the wider meshes on the outside and get trapped by the narrow ones at the centre; leastways that's the idea. Well, we'd nothing to lose so we did as he said – and fuck me if both boats didn't go half-seas over with the weight of our haul. It was all hands to the ropes and once we'd shipped our catch, we was up to the gunnels in mullet. Catfish, carp and grayling – every blessed species spawning in the Lake. Shook me up, I can tell you. I'd had no truck with Godliness to speak of and I wasn't the sort miracles happen to. I said leave me, Master, I'm a sinner, but he told me and Andy he'd make us fishers of men or some such and we found ourselves following him like sheep."

"Didn't I see the pair of you in the desert the day Johanan the Baptist pointed Yeshua out?"

"Yeah, we'd gone south for the summer festival same as others and Jo took us out to hear him for ourselves. We stuck around a space – but the Baptist never pulled a stunt like that. We went back to our trade up north till the Master started teaching at Capernaum and begged the loan of our boat 'cos the crowds were pressing on him. That's when he did our happening. I hadn't reckoned much to him – but I'm a fisherman born and bred. I know the Lake like the back of my hand, I've fished it all my life and when the impossible happened, well, it knocked me all ends up. He did it special for us, you see."

Some miracle! Everyone knows that a lake-storm churns up the surface water and sends the fish down to deeper levels where it's calm. They must have anchored above a shoal and scooped the jackpot. Coincidence playing into Yeshua's hands the way it did at Kana. It's hard for me to go on thinking of him as a con-artist, given my emotional commitment; let's say he's fooling himself and misleading others in the process...

As we sit round the dying embers with daylight fading into dusk, he chats to his oddly assorted crew about their immediate future. "As I've already mentioned," he says, "I'm going to send you out in pairs to spread my teaching and healing. I shan't be with you for very much longer, and you must learn to go it alone."

"But we'll make a pig's ear of it without you at our side," Phil protests. "We can't put things across the way you do, Master, and we've no hope of winning the crowds over by working wonders."

"My Poppa will give you guidance, Phil, and the Spirit we share will strengthen your hearts. You may take that for granted. What's more, I want you to take no cash and no extras. Folk must see for themselves that you live by the precepts of poverty and trust in providence. The well disposed will subsidize you and listen to your message; turn your backs on the rest and leave them to stew in their own juice. Does that meet with your approval?"

It doesn't, apparently. It's one thing to trail in Yeshua's wake gaining kudos from his leadership, quite another to evangelise without his support. The jolly voices go quiet. Rock tries a different tack: "We can't just – desert you, Master, You've made enemies among them Set-aparts who'll likely do you a mischief if we're not around." He flings back his cape with a theatrical gesture and grips the pommel of a rusty sword stuck in his belt – at which his mates chuckle. "You can laugh but when the chips are down, this'll come in mighty useful. You'll thank me for being prepared,"

"Those who live by the sword will die by it," Yeshua comments dryly. "Keep your blade for scaling fish, my old friend. To raise it against another human being would be a denial of everything I stand for."

Nat interposes: "Nobody's going to lay hands on the Master, Rock. Why should they? You're being melodramatic as usual. All the same, someone has to see to his needs."

"What needs, Nat?" Yeshua asks. "Foxes have holes and birds have nests but the Son of Man has nowhere to lay his head." A rueful note. Is he thinking of that arch-fox Antipas whose agents are a greater threat to his safety than any Set-apart? He continues, "Don't worry. I've Miri to look after me now. A woman's touch will be welcome for a change."

I can't conceal my glee. What a break to have him entirely to myself. A woman's touch. That's what's needed to dispel his delusions of grandeur and remind him that he's flesh and blood.

Tom's slow wits are still wrestling with his previous remark. "If you don't approve of strong-arm tactics, Master, how come Jude's one of us? No, not you, son: the other Jude who's hanging round the City with Si. He's a right yobbo..."

"I didn't choose my helpers, Tom. My Poppa chose them for me. Each of you has a part to play in his scheme of salvation, whether good or bad."

"Then why aren't they with us at this moment?"

"You know the answer. When I first stated my purpose of sending you all out into the field, they opted to do their stint in Judaea."

"And you told them yes because Si's your cousin."

"He's also a cultivated man and a Zealot. He can argue on the same level as others of his stamp but he'd make small headway with a rustic audience. As for Jude, he's a southerner born and bred."

I've been listening to their discussion in fascinated suspense. Things are clicking into place. I knew I'd seen that gruesome pair before – it was at the pool of Bethesda when Yeshua 'cured' the paralytic. If their lair hadn't been so gloomy, I'd've identified them properly. Si talked about their leader, I remember, yet it never struck me he could be meaning Yeshua, despite the family likeness. He's a babe in arms where those two are concerned and can't have an earthly idea what they're up to… This puts my prospects into a fresh, and far from reassuring, light. I've no desire to meet up with either of them again as members of his squad!

The thought keeps me wakeful and restless long after we've all dossed down on the hillside. Around me sleeping figures lie humped under their spread capes, still as boulders – though I sense that one is awake, and feel the vibes of his awareness. I close my eyes and will myself to drop off but as always, the effort defeats its own purpose. The beat of pursuing footsteps marches across my brain and a razor-blade flashes on and off beneath my shut eyelids. I open them – to see a tall silhouette leaning over me.

"Sleep seems to elude us both, Miri." Yeshua's voice quells my momentary dread. "Let's take a stroll away from the others."

I scramble to my feet and walk beside him round the mountain's flank, noticing little things: the way my head reaches exactly to his shoulder-level, our steps in unison on the uneven ground, the warmth of his arm encircling my waist. Its contact pulses through my body down to its secret places and every instinct in me cries out, "Love me, Yeshua, forget your stupid vow and take me, make me one with yourself. We'll find sleep in each other's arms." I nestle closer, willing him to respond.

He murmurs, "Miri, I did a botched job on you, didn't I?"

"What d'you mean?"

"I left one small imp to prick your flesh and blind you to my true nature."

"You made me fall for you in a big way, Yeshua. My love for Jo was nothing to what I'm feeling now."

"That's merely a transference. Love on the rebound. I want the whole of your heart, Miri, but not on human terms alone. You must learn to know and love the divine in me."

Humour him, Miri! "You're expecting quite a lot from a baggage who's no better than she ought to be, aren't you? I'll love you any way you want, Yeshua, so long as you'll take me on. There, I can't say fairer than that, can I?"

"Indeed you can't." He laughs gently. "But we're talking at cross-purposes. I don't mean a physical relationship."

"What other kind is there between a man and a woman – apart from simply being bosom-pals?"

"A union of souls."

"I used to think Jo and I had that – yet it wasn't enough."

"In the normal way of things, I agree. But neither of us is – ordinary. I am who I claim to be, despite your disbelief, and you have a rare gift which at present you discount. It's God-given, like your beauty, and one day it will bring you to a truer knowledge of my nature than most achieve in a lifetime. You're a battlefield. Miri, where sceptical reason's at war with spiritual intuition."

"You've lost me there. I'm just an average female who's gone without sex too long recently and who needs to satisfy her urges." Crudely put, but true if you come to think of it; had I guessed that my last night with Cass was to round off my sex-life for an indefinite age, he'd have got darned little sleep on that barrack-roof! Now frustration's making me irritable, causing me to overplay my hand. Yeshua's not in the mood for love-games. All the same, he's not quite as naïve as I'd supposed. I've never had the brush-off applied in such complimentary terms. At least I think he meant it as a compliment...

Change the subject. "Yeshua, I'm scared."

"Scared of what, my dear?"

"Those two guys you were all talking about – your cousin and Jude. They're on my track because I've been with non-Jews."

He shows no surprise. "Yes, they've got a great deal to learn about my cause. It's a pity they missed out on my story this morning."

"The truth is I'm none too keen to see them again – not till Jude's cooled off, at any rate. Will they be staying in Judaea?

"No, they'll be coming north when the others return to base. Don't worry; I'll be there to protect you. They're under my orders."

"We can't be together all the time, Yeshua. Say they come back earlier than expected and Jude finds me on my own? He gives me the creeps – the very thought of him makes me shudder."

"You're nervous of them, Miri, and I don't blame you. Very well. What we'll do, you and I, is to go straight to Nazrat and pay Momma a visit. She can look after you while I'm out spreading the word. I'd like you to get to know each other." He pauses thoughtfully. "It may seem odd but I haven't had a crack at my home-town so far. To be honest, I've funked it. The folk there have known me all my life as the local carpenter's son. How on earth do I persuade them I'm the Mashiah, the Lord's Anointed One?"

It's like conversing with a lunatic who has snatches of sanity – or vice versa. I remark unkindly, "Specially as we're told his origin will not be of this world."

"You spoke one true word during your diatribe last night, Miri. You called my Momma 'unwed'. I've no mortal father – lend your mind to the implication of that."

I could make a snide retort but he's moved away from me further down the slope. Moonlight sheds a bluish lustre over his dark hair and outlines his still figure against the rising ground. Watching him,

I'm suddenly afraid – not the fear I have of Jude but a different and deeper sort mixed with awe. Is it a trick of the atmosphere or has he grown taller than a man should be? Involuntarily I sink to my knees, time ceasing to exist…

I wake on my own to the full light of day. I must have passed from one of my trances into sleep. The hillside is bare and when I retrace our steps, there's no sign of him or the others. A voice hails me from above; I look up and see Jo waving. So we're mountaineers now! I climb up to them. Yeshua's gone ahead and reached the summit. He doesn't glance round as we puff and pant to his side. He appears wrapped in thought – or perhaps prayer. We gaze over a vast area of prairie like a green tide sweeping outwards from the foothills below, alive with the promise of spring. On its southern horizon the City's crenellated walls and pinnacles break the skyline, and eastwards Jordan's valley is a ribbon of lush vegetation threading the barren Midbar Yehuda. It's a bird's-eye view of half the country and it gives one an exalted feeling as if one were lord of creation.

Yeshua speaks without turning. "I was brought here once by the Father of Lies. He offered me an earthly kingdom – but his price was too high."

"Was that the time you went off by yourself, Master, after Johanan had baptised you?" queries Jo.

Yeshua nods. "It was my preparation for the ministry, a wrestling-match against hunger and hardship and the onslaught of human pride."

"Surely the Mashiah has no need to overcome temptation?"

"I'm a man, Jo, never forget that. I must share the weaknesses of other men. This world is the Devil's playground and he doesn't discriminate. He started on me with the lure of physical appetite, knowing how many fall at the first fence. The pebbles at my feet could be turned into bread if I wished, he said. Then he carried me in imagination to the Temple's minaret and invited me to throw myself down to the rocks below. That was a moment of suicidal despair when it seemed to me that my calling was an illusion. Finally, he led my steps up this mountainside and showed me the panorama we're looking at now. It's yours, he told me, if you care to win it with my weapons: sword, fire and massacre. That's what Israel expects of its Mashiah and they'll follow you into battle as one man. Do it my way – or take the consequences."

"He had a point," I remark, thinking of Zealots and dagger-men and the hatred of oppressors stored up through the centuries.

"Yes, he'd held back the most persuasive temptation till the last. How many reformers have begun in a spirit of peace yet ended with bloody destruction! They turn into dictators, an embodiment of the injustice, which they set out to conquer. But there's another way. It means directing Satan's lust for murder on oneself…" His voice is almost too low to catch.

"Did you argue with him as you argued with my lot at Bethaniah?" I inquire.

"No, if he'd grasped my scheme for salvation, he'd be doing his utmost to defeat it. I told him to get lost – and he did." He looks at me. "Never reason with him, Miri; turn your back or close your ears. It's the only way."

Never reason with a madman, either, I reflect as we go down towards the vale of Yericho once more. Given his false assumption, there's a crazy logic about everything Yeshua says, which could so easily blow the mind. It's happened to others – but Miri's a tougher nut to crack than credulous fishermen and moonstruck dreamers like Jo. My ex-paramour evidently holds himself responsible for my change of heart, as he does for my behaviour. We wrangle during much of the remaining journey.

"Look, Miri," he says, drawing me apart from the rest, "I don't think you should address the Master by his first name. It's, well, disrespectful."

"He doesn't seem to mind. Why should you?"

"Because he's not like other men. He's a great teacher and wonder-worker. You can see that much for yourself even if you doubt his true identity."

"I'd sooner think of him as a friend. Yeshua's a name I like." I giggle. "I've called him far worse!"

"And how! You know, I scarcely recognized you – even your voice sounded different. Now you've gone to the opposite extreme. You're all over him, making eyes and showing off your hair."

"Jealous, lover mine?"

"Dammit, no! You mean a lot to me, Miri, but no longer in that way. If it was anyone else, I'd be glad for your sake and wish you the best of luck but flirting with him – it's like trying to seduce a – "

"A god? You're screwy, Jo Barzabdiah, know that? I should've got wise to you in the old days when you blathered about the Prince of Heaven ringed by rainbows and crystal seas. Along comes Yeshua and you unload all your fantasies on him. O.K. so he has charisma, I'll grant that, but he's a man – he told you as much himself. He's not some supernatural being who's adopted human shape to save us from our sins. If he was, I'd hardly fancy him the way I do!"

Jo's already off on one of his mind-benders, all froth and fervour. I used to adore him in this mood with his blue eyes shining and his gestures miming the pictures in his brain; I still feel a ghost of my emotion – only the ghost, mind you, because that, too, was self-induced.

He says, "You used the word I couldn't bring myself to utter. You called him God. That's it – don't you see? Our Master, yours and mine, isn't just a man created by the Almighty to redeem his people, nor some visitant from outer space. He's both: God and Man –

divinity incarnate, the Word made flesh."

"That's blasphemy, Jo, apart from being nonsense. If you'd said that in public, the Hasidim would've stoned you. God's a spirit; we're forbidden even to make an image of him."

"I don't mean the God of Abraham. I'm speaking of Yeshua, his son."

"Worse still. You know as well as I do that God is one. Only the heathen multiply their deities, worshipping their Baals and Astartes, their Jupiters and Junos."

"No, I can't explain it but there's a difference – a vital difference. The Master always talks to us about his heavenly Father as though they were one and the same being – as if they shared their thoughts and acted in unison. It's mind-boggling, I know, yet somehow it makes wonderful sense: the Creator becoming one with his creatures and leading them in person to their predestined goal."

"It's certainly true that he's on familiar terms with Yahweh. Calls him 'Poppa' – or hadn't you noticed? I'd say that justifies my using his first name. After all, it means 'he who saves'." (Chalk one up to yourself, Miri.)

As we trudge behind the troop, I glance at Jo commiserating. "Sure you didn't swig too much of that date-wine? It's strong stuff for a weak head. Where's your evidence for this fantasy? You've only his word to go on."

"And his happenings."

"Faith-healing. Lots of folk have the gift. He's better at it than most – but then he's got a more forceful personality. He can help sick people to help themselves."

"Actually I wasn't thinking of bodily disease. That's only the outward sign of his real purpose. There was this fellow in Capernaum who'd got the shakes. Old Achaz – remember him? When the Master launched his mission in Galil, he'd got a whole lot worse than he used to be in our childhood. He was pretty nigh helpless. They brought him on a stretcher to Jonah's place where the Master was teaching. Rock and Andy's poppa is as blazing-mad as mine and for the same cause – no sons left to supplement the family wage or carry on the business, plus a deserted wife to support out of his own funds. So he'd got a bunch of Set-aparts to do their stint. Well, the house was jam-packed and Achaz had to be let down through a hole made in its roof. That pleased old Jonah, I can tell you! (He made the bearers replace the cross-timbers and roll the clay out afterwards.) We were close to the Master, looking forward to another proof of his power. One in the eye for these Holy Joes, I recall thinking. All he said to Achaz was, 'Your sins are pardoned.' That really got up their noses: they said he was claiming a right God alone possessed. They waved their fists in his face yet he didn't turn a hair. 'Very well,' he said, 'if you doubt my authority to forgive sin, I'll do something you can't deny.' And he told Achaz to get off the stretcher.

You should've seen their expressions when the old sod leapt up like a ten-year-old, grinning from ear to ear."

My mind returns to the cripple at Bethesda, to poor Sue and my own encounter with Yeshua in the Temple. In each case, there'd been mention of inward healing.

I refuse to be impressed. "Achaz was a fake. I sussed that out as a kid. He went round quivering like a jelly to attract sympathy. Once round the corner, he'd chuck his stick away."

"You're missing my point. On purpose. The Set-aparts were quite right: only God can cure a man's soul."

"Precisely. So those who claim they can do so must be liars – or on some way-out trip."

"You know better than that, Miri. You yourself were privileged to receive his mercy."

I make no answer. Now that it's no longer a barrier to my happiness, I've no desire to upset Jo's simple faith nor to hurt his feelings. Yet the conviction in his voice and manner continue to bother me. If – and I'm admitting nothing – but if there's a single grain of truth in what he believes, then I'd have one hell of a debt to repay the guy who'd most reason to condemn me for my wrong, but who spared me instead.

A lifetime would hardly be enough.

SEVEN

'Nothing good can come out of Nazrat.' That's a saying so well known it's become a proverb to describe any place whose inhabitants you happen to despise. Goodness knows why. The worst I know of them is that Nazrenes tend to be rather clannish and provincial, being cut off from the mainstream by confining hills. Their outlook on life is narrow, pious and rigidly conservative. The nearest I've ever been to the town is Kana and I'm thinking of Abi's wedding-day, the day which changed my life, as we approach.

We parted company with the missionary-team on the border of Galil, watching them drag their feet like sheep deprived of a shepherd. I felt sorry for them but Yeshua laughed at me. He can be quite tough-minded and unsentimental at times, 'They'll have to go it alone one day,' he said. I wish he wouldn't talk like that, as he did at Bethaniah. It makes me uneasy. Still, I've got him to myself for the present, which is all that matters. I'm wearing Joanna's veil like the 'nice', self-respecting girl that I'm not, because there's a winter's chill clinging to these heights. No, Miri, be honest and confess you want to make a good impression on his momma. Despite her reputation, she looked so prim and proper in her widow's weeds at the messima! I wonder whether she goes along with his Mashiah bit, or just thinks him a silly, lovable boy the way mommas do…

'Quaint' is the right word for Nazrat. It has that best-kept-village appearance, oodles of rustic charm with cobbled streets and hanging flower-pots over prettily painted doorways. Not a scrap of litter to be seen and the prettified aura, which testifies to a beauty spot. We meet nobody as we stroll past a picturesque well in the market-square except one old codger who greets Yeshua with a surly nod. He doesn't seem aware of his status – none of the 'local boy makes good' stuff; just grumbles about having to mend his own farm implements now the shop's been closed down. Why didn't Joseph's son follow in his poppa's footsteps instead of traipsing round the countryside making an idgit of himself? Why hadn't he gotten a wife ten-year back and settled down like a decent body? He gives me a speculative stare from his rheumy eyes – p'raps I'm the one to fill the bill. I've no wish to disillusion him. Chance would be a fine thing!

The shop itself is tucked away in a back street. A carpenter's sign, a mallet crossed with a saw, creaks dolefully in the breeze, its peeling surface crusted with pigeon-droppings. We go through a gate in the front yard still stacked with rotting planks. The work-area takes up the whole ground floor of the house; only a counter separates it from the yard. Tools, beautifully kept, are ranged on shelves or pegs round the walls. A piece of furniture leans against the saw-bench, its decorative scrolling half-completed as if the maker had been interrupted and never got back to his task.

"That's quite something, Yeshua," I remark. "Is it yours?"

"No, that was the last piece Joseph undertook."

"Joseph – your poppa?"

"My adoptive father, yes. He was making it as a birthday gift for Momma. We've left it there as a sort of memento. He was a fine craftsman but not the world's best breadwinner. Too much of an artist, a perfectionist. The folk hereabouts pay for practical jobs: ploughshares, yokes, window-frames. They're mostly small farmers and husbandmen who've no money to spare for luxury articles. We lived on the grain they supplied at harvest. I never held a shekel in my hand till I left home."

"Won't you finish it for him?"

"I prefer to work on living material, Miri. Besides, I lack his skill. He used to hand the routine stuff on to me."

You'd expect his momma, hearing our voices, would rush down to welcome her long-absent son, but no. We climb the wooden steps to an upper room where she's waiting. He goes across as she rises from her stool and takes her outstretched hands, roughened by woman's toil. For some reason my own Momma's soft, delicate palms, so different from these, come to mind – her sensitive features and the gorgeous hair she bequeathed to me. Why does this plain-faced, nondescript woman make me think of a mother whose love I've missed so badly over the years? It's not as if she's showing maternal affection towards her own child: no kiss, no throwing herself into his arms... It's almost as though she held him in shy veneration.

Yeshua introduces me and she smiles into my eyes. "I saw you at Kana and thought you an unusually lovely girl. Aren't you Jo Barzabdiah's special friend? Such an excellent young man." She moves forward and gives me the warm embrace withheld from to Yeshua. "You're most welcome, my dear. I'm far too much on my own nowadays."

She doesn't ask any explanation of my being here nor does Yeshua offer one. Yet the feeling grows on me as we get to know one another that I'm an open book to her. She gives me the same vibes as Joanna did – kind, uncritical, compassionate ones – but Joanna needed to be told my story to the end. She doesn't; she seems aware of it already. Maybe she has the gift of second sight and has passed it on to her son. Maybe they can read each other's mind. I don't know. Anyway, I'm happy to be here in this quiet little household, like a ship battered by waves finding shelter in some land-locked bay.

We've plenty of time together, she and I, since Yeshua isn't here for a rest cure himself. I wish he'd lay off his hot-gospelling for a few days yet that's like wishing for the moon. Every morning after a quick bite he abandons his two Miriams and we don't see him again till nightfall. Can't imagine where he gets his listeners from – the Nazrenes keep themselves to themselves and the market-square seems as empty as it did on our arrival whenever we go there to fetch water. I suspect the elders who preside over the local shul have warned them off him; backwoods communities are always under the thumb of their religious elite and this one's no exception.

When you're in love with someone, you want to discover everything about him; no detail, past or present, is unimportant. Miriam's only too glad to tell me about Yeshua's childhood, his early youth, and I'm as glad to listen, absorbed, while the hours drift by. Naturally I'm bursting with curiosity to learn his true parentage – yet it's scarcely a thing one can ask the unlucky momma! Probably some yokel got her into trouble under a hedge during the long, hot harvest-season. That appears to fit the facts as she tells them. Joseph, a kinsman of hers who'd feel obliged to hide the family's shame, wed her and carted her down south to have the baby well away from busy tongues. She says they went to Bethlehem, their tribal town, to register for a tax-census – and I don't blame her for covering up. It's her story and she's sticking to it. I'm the last to pass judgement, I should say! Trouble is, some scandalmonger did a bit of calculating at the time and the truth got out. Neighbours never let a juicy item of gossip die the death for want of spreading around. No wonder she has to live alone and friendless. Poor Miriam.

She's more forthcoming about his infancy. "When we got to Bet-lehem the place was crowded with our fellow-tribesmen signing in. D'you know the village?"

"I've never been there."

"Well, most of the dwellings are built from natural rock above caves where animals are stabled. We had to make do with one of those and use its trough as a cot."

"Tough," I say.

"Not at all. Lovely soft hay and the comforting warmth of the oxen. It was a birthplace fit for a – king. Besides, we'd plenty of help, the people were so kind. They adored Yeshua and piled necessities on us." She pauses. "There was one bad moment, all the same. Soldiers came to the district and rounded up every baby under two years they could lay hands on. We got out just in time. I heard afterwards that the little mites were killed by Herod's order."

So it happened there, in Bet-lehem, and at the time of Yeshua's birth. An odd coincidence – in view of his later claim. 'Fit for a king.' she said. Can it be that she, too, credits his claim? I won't press her for details. I mustn't let myself be caught up further in this web of absurdity. If he hopes that his momma will infect me with their shared make-believe, he can think again. I admit she seems perfectly balanced – just as he does most of the time. Her grey eyes, so like his, are serene yet touched with sadness, and her whole being is so gently unassuming. When she talks about Yeshua's boyhood, she sounds like any other momma, convinced that he was the manliest and handsomest son ever born! Not to mention the best-behaved – well, apart from one episode…

"It was the year of his bar-mitzvah," she recalls. "We'd gone south to celebrate Pessach with the usual crowd of pilgrims. After Holy Week we started back. Yeshua wasn't with us but we presumed he was larking with his pals somewhere out of sight. He was always the popular one, you know, telling stories and thinking up new games to play, a real bright spark. We didn't worry till we were way out of the City and still no sign of him. We searched the throng, made inquiries and finally had to turn back. I was really anxious by now and Joseph was upset for my sake. Guess where we found the rascal! He was standing bold as brass in the Temple court, being put through his catechism by the Sephorim. They were open-mouthed at the answers he gave them and I heard one say he was a marvel and deserved special training in the Law." She smiles to herself as though the comment had amused yet not surprised her. "I was proud of him, of course, but his independence had shaken me up. A mother dreads the day her son will leave the nest. This was a foretaste. I asked him why he'd acted so; he said, 'Now I'm a man, I have to do my Poppa's work.'"

"Cheek. I'd've smacked his backside for him."

"No, he was speaking the plain truth and I knew it."

"What has arguing with doctors of the Law to do with carpentry?"

She looks at me steadily and I'm tempted to lower my eyes. "I think you know his meaning as well as I did, Miri. Joseph wasn't his father."

"Please, Miriam. I - I don't want you to tell me things that are your private concern."

"Private? Every race on earth will learn his origin one day – and marvel at it. Yeshua's father is not of this world."

"You can't believe – "

"It's not a question of belief, my dear. His conception was announced to me beforehand. I was singled out as the mother of God's son."

Second line of defence – a mystery birth from on high. Superstition is rife in the rural outback but this is going too far. I don't know where to look: the shelf with its lovingly carved knick-knacks, more presents from a husband whose chief gift she'd pre-empted, the prospect of placid hills framed by the window or the mezuzah nailed to the doorpost inscribed with its shema: 'Hear O Israel, the Lord our God, the Lord is One.'

"Don't be embarrassed, Miri." She leans forward and puts her hand over mine. "You've heard allegations made against me – who hasn't? – and you suppose I've invented an extravagant lie, or else that I'm mad... Of course I don't blame you. You've moved in a world where the facts of life are only too obviously sordid, where the idea of a virgin conceiving would raise a cynical laugh. I've told you this simply because my son assures me that your spirit is searching for truth although your intellect resists it."

"He's barely said one word to you since we came."

"There was no need. We've – other ways of communicating between ourselves."

"Are you suggesting I ought to deny my common sense, Miriam?"

"Certainly not. You're a levelheaded young woman with a mind of her own. But there's a kind of understanding only God can plant when He judges our souls to be ready for it. You may already possess its germ without realizing it."

I must keep playing up to her nonsense. It would be sheer cruelty to tear down this tissue of self-deception she's woven. My best plan is to stay right off the subject yet that doesn't prove easy. She's lived on her own so long with this one belief to console her and now I'm in her confidence, she can't resist pouring out her heart to me. We read Scripture together during the day – I who haven't studied a page since childhood under Mart's eagle eye! - And she takes me back to the very start: the serpent's mastering of Eva and God's promise that a woman's heel should crush him, the Covenant with Abraham, Israel's faithlessness, and the forecast (constantly renewed) of a Saviour. For her its fulfilment is Yeshua, her God-begotten son. "*A child is born to us, a son given. Government is upon his shoulder and his name shall be Wonderful, Counsellor, God the Mighty, Everlasting Father, the Prince of Peace.*" Her low voice thrills to the words yet sorrow steals into it. "I remember an old man who was present when we offered Yeshua in the Temple; he told me men would reject my son and a sword would pierce my soul. That troubled me deeply and I found his warning echoed in other texts." She turns the pages, though I'm sure she knows their message by heart. "*Woe to the sinful nation; they have rejected the Lord and blasphemed the Holy One of Israel – He shall be led as a sheep to the slaughter, dumb before the shearer, for my people's wickedness.*" She gazes out of the window as the sky deepens into dusk. "When Yeshua was a child, there were men in Galil claiming to be the Mashiah. They killed those who opposed them – but Rome was efficient. Two thousand of their followers who'd rebelled against taxation-laws were crucified round Sepphoris not ten miles from here. I remember how the wind carried the stench of their rotting corpses to my nostrils. That gave rise to a double dread which time hasn't dispelled: the fear that his triumph might prove a deathly one for others and the greater fear that it might prove deathly for himself.

The first I know to be unfounded; as for the second – Oh, Miri, when I hear about the hatred he stirs up among those who should flock to him, it terrifies me."

Emotion is catching. One of her fears at least must be fulfilled. Either he crushes his enemies by force of arms or they'll crush him. And all for a chimera! He needs a woman's weapons, love and tender persuasion, to overcome his mania before it overcomes him.

Every evening he comes home drooping and dispirited. "I've not achieved a single cure," he says, toying with the meal we've prepared with loving hands for him. "The folk I grew up among haven't a scrap of faith in my powers. They call me 'the bastard' behind my back and accuse me of pretension to my face."

I redden, thinking of my own abuse at Bethaniah. "You told your mates to ignore those who didn't welcome them," I say. "Perhaps we ought to write off your home-town and return to the Lake."

"Good thinking, Miri. The others will be gathering there soon to report their doings. They'll need our moral support."

"I'll miss you, son." The words seem to be wrenched out of Miriam; almost at once she puts a hand to her mouth as if regretting them. It's the first display of spontaneous feeling that she's allowed herself to make in his presence.

"You could sell up and come to Capernaum, Momma. Cleophas would be glad to take you in. After all, he's your cousin by marriage and his two sons have thrown in their lot with me."

She shakes her head. "No, Yeshua. Once a man goes out to begin his life's work, he doesn't want his momma hanging round his neck. I'd be a burden to you." Her tone implies that she wants him to overrule her yet he makes no answer. This angers me. Has he no pity for this lonely woman, his own mother? His whole teaching is centred on love but he shows no sign of a sentiment, which every guy, however depraved, should feel towards the one who bore him and who watched over his earliest years.

On the Shabbat Miriam sets out to shul at dawn. We follow later for the service. I've looked for opportunities to get him on his own yet now that one's occurred, I feel bound to talk about her, not us.

"You must be aware how solitary her life is, Yeshua, and the reason for it."

"We're both tarred with the same brush," he replies bitterly." Naturally I know – but she's a strong character and is willing to accept her state."

"I'm sure she wants to be near you and see to your needs as she used to do, it's a mother's instinct."

"My need is for her prayers and her self-sacrifice to help me in my cause."

My turn to be bitter. "That's exactly how Jo felt about me. He expected me to grin and bear it while he went chasing after some abstract ideal. Men are like that: they set up slogans for themselves – POLITICAL REFORM – SOCIAL JUSTICE – UNIVERSAL PEACE – and neglect the human misery on their own doorsteps."

"No, Miri. There's nothing cold or abstract in Jo's faith. He's made himself over, heart and soul, to a person in whom every ideal has become reality. That person is myself. If anyone hopes to win salvation, he must give up mother, father, wife or fiancé for my sake."

"That's inhuman – and terribly self-centred of you... I'm sorry, Yeshua, but it is. Can't you see that?"

"With your eyes, yes. I'm inviting those who wish to be my friends to cut off every tie of earthly affection as well as worldly pleasure – to attach themselves entirely to me. Yet one day they'll rediscover all they thought lost within this single love, no half-measure but brimming-over. Divine truth is a paradox. It asks that you give up your life in order to find it!"

Much good my intervention on Miriam's behalf has done. I join her in the screened gallery provided for womenfolk, where she's kneeling in prayer. This segregation of the sexes adds to my resentment. Why should we be here on sufferance, swept into a corner while men occupy the main seats below us? From bar-mitzvah to burial, the male takes pride of place, manipulating the rules to suit his own interests. No female may preach or aspire to the priesthood – it's a masculine preserve. And come to that, no man admits that God may not be 'he' or that Eva was the equal of Adam though she's blamed for mankind's fall. Who wrote the Torah? Men did! Apart from these feminist grudges, I feel thoroughly out of place here as I watch the worshippers enter and the shammash taking the sacred scroll from its ebony cabinet to put it on the reading desk. Self-important elders settle in the front rows, facing the riff-raff. They wear their prayer-shawls and teffilin with an arrogance unbecoming to servants of Yahweh. Yeshua's height singles him out though he makes no move to occupy one of the privileged seats.

After the opening hymns, the hazzan walks across to him, however, and invites him with ironical courtesy to choose a text. The elders smile frostily; they're willing to pay lip-service to this comic pretender so long as he fails to loosen their stranglehold on Nazrat. He goes forward to the desk, but not to read. Like his momma, he can quote Scripture verbatim. He surveys the congregation, his glance sweeping upwards to include us unworthy women.

He begins: "*Behold my servant. I have put my spirit upon him. He will bring justice to the nations. He will not raise his voice or make it heard in the streets.*" He interrupts Isaiah's words to add a comment of his own: "That's true for the streets of my hometown, You've made it clear that no man who calls himself a prophet gains a hearing from his own kind."

There's a shuffling of feet, a half-suppressed mutter. He continues unperturbed: "*I have given you a Covenant, a light to all nations to open*

100

the eyes that are blind, to set prisoners free and to proclaim a year of acceptance to the Lord." He pauses, measuring the silence. "I'm here to tell you, very simply, that this foretelling's come true. I am he who has come to heal Israel's blindness and free you from the Law's oppression."

Someone bawls out, "Blasphemer! That was said of the Mashiah whose source of being no man shall know. You're a Nazrene like the rest of us, son of our late carpenter – to stretch a point!"

The innuendo raises a snigger yet doesn't dissipate the underlying fury. Yeshua fastens his heckler with a steady eye and says, "Your last comment proves your ignorance of my origin, doesn't it? I tell you once again: I am the Lord's Anointed One sent to redeem the nation – but my Father in Heaven withholds belief from your hearts because you're not worthy of it." Again he pauses, as if searching for a barb, which'll really get through to them. "Remember how Elijah was sent in time of famine, not to comfort his fellow-Jews but Zarephath, a Sidonian – and how Elisha cured a Syrian leper, Naaman, instead of the stricken in Israel?"

The crowded shul seethes and steams with outrage. These are no sophisticated listeners, like Benesdra and his ilk, ready to string Barjoseph along for their own sport while building a watertight case against him; they're hidebound reactionaries whose response to sacrilege is likely to be one of instant violence. I shudder for Yeshua and sense his momma cringe beside me, huddled in a paralysis of dread. Is her 'sword of grief' about to be plunged – and shall I feel it too? Even the gentle souls around us are shaking their fists and screaming for his blood.

The elders make the first move, ringing him and hustling him down the central aisle. Have they preplanned this strategy in the hope that he'd justify it? Massed spectators surge from their places and lend impetus to the lynching-party. I'm sickeningly reminded of the audience in the stadium at Tiberias baying for a kill...

"I know where they're taking him," Miriam whispers to me tremulously. "There's a cliff on the edge of town with a sheer drop. They're going to throw my son over it."

"Let's get out of here. It may be possible to do something – change their minds."

What a hope! A mob is a mob. It won't listen to the voice of moderation or be thwarted of its will. I help his momma to her feet and guide her out of doors. It's a lovely morning, fresh and sunlit; nature seems to put man's darker side to shame. Far ahead, a tall figure is already close to a projecting spit of land high above Jezreel's plain hazed with the carpet of ripening crops. Yeshua's about to suffer the fate he once saved me from – and there's nothing I can do. I've never felt so helpless, so tense with anticipated heartache. We're the last of the human trail, which swarms across this intervening space... But no, I hear feet thudding behind us and tear my gaze from

101

what may well be my last sight of him, alive, turning to see two blokes race past . One of them limps yet I know his determination will keep him going! Jude the Siccarioth and Si the Zealot – my private enemies but champions of today's least popular man.

Have they a chance in hell of rescuing him? While Jude staggers on, Si pulls up and shouts, "You Nazrene scum! Would you dare proceed against the Almighty's purpose? Would you slaughter his Chosen One, destined to lead our nation to victory over Alien oppressors? You should be praising him with psalms and strewing leaves before his feet instead of threatening his life!"

His diatribe takes effect on those in the vicinity. This assertion by an outsider baffles them, erodes their certainty that justice is being done. Might not Nazrat, after all, be honoured as the hometown of Israel's Mashiah? Jude's grim obduracy also makes an impact. The crowd falls away to let him pass, his cut-throat glinting in one fist, the other belabouring left and right. Surely they've arrived too late? No change of mood can influence the vanguard, two hundred yards ahead. I shut my eyes as Miriam has done and wait to hear the distant thud of a body, the howl of vindictive triumph. I hear neither. Unbelieving, I open them once more. The scene before me is uncanny: a concourse, which a moment ago crawled like maggots over dead meat, is frozen to the spot. Jude stands in arrested movement, his razor lifted. Beyond, the killers are a sculptured group, their hands stretched out to grasp – nothing. O God! They've sent Yeshua to his doom. His momma's first to break the spell. She rushes forward and I follow her. In mortal fear of what I'm about to see, I peer over the cliff's ragged edge. The earth far beneath lies empty, innocent of blood, its growing wheat uncrushed.

My legs give way. This time it's Miriam who supports me, the younger woman, with her work-hardened hands. She murmurs thankful words that I recall on the Baptist's lips: "His time has not yet come."

"Wh – what happened?"

"My son has delivered himself from danger. He has no need of earthly rescuers – those who rely on battle-cries and blades. I should have reminded myself of that and remained calm. Remember, Miri, whatever the future holds for him, it will happen by his own will. His life may be given but not taken."

The assembly, restored to motion, simmers with bewildered agitation. Gradually the second thoughts aroused by Si's speech spread through its ranks, and now the instigators' lives are threatened. Nazrat has jacked in its chance of everlasting glory; the Mashiah will disown it! For me, the greater crisis has given way to a private one. Inevitably Jude has recognized me and I try to dodge his baleful eye as he approaches us. Thank God for Miriam's presence. He ignores me loftily and addresses her: "Ma'am, may I congratulate you on your son's escape? Permit us to escort you home, away from this murderous rabble!" Such deference from a foul-mouthed gangster – but of course he ingratiates himself with Yeshua's mother while no doubt despising them both. I'm sure he's disappointed there was no fighting and to be fair, he'd have taken on the lot single-handed. He continues to behave as though I'm not here (which suits me fine) and we return with him and his crony on either side of Miriam, myself dragging in the rear. I'm not fooled by his smarmy performance to Miriam nor his highhandedness to me: he intends to get even for that mortifying chase when the moment's ripe. Pray God Yeshua's there to greet us at the house.

It's empty. Wherever he's got to and by whatever means, he's not here. No doubt he's crouching in some covert or in some cave recalled from childish hiding-games. Once the coast's clear, he'll slip away over the slopes to Capernaum. His momma may choose to think otherwise, not me. I haven't yet lost my marbles... She bustles round, setting the table for a meal to serve her guests. We're hardly a convivial group. I'm in no mood to socialize and she, though polite to her nephew, evidently sees through Jude's phoney politeness. After a while, she senses my constraint and tries to draw me out by accounting for their presence.

"This is Simon, the son of my sister Rakel who passed away last year. His poppa is an influential man who had him well educated in the Law and he joined a most exclusive political club before affiliating himself with Yeshua."

"Oh, we've already met," remarks Si, not sparing me a glance. "I must say it's surprising to find this girl in your company, Aunt Miriam – or in your son's, if it comes to that. She's a traitor to our people."

"A randy little slag who beds with Roman filth and deserves to be carved up," growls Jude, reverting to style.

Miriam refuses to look at him. "Your friend is ignorant of his Master's teaching," she tells Si, "Yeshua would sooner befriend a foolish girl than have his so-called disciples entice her to their hide-out and rob her of her beauty." She comes over to me and runs her fingers through my hair. "It's so lovely, my dear. I'll be sorry to go without the pleasure of gazing at it in this dark room. You must let me brush and comb it one more time before we say good-bye."

She must have got the facts from Yeshua, I tell myself as she grooms me for departure. That settles it; I *was* delirious when they took me in that night. Aloud I say, "Thanks, Miriam, but why must I leave you?"

"Because you're going back with these two. Yeshua's already waiting for you by the Lake." She puts her lips close to my ear and adds, "Don't be scared, Miri. He'll make sure you come to no harm." Then she lays them softly on my cheek and her kiss is like Joanna's.

We set off shortly afterwards. Jude is predictably bad-tempered.

"So you grassed on us, you little whiner! Not to mention worming your way into the boss's favour. I should've done for you while I had the chance."

My thoughts are still with Miriam in her doom-ridden solitude but I find the nerve to say, "Didn't fancy a midnight dip, eh? I s'pose you can't swim with that club-foot of yours."

He wheels on me savagely. "Don't ever mock my deformity again, slut! The last one who did that ended up worse than me."

"Leave her be, Jude," says Si loftily. "Now that she's in the Leader's good books, we'll have to handle her with kid gloves. In point of fact, her – connections may come in quite useful to our plans."

"What plans?" I question suspiciously.

"Our campaign to rid Israel of Alien occupiers and set the Leader on his rightful throne. You're in a position to infiltrate the enemy, mislead them as to our intentions and report their movements back to us."

"I haven't slept with the whole bloody legion."

"I should hope not though I wouldn't care to wager on it. Your raunchy playmate Longinus is as good a contact as any. You've blown your cover with Antipas, more's the pity, but he's in the Tetrarch's pay besides being first on the short-list for promotion to the Procurator's personal bodyguard. We do our homework, you observe."

"And if I don't co-operate?"

"I think you will. You'll be serving your own best interests by doing so. I presume you want our Leader's cause to succeed?"

"I don't give a damn about Yeshua's cause, as you call it, but I do about him."

"I see that you and he are on quite intimate terms… 'Yeshua' indeed! Even I, his cousin, no longer address him by name. I trust you haven't designs on his chastity?"

"That's my business."

"It certainly has been in the past. I must tell you for your own benefit that you'll be disappointed. Like Jude and myself, he's dedicated to higher things. However, since you value his survival, I'd point out that our personal labours are vital to this. As with so many idealists who preach the merits of peace and simple virtue, he depends on realists like ourselves working behind the scenes to boost his image."

"You make him sound some sort of – commodity."

"Not at all. He's got the right sort of charisma and an excellent line in propaganda. If I hadn't appreciated his potential, I shouldn't have taken him on. Yet he's a liability left to his own devices. You saw what happened this morning. We missed the build-up but somehow he'd managed to aggravate his fellow-townsmen to the point of attempting his destruction."

"He told them he was the Mashiah though they weren't worthy to believe it – all in one breath."

"I might've guessed. Hardly the most subtle approach, you'd agree? If we hadn't learnt of your whereabouts and gone after him to report on our activities in the south, the whole enterprise would be at an end."

I let this go. "And what were your activities – apart from putting the frighteners on an insignificant street-walker?"

"Basically, we diversify. Jude here concerns himself with the militant aspect. He has contacts with the heavy mob, men like Yeshua Barabbas, and together they're working on a strategy for the Leader's take-over bid. Tell her, Jude."

Jude's sulking, still narked by my reference to his handicap. He grunts, "I don't trust her. Why blow the gaff, Si? She'll put her soldier-boy wise to what we're doing."

"I doubt that. You heard her – she's besotted with the Leader and only wants what's good for him. Unless we put her in the picture, she'll be no help to us."

"If you breathe a word, sister…" Jude's hand grapples under his cloak; there's no need to extract the weapon which I know lurks beneath its folds. "Right, so we start at flash-point and work backwards."

"Flash-point?"

"Code-word for the take-over. First items to sort out: time and place. Timing's critical. It has to be soonest 'cos the Sads are up in arms against him and they'll waste him if we don't act fast. Antipas ditto. Centre of ops: the City. Put the two side by side and you come up with the answer. Twelve months from now, when the boss goes south for Pessach, we make our move."

"You and whose army?" Frankly, I can't take him seriously. "What are a handful of agitators against the might of Rome?"

He scowls at me. "These guys are pro's. They've got ironware stashed in Solomon's quarries and they'll neutralize the key-points – Antonia, Herod's citadel, the Temple – soon as we drop the flag. They need to be paid, of course." He grins at Si. "That's why I volunteered to take charge of party funds. You'd be amazed how much the fat chicks who sub up secretly to the cause hand out – so would the boss if he knew! But we don't have to bribe our fighting-strength: the Am-haretz, the nothing-to-losers. They're already rooting for him and, with a bit of arm-twisting – rabble-rousers, demos, and suchlike – they'll carry him to the top on their bleedin' shoulders."

His partner takes up the tale. "My province is public relations, as perhaps you've guessed. I'm a man of peace, like my cousin, and I'm not in entire accord with Jude's modus operandi. The employment of muscle may be necessary in the end yet I'd prefer to achieve our common aims with the approbation and support of the religious establishment. That's where promotion comes in. It's my job to publicize the Leader's credentials as Mashiah among the arbiters of public opinion."

"I'd have thought he does a pretty hard sell off his own bat."

"Yes indeed, and with the deplorable results we've recently witnessed. The bald assertion of his status is ill-advised; we must ensure his acceptability to the intelligentsia by presenting them with a fool-proof case."

"Tell me, d'you believe he is the Mashiah?"

He seems taken aback. "Your question is irrelevant. It's my purpose to make him the Mashiah. Don't imagine that's an easy task. These Scripture buffs study every last detail of the prophecies and I have to make the facts fit. As a member of his family, I'm able to confirm certain coincidences: his descent through both parents from the line of King David, for instance, and his birth in Bet-lehem. Such biographical data are announced by Yeremiah and Micah, respectively." He's pulled a minutely scrawled parchment from his pouch to check the references – another compulsive scribbler like Matt, it would appear. "The problem of his conception is more delicate. There's an unsavoury rumour that – "

"He's illegit. I know. Not much of a start-off for the Saviour of Israel, is it?" I'm being mischievous but his pomposity screws me up.

"Er – precisely. The imputation is so firmly rooted that it can't be shrugged away. Instead, we make capital from it by emphasizing the mystery of his fatherhood. "He smiles at his own cunning complacently then consults his scroll again. "Ah yes, here we have it. *'A virgin shall conceive and bear a son whose name will be God-with-us'.* Isaiah, chapter seven, verse fourteen."

His quotation jolts me. Miriam kept quiet about that one! Yet surely it's hooey, the stuff of myths and fairy-tales? Odd, all the same, that Si the cynic should come up with her version of the truth. Clearly he doesn't credit it himself or recognize its implication – and I'm not sticking my neck out, either. I think I'll test his self-assurance: "Yeshua's momma read me messages from the same prophet which forecast a pretty grim outlook for the Mashiah. Nothing about take-overs or victory celebrations in the capital. He calls him the 'suffering servant'."

Si shakes his head sagely. "Negative input. Not at all the sort of image we have to promote. Enoch is my prime source on that score, even if he's acclaimed as their inspiration by those Salt Sea heretics, the Essenes. He speaks of banners waving and trumpets blowing, the City paved with jewels and a rule-book to keep the Gentiles in order. Pure metaphor, of course, but splendid, soul-stirring stuff to keep the proles at fever-heat until we've got him safe and secure on the throne."

Jude cuts across his fluency. "All this fancy talk gives me a pain in the arse. My foot's playing up after the miles we've been traipsing and listening to your blather's made my throat dry. Let's stop for a skin. We'll try this tavern…"

The smoothy and the thug. They're a right pair. If they don't fall out over their tactics, it's odds on they'll rubbish Yeshuah's cause between them. Jude means to organise one of those periodic bloodbaths which always end with the Aliens in a stronger position than before, while Si's certain to trip over his own cleverness and discredit his cousin's mission. Neither of them has the slightest inkling that Yeshua means what he says when he talks of peace and honesty; neither is concerned with whether he's really who he claims to be. For them, he's a convenient front-guy behind whom they hope to attain their private ambitions.

I owe it to Yeshua to warn him about their devious schemes. With friends like these, who needs enemies? And he's got a plentiful supply of them already.

EIGHT

Our yearly coming to Galil during my childhood often coincided with its 'magic days'. The warm, damp weather and fertile soil combined to produce a feast of colour. Hyacinths, narcissi, irises and anemones starred the meadowland, almond-blossom and oleander flowers shimmered against a powder-blue sky white-flecked with the flights of cranes wheeling above the Lake's placid looking-glass. The winter crops were already ripening; barley-fields gleamed pale gold and the wheat was almost ready for its first wave-offering. All these hues – mauve, yellow, pink and scarlet – sang out against the silver olive-trees and the startling green of densely planted fig-trees. It was as if every season's livery had gathered together for display in an enchanted garden.

Whenever the sight met my eyes, glazed by Judaea's stony sameness, I took it as a lucky charm for the future. Yet it wasn't always there to greet me. Sometimes a drought would have blighted spring's promise and threatened its harvest. Corn must be reaped at first light when still drenched with dew since, by mid-morning, the dry ears would fall from the husks and be stamped underfoot. No grain, no flour and eventually no loaves to fill peasant bellies.

As our ill-assorted trio approaches the region I know so well and have missed so long, I look in vain for past splendour. In Western Galil the vapours from the Great Sea spread lushness through the hills and valleys but here the soil is starved beneath a burning sun. Many will go hungry before summer's over. My talisman has let me down – but then I don't believe in luck any more. I deal in practicalities: the likelihood that we may find Yeshua gone and his flock dispersed. The crisis at Nazrat and the antagonism of his own community could have been the last straw for him. He wouldn't be the first mountebank to retire from an unequal struggle into obscurity.

Yet my fears prove unfounded. We track him down at Zabdiah's house in Capernaum. Salome is presiding in her husband's absence. She's a different person freed from his blustering domination, no longer the submissive wife but a warm and eager woman, as deeply attached to Yeshua as her sons. She sits with Jo and Jim on either side among his followers who are recounting their adventures to the Master. My heart leaps at the sight of him, so calm and seemingly unaffected by his narrow escape. A single day's uncertainty has been a torment to me. He greets us without ceremony, awarding me a

108

smile, which barely extends to my escorts. The others clamour for his attention like children as they spill out their tales of woe.

"I couldn't make 'em hearken to me like you do, Master," complains Andy. "They jeered at me and argued among themselves."

Honest Tom, the moaner, adds, "I felt a right shmuck most of the time. If only I'd had a few tricks up my sleeve – but I couldn't do a single cure."

Yeshua laughs. "I – I – I... There's your mistake, Tom. You must get it into your thick head that you can do nothing without my Poppa's help. He'll put words into your mouth and healing power at your fingertips. Forget self-glory – and lean on Him."

"It'd be a lot easier preaching to strangers," sighs Jo. "If I've been told once to go back to mending my nets, I've been told it a hundred times. They won't take instruction from a fellow-townsman."

"Don't I know it!"? Yeshua glances in my direction. "These are teething-pains, Jo. One day you and the rest will be spreading the good news in cities you've never heard of. Then you'll be really up against it."

"Won't you be with us, Master?" Rock sounds disconcerted, a kid dreading to be deprived of adult protection.

A long pause ensues before Yeshua's reply. "I'll be – at your side, you can be sure of that, yet not as you see me now. Not in mortal form..."

General consternation. He goes on, "If you'd studied Scripture, my words wouldn't hit you so hard. The Mashiah's purpose is mankind's redemption. Were I to remain among you, teaching and healing, I'd achieve no more than the prophets. My Poppa has sent me to open up the gates of his kingdom."

A hush has fallen over the room. Not one of us gets his drift but we sense a deep seriousness in his voice and manner. He says, "This is the season of Pessach, Israel's deliverance from Egypt. How do we celebrate the feast?"

"By offering a slain lamb, Master," answers Phil.

"Yes, the lamb whose blood spared our people from the killing of the first-born by Pharaoh. Animal sacrifice was sufficient to save earthly lives. What victim is worth enough to pay for the saving of men's souls?"

His question hangs on the air, Can he be meaning – what does he mean? Daylight has given way to gloaming and his face is in shadow, eyes veiled and only its strong bones prominent. A death-mask. Nobody feels inclined to pursue these troubling speculations now that we're a happily united band once more. Matt changes the subject by asking, "Why didn't we stay down south for Pessach, Master?"

"Because I mean to keep it among those who've given me most welcome. I want to bring home to them the true mystery of desert manna and unleavened bread – the providence of my Father who feeds both body and spirit. You'll see what I'm driving at in good time."

"It won't be the same, though," grumbles Matt. "I like watching the money-changers in the Temple – rascals, most of 'em – and the crowds queuing up to kill their yearlings. It's all go in the City at this season."

"Speaking of which," Jim remarks, turning to Si and Jude, "what fun and games have you two been up to while we've been slogging our guts out in the north?"

The devious pair are scarcely more popular with their mates than with yours truly; I can tell that by the way no one looks them in the eye. Instead of replying, Jude scowls and his buddy contents himself with a lordly smirk as though his brilliant machinations would be lost on such primitive beings,

There's no problem of accommodation on this home-territory, that's one comfort. Everyone has sleeping-quarters to go to – except Yeshua and myself. The others vie for the honour of putting him up but an idea hits me. Why shouldn't we take advantage of my family's villa at Migdal? It's only a mile from here and I've as much right to use it as Mart and Laz. I suggest this tentatively.

"Out of the question," retorts Si promptly, breaking his superior silence, "The Leader spending his nights under the same roof as a notorious woman? Preposterous! His reputation would be torn to shreds."

Surprisingly, Rock speaks up for me. "You're pig-ignorant. The Master doesn't give a sod for tale-bearers and their dirty little minds. Girls like Miri who don't pretend to be better than they are come higher on his list than self-righteous humbugs – Zealots, for example, not to mention their hatchet-men."

His seniority, or perhaps his plain speaking, wins the day and we set out, Yeshua and I, for Migdal. It's dark by the time we get there yet I could find our place blindfold. Householders never lock their doors in our village so we've no difficulty getting in. We borrow flame from a neighbour who asks no questions and when lamps are lit and a fire crackling in the hearth, I survey my familiar surroundings. As at Bethaniah, nothing's altered: apple-pie order and hardly a speck of dust to be seen – as if Mart's flying broom had only just finished sweeping it out. Would it dare look any different? How angry she'd be if she knew that I'm taking it over - but equally annoyed if I'd failed to offer hospitality to her idol! You can't win with Mart...

As on that evening in Yericho, neither of us is sleepy. We settle down on cushions in front of the fire, contented with each other's company. In my case, more than contented! Here's my chance to warn him about his misguided 'helpers' as well as Herod's designs, remote though these seem so far from El Mashnaka.

"Yeshua," I begin, "may I tell you what I've been hearing from Si and Jude? You'll think it's because I fear and dislike them, but it's not.

I'm worried about the harm they may bring to you."

"There's no need, Miri. I know. They're determined to place me on an earthly throne from which I shall hand out the spoils of victory to those who have put me on it."

"So they've come clean with you? I can't imagine you approve of hiring bully-boys or organizing nationalist rallies. It's not your way. Why don't you bring them to heel or disown them?"

"Because they're essential to the unfolding of events, one of them in particular, and I must leave them to operate as free agents. Wasn't it they who unwittingly brought us together, Miri? My Poppa uses the men at his disposal. He doesn't impose his will on a passive world, compelling its acceptance. My life is a human drama staged in human terms."

"Then you concede that you're no more than a man?"

"I didn't say that. Reality's a matter of definition. You see it reflected in what you touch and taste and smell, and you suppose that any other dimension of being is fantasy. Try thinking of it the other way round. The supernatural lends a half-life to the world of creatures; without God's indwelling spirit, they'd melt into thin air. I'm here to turn assumptions on their head – to extend men's limited vision. I must, therefore, belong to both orders of existence. God's nature and man's meet in my essence."

A crackpot talking with calm, persuasive reason. I say despairingly, "Whoever you are or think yourself to be, Yeshua, I love you. I always shall – and I want to save you from your own death-wish. You nearly got bumped off in Nazrat and it won't be long before the Sads and Set-aparts are screaming for your blood. At Jo's house you were talking about sacrifice, and a ghastly thought came to me that you meant yourself to be the victim." I move closer to him, rest my hands on his lap. "You're a fine preacher who's given hope to sinners like me and helped cripples to cure themselves by trusting in you; you're something rarer still – a guy that's good all through. Why can't you throw off this fixation on being the Mashiah, the son of Yahweh, and settle for being the decent bloke you are?"

"Every life has a foreordained pattern, Miri. We must all follow the path mapped out for us by my Poppa."

"Then ask him to spare you this fate. Ask him to let you live out your life as others do – to marry, have children to your name and glorify him by your deeds."

For the first time, I hear a sound of human distress from his lips and it goes to my heart. "At times I feel – wrenched apart by my double self. I come from my Heavenly Father and must return to Him, yet I've learnt what it is to be part of creation. I've romped as a child and toiled as a man, given love and taken it, known human joy and grief. It's anguish almost past bearing to be aware of what lies ahead and see all this ending in hatred and betrayal. A cross against the setting sun at the meeting of two ways..."

I shudder, thrusting from my brain the image that his momma can't escape. Then I feel sudden anger at the violence he's doing his own humanity, the fatalism which resigns him to a cruel, unnatural death. It's – obscene. How can he reconcile such a sick outcome with the glory of God's Anointed descending on clouds to begin his thousand-year reign? This momentary weakness on his part fires my first resolve: if I can't argue him out of it, I can use my feminine wiles to seduce him from a self-imposed nightmare. One chink in his armour of chasteness, a single lapse from the impossible standards he's set himself, and his illusion will vanish into air like a burst bubble. It's been the project uppermost in my mind all along, the tactic I once tried with Jo, yet (although it failed me then) I've never been entirely self-seeking, and it's good to realize that I'll be employing my hard-won skills to bring Yeshua to his senses. I need only reach up to caress him, letting my fingers smooth away his burden of care and send their message through his bloodstream. The art of foreplay is one I'm well practised in. Some influence seems to stay me, however.

He says gently, "You think you can deter me from my course by rousing my sensuality? Attractive as you are, dear Miri, you overrate your powers of seduction."

Once again, tact robs the brush-off of its sting. I answer, "If they're so feeble, Yeshua, why wall yourself in?"

"The wall's round you, not me. I'll prove that if you like."

He draws me into his arms, fondling me with tender urgency. I feel his mouth exploring my own, the heat of his body – but it's odd; I can't rise to the occasion. I'm dead meat.

"You see? Your limbs are wiser than your head. They won't obey the impulse of a disordered will. Don't force yourself, Miri, confess your error of judgement."

"I want you so badly, Yeshua, but I can't make myself respond… Take me, damn you, take me!"

"You're asking me to commit rape. Even if I weren't bound to a Nazirite's vow, I couldn't do that. I honour your beauty with my hands and my lips yet I don't seek to possess it. You also mustn't seek to possess me – not at least by means of human intercourse."

"What other way is there?"

"The way of self-surrender. It bypasses carnal appetite, ignores every signpost which shouts 'ME' – and leads to a consummation beyond one's wildest dreams. Believe me, Miri, you're already treading it at the deepest level of your being. That's why your body lets you down."

"Don't unsex me, Yeshua. Don't rob me of my womanhood!"

"Gender's a superficial thing. The ground of existence is neither male nor female. With the coming of my kingdom there'll be no sexual distinction, no giving or taking in marriage. Soul will be united with soul in the oneness of my Father's love."

He's turned the tables on me – nudged away my pitiful attempt on his virtue and improved the lesson with a visionary flight worthy of Jo! Water off a duck's back, so far as I'm concerned. I can't make do without the sort of loving he despises, the sort I've had with Cass but can't turn on right now when I need it most. Yeshua's embrace is a reproach to my frigidity and seeing this, he releases me. After a silence he gives a sudden chuckle and remarks, "Remember how I spoke at Yericho of the Devil's testing? I've wondered since why he didn't have a shot at the most obvious ploy of all. Now I know the reason – he was leaving it to you, Miri."

"So I'm the instrument of Satan. Thanks a lot!"

"Like my Poppa, he works through human agency. Didn't I say that I'd left one of his lesser minions inside you? Perhaps it's for the best. By fighting your last enemy on your own, you'll prove yourself the victor."

His choice of words reminds me yet again that I've failed to touch on the matter of Herod. All this has pushed it right out of my mind and it's too late into the night for the recounting of my court experiences. Maybe I'm destined to fight that devil on my own as well – though who will be the victor and who the vanquished only time will tell. We kiss before going to our separate beds and my lips, freed from a previous tension, yield softly to his. They tell me that this botched attempt on his virtue hasn't impaired our friendship – but they tell me nothing more.

The morning brings tragic news, reinforcing my anxieties and robbing me of one who earned my hatred, then my pity and regard. Joanna, directed here by Salome, has paid us a visit and her presence means that Antipas has returned north to Tiberias. Yeshua is as much in danger as he was in Judaea – more, indeed, since this is Herod's territory and he'll feel entitled to arrest the man whom he sees as aiming to usurp his throne. Naturally my first thought is to inquire after Cass's whereabouts and fortune yet even this is blotted from my mind by what she has to tell us. The poor soul is in tears.

"Your cousin's dead, Master," she stammers. "His Majesty was duped into consenting to his execution. He held a banquet before we left El Mashnaka to celebrate the ending of hostilities with Aretas, and his stepdaughter danced for him. It seems he was bowled over by her youth and grace; he promised her any reward she might care to receive. That was the drink talking, of course. Her mother leapt at the offer and persuaded little Salome to ask for the Baptist's head. Herod wouldn't go back on his word so they beheaded Johanan in his cell."

The beastliness and my unintentional share in it twist my guts as I listen to her. Why did I give in to the brat's pleading and teach her that infernal routine? The death of a good man in exchange for a pederast's lust – it's the kind of bargain, which would appeal to

Herod's Arab barbarism, no doubt.

Joanna continues, her voice muffled by the veil's fringe she's holding to her tearstained face. "I was supervising the waiters when they brought his head in on a silver dish. It was presented to the king and his wife took a pin from her coiffure and stuck it through the Baptist's tongue. She was smiling as she did it. Horrible…"

I steal a glance at Yeshua to see how he's taking the news. To my amazement he shows no reaction, other than commenting, "Only yesterday we spoke of sacrifice as atonement for men's crimes. You thought I meant myself as victim, Miri, yet you were wrong. My cousin leads where I – and many more – shall follow."

"How can you be so unfeeling, Yeshua?" I gasp. "Doesn't it break you up, hearing about Johanan's murder?"

"I was already aware of what had happened. I've done my mourning in private."

Once I'd have sneered at his claim to second sight. No longer. Now I realize what lay behind his sombre words at Capernaum. He was referring to another – but this hardly allays my fears for him. A nobler man than Herod would have swallowed his pride and retracted his promise rather than order such an atrocity; now committed to the shedding of innocent blood, however, he won't scruple to continue on that course.

I turn to Joanna. "Can't you make him see that he's got to keep shtum till all this blows over? The evening we had that show-down, Antipas told me in so many words he had put out a contract on Yeshua."

She shakes her head in an agony of indecision. He's the Master, after all, and who shall dare advise him? I think she's shocked, like Jo, at my familiarity but too fond to frown at me. Yeshua answers for her: "I'll go on as I've begun. A lit lamp mustn't be kept hidden but, rather, shine out to shame men's darkness."

Joanna has to return to her duties. She leaves a purseful of gold pieces with me for his benefit and whispers encouragement: "I'm so glad you've found your niche at last, my love. I felt somehow that one day you'd be the Master's hand-maiden."

Maiden's the word. I don't enjoy its unmeant irony as I watch her mule vanish among the trees. I'd not thought ever to see her again but I'm content to have done so, despite her horrific tale. There are those whose path keeps crossing one's own by happenstance – and who knows? We may meet up in the future.

Yeshua and I make tracks back to Capernaum. Well before we've reached it, a swarm of his fans come out to greet him, jostling and beseeching him for miracles, fairy-tales in which the lowly come off on top and the rich get their noses rubbed in dirt, crumbs of consolation for their grotty lives. The main street is awash with human flotsam, its air heavy with the foul breath and reeking garments of his supplicants. As for our merry men, they're charging about self-importantly in an effort to clear his path. Rock chivies a bunch of inquisitive youngsters: "Scram, you varmints," he roars at them ineffectually. "The Master's not to be bothered by the likes of you."

Yeshua turns on him abruptly. "Leave them be, Rock. Their simplicity is nearer to my truth than all the prayer and fasting of the Hasidim." He bends down from his great height and picks up a jammy-cheeked toddler, cradling her in the crook of his arm. Could've been myself, in another life, could still be a child of our own – a little Miri, a little Yeshua – if only that barrier hadn't come between us… Stop brooding, girl, and face the facts: marriage doesn't enter into his scheme of things. It's a non-starter.

Matt says, "They've waited since before sun-up, Master. Word of your return got round and this is the result. You won't be able to teach on this side of the Lake. There's no space big enough for your audience."

"Very well," answers Yeshua. "We'll cross over in Rock's boat and meet them on the far shore. Plenty of room to spread out there."

Gergesa is wild country inhabited by drop-outs: antisocial types who've been banished from the community for crime or dangerous forms of lunacy. Sailing before a scudding breeze that holds promise of dirty weather to come, Rock and his brother recall previous trips to the northeastern coast of the Lake with Yeshua. "How about that maniac who was chained to a stake dug in the ground?" exclaims Andy. "Did his act when you came into view, Master, thrashing around and foaming at the mouth. We gave him a wide berth but you went right up to him and ordered his squatters out of him. He gave a screech and went down like a pole-axed bull. Thought he was a goner, myself."

Rock, at the tiller, adds, "I didn't see the bugger fall. I was watching that herd of pigs. Remember how they stampeded all on a sudden and went straight over the cliffs into the drink?" His gnarled finger points to our left. "Pigs are under a curse. I know, but you don't expect them to freak out just like that. It was as if the nutter's evil spirits had got into them and driven them round the bend."

"Or rather, over the top," amends Jim to a general laugh. "Seriously, though, it gave me quite a turn."

"I thought it a great pity at the time that only your immediate followers witnessed it, Master," remarks Si. "It would have made first-rate publicity material. No doubt there'll be further opportunities – yet we must ensure a sizeable number of spectators."

"Shame we can't lay on a loony for you today, Si," says Phil, faintly sarcastic. "Just look at that little lot…"

The northern shore is a solid mass of humanity hurrying to accost Yeshua at the landing-place. Rock and the others are bucked at the sight, proud of the Master they serve, but my heart sinks. How many faces in the crowd are those of Herod's spies, keeping tabs on

Yeshua's rise to stardom? Thank God this area is ruled by Philip, his peace-loving brother. Sometimes Jo used to row me across during our courting days and I grew fond of these vast, deserted grasslands, dreaming that we'd build ourselves a secret refuge here, away from Mart's scolding tongue and Zabdiah's uncertain temper; but its secluded atmosphere is totally dispelled on this occasion. The people congregate around Yeshua, settling to rest like a flock of tropical birds in their plumage of gaily striped shawls and colourful tunics. The scene brings back to me that day I watched his cousin preach. Didn't Johanan say another would supersede him and bring his labours to fulfilment? Strange that it was also my first, unconscious glimpse of Yeshua... As though echoing memory, he talks of the wilderness – not the Baptist's stamping ground but Sinai, which stretches between Palestine and Egypt where our ancestors wandered. Yes, he's reminding us of God's benevolence, the manna dropped from the sky, as he said he would. (A travelling rep. I entertained one night in my Eleazar days told me the story was complete bunk; he'd seen the stuff himself and said it came from the bark of tamarisks – a sweet, flaky deposit which fell to the ground and melted in the sun's rays. Still, we'll let that pass.)

As the day wears on, I hear stomachs appropriately rumbling left and right. Many must have been empty when this exodus started and by now their owners will be feeling the full force of Yeshua's reference. "Come to me, you who are hungry, and I shall make you full!" he cries, rather unwisely in my opinion. Phil's rustled up some urchin with a basket of provisions: five-minute loaves and a couple of pickled graylings.

"What's the use of that?" asks Matt who's been calculating the cash that would be needed to feed this rabble, from force of habit – a wasted effort since there aren't any pastry-shops in this neck of the woods.

Yeshua is unperturbed. "I was talking of spiritual food," he says to us, "yet my Poppa sees to the body's nourishment as well. Split the crowd up into roughly equal groups, some of you then distribute the contents of this basket to each."

Phil's mouth falls open. "It'll scarcely feed the front row," he objects. "They'll fight over it like dogs."

"Do as I say."

The habit of obedience, rather than trust, operates and we persuade the people to form five sections. Then, feeling perfect idiots, we apportion one loaf to each. What happens next is beyond me to understand or explain. Within minutes, every man jack of them is guzzling contentedly with a huge hunk of bread in his hand – yet at no time have I seen more than the original five loaves! The sound of champing jaws has replaced the rumbling and grumbling. I hear someone call out, "Durned it it ain't the best bread I ever tasted!" followed by a chorus of enthusiastic agreement. Our satisfied customers seem unaware that a happening has occurred, just as the new wine at Kana went unnoticed except by the few.

Even Tom, whose appetite is proverbial, displays gratification. "It's a ruddy marvel," he says. "If his poppa can make grub appear out of thin air, we're quids in. I'll never grouse about giving up my livelihood again."

Jude is equally impressed. "Why don't he work the same wheeze with cash? We could swamp the market and buy out the finance-houses. It'd be a short-cut to the top…"

Matt shakes his grizzled head. "Money isn't everything. I found that out the hard way."

They react like children to a tale come true. I'm starting to sense a pattern in Yeshua's deeds. The blind who are made to see, the healing of deformities (why hasn't he cured Jude's?), water turned into wine and loaves multiplied: don't they all suggest some deeper transformation to come, the foretaste of an unspoilt world of health and plenty? I've been able to rationalize his happenings to date but this one I can't explain away – and if you allow for one, why not the rest? I wish I didn't have to. I'd so much sooner he could be a normal guy with normal limitations and let me turn my back on all this strangeness, these implications I daren't face up to because they frighten me and threaten to disrupt the life I take for granted. I know it's been a shabby one so far but it's mine, I've called the shots myself. Please, Yeshua, don't take it from me, don't shape it to your ends.

By now the guzzlers are sated, lying back on the grass like happy picnickers in no mood for further moral uplift. We circulate, picking up the scraps – enough to fill twelve of the urchin's baskets, I'd say. He beckons to us and we follow him dumbly out of general earshot.

"The people have been taught their lesson at a simple level," he says. "From you, my friends, more is required: understanding. Nat and you, Rock, do stop gawping at me as if I'd pulled off a bigger stunt than the parting of the Red Sea."

"We're homespun folk, Master," protests Rock. "We've just seen the impossible."

"More impossible than evicting evil squatters or restoring atrophied limbs? More impossible than the growth of cereal from a tiny seed? All my Poppa did was to speed up the process and take man's share in making the final product for granted. Let me remind you of my purpose: to show that He who feeds the belly also feeds the soul. I shall give you food that will never decay or fail you."

"Land's sakes," groans Tom. "We're back to the spirit-talk – pious mumbo-jumbo a man can't get his head around."

Yeshua overhears him. "Don't worry, Tom. The food I mean is real enough; so real that you're going to doubt my sanity." He pauses. "I'll give you my own flesh to eat, my own blood to drink."

Dismayed silence ensues. I can't believe I've heard him aright.

"You're asking yourselves how this can be?" he continues. "Yet none of you questions the greater mystery underlying his whole existence. You must take my word for this one."

The sky, as if reflecting our troubled minds, has gloomed over and crosscurrents are churning the Lake's leaden surface. One by one, Yeshua's pals start drifting away from him towards the beached boat in which we arrived. Momentarily I hold my ground. Yeshua stands alone, abandoned, and I long to show him my loyalty – yet how can I in this instance? Of all his followers, I'm the most sceptical; even those who've taken his claims in their stride can't swallow this latest assault on their common sense, such as it is. I turn finally and go after them, without speaking. Rock and Andy push the craft out; we climb aboard and almost at once the restless tides sweep us westward, while a thickening haze obscures the land-bound figure.

"Does he think we're cannibals?" asks Jim defensively, breaking our silence.

"I just don't get it," Jo mutters. "Everything he's said and done has made a kind of marvellous sense to me so far. This is grotesque, unimaginable…"

"He has fancy ways of putting things sometimes," suggests Nat. "P'raps we took him too literally."

"No." Andy sounds positive. "He said it deliberately. I was watching his eyes. I know how he looks when he's testing our faith in him."

"That's it, then. He said it to put us on trial. Like a gang-leader telling his mobsters to kiss his backside."

The analogy appeals to Jude. "Yeah, we're right shmucks to be letting him down like this – eh, Si? One day it'll be the Aliens licking his arse, and ours as well. Let's turn back, I say. I'm no seaman and this cockleshell's makin' my guts heave!"

It takes slow-witted Rock longer to make up his mind yet it's his decision we're waiting for. He says nothing, simply yanks the tiller round. He's left it too late, though. The sea-monster lurking in Kinnereth's depths has woken and its tail is lashing the water into waves. The boat teeters on their foaming crests, slithers sickeningly down their sheer sides and wallows in their troughs. A gale-force wind forbids us to raise sail; three men strain to each oar in an effort to keep us on course – or at least afloat. Someone (I think it's Rock) puts a brawny arm round my shoulders as I'm flung helplessly from side to side.

"Ship your oars!" he yells above the storm's thunder. "They'll splinter like matchwood. Shift your weight to hold us on even keel or we'll capsize."

"If only the Master was with us," moans Phil, the landlubber. "He saved us once before…" Oh yes, now we're all in shtook, we'll forget Yeshua's little indiscretion – so long as he gets us out of it.

Rock beside me is praying, tears or salt water streaming down his cheeks. He shouts at the top of his voice, "Rescue us, Master, rescue us and I'll never doubt you again!"

"I'll hold you to that, my friend."

Yeshua's reply seems no louder than when he spoke to us in Zabdiah's house last evening but it penetrates the turmoil of wind and wave. We must be far off shore by now – and a superstitious dread assails me. I narrow my gaze, trying to see through the unnatural darkness of the afternoon. Then I catch sight of him (it can be no other) standing unmoved on the threshing surface of the Lake as he stood on the mount at Yericho. Is it this eddying fog, which makes him appear to loom over us, an elemental being?

"Come on, Rock," he invites, extending one arm. "Come to the Master you'll never doubt again."

Rock grunts, incredulous, forcing air out of his constricted lungs, then swings a slow leg across the gunnel. Pure bravado. We watch him tread the foam, arms outstretched like a tightrope walker, eyes fixed on the spectral form ahead. He's more than halfway there when he falters, stares down at his feet and starts to go under.

Andy moans, "It's a trick of Satan. He's had it…"

"Help me' Lord," Rock screams. "Help me. I'm sinking!"

And seconds later, Yeshua's beside the boat, carrying the dead weight of our brave adventurer as easily as though he were a babe-in-arms. He tips him over the side and Rock lands on the boards like some huge porpoise flung up by a wave. Unhurriedly, Yeshua climbs aboard and I put out a cautious finger, touching solid flesh and bone. You're shaken, Miri, admit it; the world of predictable events is crashing about your ears… Above and below, the tempest's fury has abated and he speaks through the ensuing hush: "Has your faith in me come back?"

A chorus of assent.

"For the moment," he goes on sternly. "Until you doubt my power to sustain you – as Rock did just now. I don't want belief that's intermittent and I shouldn't have to put on vulgar displays like this one to convince you of my status."

"Vulgar?" queries Jude. "Bloody terrific, if you ask me! A bloke walking on water and calming a storm with a click of his fingers could have the whole world grovelling at his feet."

"You all witnessed what happened," adds Si in his best executive manner. "I'll record the facts when we reach base and ask for signatures or, in certain cases, your marks. A cross will do."

Yeshua repeats him as if he's talking to himself. "A cross will do. Yes, that'll be the true test of their loyalty…"

Rock is beginning to recover. He sits up, shaking a bewildered head. "I felt so sure I'd reach you, Master. It came to me, like; as if you were beckoning me in a dream – then it went out and I was back in the real world. Talk about panic! I lost my bottle, I'll admit as much. You see, I can't – you tell 'em, Andy." He hides his face.

"My bro can't swim," Andy says shortly. We burst out laughing.

A fisherman who can't swim!

Yeshua smiles. "You've made amends, Rock. It took more guts to acknowledge that than to challenge the waves, didn't it? Human respect is virtue's most stubborn enemy. We can't abide making fools of ourselves – or being despised for supporting an unpopular cause. As for you, Jude, you think you're on to a good thing at this minute but how will you act when all hell's let loose? Not you alone: I'll be counting my friends on the fingers of one hand before my mission's completed."

"Whatever happens, Master, I'll never let you down." Rock's his old, impulsive self again.

"Don't make rash promises. We've almost reached dry land yet there are bigger storms, bigger crises to be weathered. Next time you go under, Rock, fight your way back. Learn to swim."

NINE

Springtime gives way to summer. The harvest's a poor one, as predicted, but the peasants are fatalists; they shrug their shoulders, reap and winnow and store what little there is. Only the priests and landlords carp at their reduced tithes. The sunshine has blessed our vintages at least, with grape-clusters purpling on the terraced slopes, olives and figs ripening in the valleys. Even an itinerant preacher and his disciples can live off their abundance for by law a tree's fruits may be picked once by its owner, its second crop being left to the passer-by. Needless to say, Yeshua lets us scrump on the Shabbat, bringing the Set-aparts' wrath down on his head. Every fresh spat he provokes is another nail in his coffin, so to speak, yet the rhythm of country life, this peaceful interlude after my chequered past and before an uncertain future have dulled my concern on his behalf. Antipas has made no move though Joanna, who visits us as often as she dares, tells me he has regular bulletins on his activities. The City, his other source of danger, seems far away, Yes, I'm happy.

The one fly in the ointment has been Mart's arrival. She's come north to give our villa a real airing and doing-out, as she puts it – and I didn't need Yeshua's fortune-telling to anticipate her reaction on finding me in residence. Actually, it's the fact that I'm living here with him which riles her. She swoops round us as we sit together, clattering her mops and pails, dusting and sweeping like a dervish, only stopping to make acid comments about slatterns who lounge about all day leaving others to do the chores. I take a leaf out of Yeshua's book and manage to keep my cool but it's aggravation almost past bearing – because I value these quiet moments in his company. He no longer raises his smokescreen of divine authority, finding my laid-back attitude less of a drag than Mart's veneration, and I feel more in tune with his practical human wisdom. He's advising me how I should pray, not as the Set-aparts do with breast-beating and an eye on their admirers, but simply, like a trustful child.

"Just talk to my Poppa as you would to a kind parent," he tells me. "Something on these lines: 'My dear Poppa in heaven, I bless and praise your name. May you reign in our hearts and may your will be done. Please give me and my fellow-men what is needful to us. Pardon our sins as we pardon others. Don't let us be tried beyond our strength and protect us from the Evil One.' That covers the essentials – you can leave the small print to Him. The great thing is believing there's Someone at the other end listening to you, a Father who cannot, and will not, refuse his own child."

"When I'm alone, thinking about you, Yeshua, I seem to pray without words."

"Better still. That's the truest form of prayer yet it's only granted to a few. After all, my Poppa hardly needs to be told your wants, does He? If you chat, chat, chat, you'll drown his voice – just as your sister is interrupting us now with the banging of her broom..."

Mart snaps, "If Miriam would help me with the housework, it'd be done by now. I work my fingers to the bone while she sits at your feet, forcing herself on you, Master, demanding your attention."

"Mart, my dear, your diligence is admirable. All the same, your younger sister does well to be quiet in my presence and give her mind to priorities. There'll be time enough for trivial matters after I'm gone."

Mart, irritated by his mild reproof, misses the sombre note in his last sentence. Flushing, she throws down the broom. "You'd think she was the one who'd given up her life to the care of a sick brother, instead of which she turned herself into a tawdry little street-girl, sold her flesh to all and sundry and abused you to your face. I've served you from the start, Master, whereas Miriam came whining for your protection as a last resort – yet now she's monopolizing you and getting every encouragement to do so. It's not fair!"

Yeshua looks at her gravely, his eyes as bleak as the Lake under storm. "You'll serve me better by learning to forgive. That's the ground of my whole teaching and the reason I came to earth. My Poppa's arms are open to all, sinners and just alike. Whether they come to him late or soon, his mercy is unreserved. I've a story for those who imagine, like you, that He measures out his love according to men's paltry standards. I've told it before, but it'll bear retelling."

Mart grumbles about having her precious time wasted, so much to be done etc. etc., but she settles down to listen. (I know she'll take this out on me later when she gets me to herself!)

"Since you disapprove of idleness," Yeshua begins, "What would you say to the loiterers who hang around in the streets and squares at this time of year?"

"That's different. Everyone knows labourers get laid off between wheat harvest and fruit-picking. They can't help being redundant."

"Agreed. It's a thin time for them and their families. Well, a certain good-hearted landlord felt the same and sent a batch of them to work in his vineyard. He offered them a fair day's wage and they were delighted to accept. That was at first light. Every three hours he sent a further lot, on similar terms, until the town was empty of layabouts. When it got dark, he blew the whistle and handed out their pay. The first bunch got quite stroppy: 'We've toiled throughout the day,' they complained, 'yet we're getting no more than these slackers who mucked in at the last moment.' The landlord answered, 'I'm paying you the sum we agreed on in the first place – so what's your beef? If I choose to show generosity to others, that's no business of yours. Be glad for their sakes.'" He pauses. "Got the message, Mart?"

She remains sulky. I can guess what's going on in her mind: that Yeshua's giving me, not as much as, but a hell of a lot more than, she ever had from him – she's sure that I fancy him rotten and afraid that he's falling for my charms. She's right about the first, of course, yet not in the sordid way she supposes. My lech for him is giving place to a feeling I can't define. No, feeling's the wrong word; it's more a kind of intimacy which links us even when we're not in physical contact, almost as though he were taking over my inner self, That sounds vague and unreal, I know, yet it's not. When you make love you try to meld with your partner but for all your efforts the separateness remains and, after climax, two bodies roll apart. My bond with Yeshua has no breaking-point. It grows firmer, more tightly meshed from day to day. There's this odd, inexplicable faculty, which used to take me unawares and transport me to a private universe. Now Yeshua fills it, seeming to gather all my dreamy yearnings into his single presence and waken a sleeping self at the very centre of my being. I switch right off, time loses its momentum while life goes on around me and Mart hits the roof with exasperation!

These trances help me also to recapture a whiff of the past. They take me back to the days when I strolled along the Lakeshore or sat in summer meadows listening to Jo's crazy ramblings, letting my own imagining unwind like a golden thread. Memory's cast its spell over him, too; we've resumed many of our former habits, standing hand in hand at the water's edge, older and (perhaps) wiser versions of our vanished selves, recalling infantile scrapes – even our vows of eternal fidelity… Does he regret the way things have turned out? I doubt it; for him the change of circumstance has led to a fulfilment, but my deepening love for Yeshua still battles with the need for carnal satisfaction. My imp of Satan won't let me go!

We discuss the guy who occupies our thoughts. Like me, Jo's worried by Yeshua's presentiments, his tendency to retire into himself. "He's always been so positive, Miri, so full of hope. Nowadays he goes on about a 'necessary sacrifice' and leaving us to carry on without him. It's morbid."

"Maybe he only means it in a figurative way, like when he told us we should eat his flesh."

"I wish I could believe that. You know I've gone along with everything he's said and done but I don't understand this latest mood of his. The Mashiah is destined to an everlasting reign. He's divine, imperishable. How can he submit to death?"

"You're a man, Jo. You have to have facts fit neatly into place. I'm a woman and logic bothers me less. I've given up asking myself exactly who or what Yeshua really is; my intuition tells me he's unique, a world-beater, and that's good enough for me."

"World-beaters don't bow out before their time."

"We've all got to die. The thing is he's become part of us and whatever happens, he'll go on living and working through us – you, me, Rock and the rest."

That's cold cheer. It brings Jo small comfort when I say it; yet a few days later he's back to his old excitable self. The others were slightly put out when Jeshua invited him, his brother and Rock to keep him company on an expedition. They set off southwards with smug expressions while their pals pretended not to care. (They bicker interminably about which of them rates highest with Yeshua, like schoolboys competing for Sir's favour.) There's a lot of moping and aimless kicking of heels till the privileged three returns at evening, alone. Naturally we wonder at Yeshua's absence.

"He said he'd be staying overnight where we left him," Jim says. "He'll be back tomorrow." There's something peculiar in his manner and that goes for the other two as well. Rock was swanking his head off beforehand but now he's all subdued as though a slow brain is grappling with a teaser beyond its powers, while Jo's bubbling over like a kettle on the boil. He's in a fever of exultation and can't wait to spill the beans.

"The Master led us right away from the beaten track," he tells us. "I thought we were in for a long spiel about our responsibilities – he looks on us as his specials, you know – yet he said very little."

"Did he do a happening?"

He shakes his curly head. "No, we were on our own, I tell you. All the same, there was one. It happened to him, you might say."

"He's drivelling," says honest Tom. "Making mountains out of molehills…"

"Mountain! That was it, Tom. We'd reached that great hill in the middle of nowhere, the one shaped like a pudding-bowl upside down, on the route south – "

"Or like a woman's breast," remarks Phil more poetically. "They call it Tabor, don't they?"

"Who cares? It's a good way from here and we were absolutely whacked so he told us to take it easy. We settled down for a snooze in the sun and almost at once we were spark out. You were the first to come to, Rock. You shook Jim and me awake. I'll never forget how you looked – I'll swear your hair was standing on end! You pointed up the slope and your arm was trembling like a leaf. I looked and saw – and saw – "

"A sort of fog wreathing round the summit," Jim takes up the tale. "Clear sky above and clear ground below. It was uncanny. Slap in the middle was a blinding light – it dazzled me and at first I thought a fire had broken out, you know the way dry scrub catches when the sun focuses on a splinter of quartz…"

"It hurt to look at but I sort of squinted and made out three figures standing inside it," continues Jo. "The brightness seemed to be pouring from the central one."

"Shepherds? Fire-fighters?" queries Matt, licking his finger to turn a fresh page,

"They'd have shouted for help, wouldn't they? These were more than life-size, the outer ones bearded and robed in old-fashioned garments – no, we're not having you on, honest!"

Thaddeus says, "Where was the Master?"

Jo's voice drops an octave. "It was him, the one who radiated light. I didn't twig right away because he looked so different. He seemed to have grown and his body was all rigid."

"He's got a good height on him as it is."

"Sure, yet I was staring at a giant. Once I saw an artist's sketch of some Egyptian statue stuck in the Great Desert. He looked the same. Majestic and – "

"Frightening." Rock's found his voice at last. "I was bloody terrified, pissing my pants. He wasn't the bloke we know and love; he was like a stranger from another planet."

As their phrases tumble out, I recall that midnight at Yericho, the Yeshua who withdrew from me, a magnified, visionary form. It wasn't fright I felt so much as awe.

"They spoke among themselves as we watched," Jim's saying. "Their voices sounded like a wind blowing though everything was dead-still. I scarcely caught the words."

"I did," says Jo. The light's gone out of his blue eyes and his own voice is almost a whisper. "It was about death – the Master's death. I put my hands over my ears to shut them off but the sound crept through like the fog that curled round us. It blotted out the whole landscape and a thunder filled my brain."

"The thunder had a voice, too," Rock adds solemnly. "Whatever real thunder is, it weren't that. I remember I went spare for a minute and babbled some nonsense about building booths. God knows why…"

"You were beside yourself, out of your skull…. I pulled you down and the three of us fell on our faces, hiding from the unknown. When we lifted them again, the Master was beside us, his own height and perfectly normal – just as if nothing had taken place."

"Who on earth were his visitors?" asks Nat.

"I can't be sure but I think he addressed the older-looking one as – Moishe."

"You're kidding, Jo. I'll bet it was all a dream."

"A dream shared by the three of us?"

"Well, I'll check with the Master once he gets back."

"No." Jo pauses. "He told us to say nothing. I just couldn't keep it in – it proves I've been right to trust in him, the Chosen One – divinity incarnate."

"Divinity incarnate?" repeats Si thoughtfully, "You really believe that, do you? It's a surefire promotion-ploy – and I begin to see how it could be worked into the facts as we have them." He makes an entry on his well-thumbed sheaf of notes. "All the same, I do wish he'd keep these spectaculars for more public occasions. They're wasted on a trio of illiterate fishermen."

Which leads to an unholy squabble. I withdraw from the fracas and meditate alone. Death, death, death. Why does everything point to Yeshua's dying? He appears so indestructible yet I've heard of those who've died by self-persuasion while at the peak of health. I haven't Jo's assurance that, being divine, he can't peg out. Is it, maybe, that he's started to doubt his own proclaimed identity and contemplates taking his own life? Or does he mean to use his enemies' wrath for a suicide-weapon, baring his breast to them as Antony, Black Herod's bosom-friend, did to his slave's spear? They'll be more than ready to oblige...

Next day the crowds are as dense as ever, milling in Capernaum's streets for a glimpse of Yeshua, some saying or story to take home or a cure to witness. Since he's not on tap, they're disappointed – and far from appeased by his followers' efforts to stand in for him. It's as well, perhaps, that there's no one to challenge their abilities. The Sephorim disdain to argue with pea-brains and those who come forward to be healed of minor ailments are content with a blessing, the promise of health restored. Any magical incantation would have done the trick as well.

Idly I survey the many-headed throng. This is the scene which greets Yeshua's gaze day after day; how weary he must get confronting these wistful faces and outstretched arms – yet the moral force he transmits never seems to flag. My eyes are drawn to one pair: a man and a teen-age boy standing a little apart from the rest. There's something arresting about them. Is it the tenseness in the youngster's features or his senior's nervous, protective gesture and look of desperation? I may have spoken too soon; Rock and his mates could have a crisis on their hands. Suddenly the lad utters a blood-curdling shriek, tears himself from the man's grasp and falls writhing to the ground. His eyes roll upward, showing their whites, and a scarlet-flecked spume dribbles from his lips as he scrabbles in the dust. The screams rise to a climax, which shatters my nerves and fills me with helpless pity. Rock shuffles forward, glancing uneasily at Jim and Jo, then goes into a sort of pantomime imitating his Master's technique. It has no effect whatever on the possessed child.

"Try harder, for God's sake," pleads the man. "This will kill my son!"

I breathe a prayer. For a second the convulsions cease and the boy's eyes fix themselves on me as though in response. Then my sense of purpose wavers and he starts screaming once again. Yet my prayer is answered in a different way. As abruptly as Yeshua vanished from the cliff at Nazrat, he appears among us, his full attention on the father, not the epileptic.

"How long has your son suffered from fits?"

"As far back as I remember, Sir. The – thing inside him has no mercy. It throws him into fire and water. It'll do for him unless he's cured."

"The child can't hear or answer me. You must supply the faith required to heal him. Do you believe?"

"I – I'm not sure. I want to, but…" The guy's honesty conflicts with his need. "Lord, help my unbelief!"

Almost casually, Yeshua raises his hand commanding the squatter's obedience. In a burst of malice it yells its impotent defiance at him then throws a final, climactic fit before leaving its victim inert, a discarded doll in the roadway.

"He's a goner, poor lad," someone mutters.

Without comment, Yeshua bends and helps the boy to his feet. He stares about him dazedly then seeks refuge in his poppa's arms. The man's sobbing with relief and gratitude – my eyes prick with unshed tears. When the rabble's dispersed to spread the latest headlines, Rock asks ruefully, "What did I do wrong, Master? I wanted so badly to pull that one off."

"And win general applause? Wrong attitude, old friend. You tried to go it alone, forgetting that the healing power is from God, not man." He pauses, looking round at us. "One of you had the right idea. I felt the vibes on my way here and I projected, but the contact went dead."

"Was it me, Master? – "Was it me?" They all want a share in his glory or at least some commendation. Yeshua's glance rests on me. "Let's say it was someone who has a deeper intuition of my nature than most of my longer-term followers."

This episode proves the crown of Yeshua's achievements to date, so far as his public's concerned. Even Si is satisfied with the resultant propaganda. Needless to say, the reaction of the oppo is exactly the reverse. They step up their anti-Barjoseph campaign, adding a new and more sinister twist to it. In order to eliminate him once and for all, they must invoke the power that belongs to Rome alone. The Nazirite must be trapped, therefore, into uttering sedition against the Emperor himself. One of the Set-aparts approaches him with a guileless expression and says in his colleagues' hearing, "Master, we know your egalitarian views. You claim that we're all alike in the eyes of God and that no one merits being honoured above his fellows. Then tell me, should I pay tribute to Caesar – or Yahweh alone?"

Yeshua looks at him narrowly, sensing the obvious pitfall. Whichever way he replies, he'll offend against Roman rule or Jewish orthodoxy. He borrows a denarius from one of the bystanders and holds it up. "Whose image is this?" he asks.

"The Emperor's, of course. Read the inscription for yourself."

"Right. Then give Caesar what is due to Caesar – and God what is due to God."

His answer silences his interrogator but it earns Si's disapproval. "He'll be kissing the Procurator's toe next," he grouses. "There are moments when I despair of the Leader. He's just thrown away a golden opportunity to declare himself."

"Hold on," says Jude. "Aren't you cutting a few corners, Si? We've got it all laid on in the City. Shouting bloody murder and waving banners in this one-horse joint ain't' to get us anywhere. There's nobody to sit up and take notice."

That's where he miscalculates. Antipas has no apparent need of Rome's permission to execute, judging by the Baptist's death. One piddling, small-time revolutionary won't make the mighty Pilatus sweat under the collar yet he poses a real threat to Herod on his own territory. It doesn't take the Set-aparts long to appreciate this. They're aiming to rid Galil of Yeshua's presence and they tempt him to his doom down south by hinting at royal displeasure. "Antipas is out to get you," they tell him solicitously. "He's made up his mind that you're a menace to his throne and he'll pounce at any minute."

Trouble is, they could be so right! Their insinuations reflect my own fear but bother Yeshua not at all. "Tell that fox," he retorts, "that his authority is conferred by Rome – and ultimately by a still higher source. He can do nothing to me without my Poppa's consent."

His refusal to face facts is all of a piece with his unshakeable self-belief – unless it's plain perversity, the obstinate bluffing of a man who has lost his way. I'm inclined to believe the last in view of his pessimism about the future. Tiberias is so close, though he's persistently skirted it on his walkabouts (as a good Jew should), and Herod's stooges are all over the shop sniffing out local talent to tickle his fancy or cheap labour to staff his palace. I know because I recognize them – and keep my headscarf in place to avoid being recognized in turn. Joanna hasn't shown up for a fortnight on the other hand; perhaps she's been sussed and forbidden to hobnob with Yeshua? The last item I learned from her was that Cass is back from the wars with fresh scars and medallions to parade. She thought he might be due for a transfer, which ties in with what Si told me on the way home from Nazrat. Anyway, I'm keeping a look-out for soldier-boy; it seems an age since he held me in his strong arms and, while he hasn't been Number One on my rating-list for a fair time now, my body continues to hunger for his touch. He's the one bloke who's loved me as a woman should be loved, sexually yet with genuine fondness. Jo's written himself off in that respect and my relationship with Yeshua's on quite a different plane – yet I still need what Cass alone can give me. There are moments when I give way to a kind of panic, feeling myself being sucked into a vortex, swept along on a dark tide of nothingness towards some uncharted goal. It's the same

128

sensation that I had in Hezekiah's tunnel. That dreadful journey returns to me in dreams and I wake sweating, with Cass's name on my lips. Then I know for certain that I want him: his warmth, his reassuring earthiness – even his ghastly jokes and schoolboy slang. Only he can save me from myself...

Our meeting's inevitable. Patrols are rarely seen in these peaceful Lake-villages yet the military presence has hotted up recently. So the Set-aparts' warning wasn't unfounded after all! Herod's troops are keeping a low profile but there's no doubt they've got their eye on Yeshua. They may make their strike at any minute – or bide their time until he compromises himself as Johanan did. They're mostly Syrians, privates and N.C.O.'s I catch a glimpse of Abenadar's dusky, good-natured face some days before that of his immediate superior.

Cass is standing in the shadow of a curtained stall across Capernaum's market place when I first sight him. My impulse is to run to him yet something holds me back. Is it the fear that I might implicate him in my disgrace at court or the greater one that he might disown me out of hand? Leave the first move to him, Miri; take off your silly headscarf and let him know you're in the vicinity – then he can decide the issue. My hair floats free, blazing out among the dark heads round about, and I go on walking from stall to stall as if intent on my purchases, then turn into an unfrequented alley. I hold my breath and listen for the tread of hob-nailed legionary boots. Thump, thump, thump.

A moment later, he has me in a bear hug. No inhibitions, no second thoughts. How could I have doubted him? When he lets me go, holds me at arm's length with a huge grin splitting his face, I observe a new scar down the left cheek which blends with his battered beauty. I stroke it with one finger. "Aretas?"

"Not in person. One of his dagoes took a swipe at me before I spitted his guts on my sword."

"Did you bully-boys win your war-game?"

"Not so's you'd notice. We conquer on the plains but we're not hill-fighters. Aretas had the upper hand and made terms which don't suit Herod's pocket or his pride – so his officers carry the can."

"Joanna, Chusa's wife, told me you were on the move, Cass,"

"Believe it, babes. Abenadar and me's posted to the Third Cohort under Pilatus's command. The king, thank Jupiter, is delighted to be losing us."

"Won't that mean – Caesarea?" Reunited, and about to be split up once more; my heart misses a beat.

"Yup. And the City when Mister Big puts in an appearance there." He pauses, always a trifle slow on the uptake. "See what you're getting' at, sweetheart – though it won't be right away. No sweat. I can take you along with me."

His unquestioning assumption that he's still my Mister Big is typical yet I'll forgive him anything.

"I've missed you, Cass."

"Me, too. Ab filled me in on your vanishing act plus a few other items besides. It seems you rubbed Herod up the wrong way after your surefire start – which makes two of us. I've been asking myself if we'd get together again. When I saw the flash of that gorgeous crest just now, I felt like the sun'd come out after a year of steady rain."

"I'm sorry. There was no way I could get in touch with you, explain my position. Did you know I was here, up north?"

"Not till Chusa's better half tipped me the wink. She thinks the sun rises outa your butt, by the way. Soon as she told me, I cadged a spot of leave and came out to this dump to track you down."

"I'm glad. Not simply that we've found each other but because it occurred to me that you might've been sent officially to nick Yeshua Barjoseph. I – I've tacked on to him, as Joanna must have mentioned."

"She sure did. You could've knocked me silly with a palm-leaf! I'd had the impression he was really bad news so far as you were concerned."

"I changed my mind about him – or had it changed for me. He's a great guy, Cass."

"So they tell me. Buddy of my pater's, one Cornelius, looks me up now and again at the palace. He's a centurion like me, higher grade, retired when he cashed in on a lucky investment and came to settle in these parts. One of his servants fell ill. He's a caring sorta guy and he found out Barjoseph was performing in the district, so he went out and asked him for help. Knowing no Yehudi will enter a Goy homestead, he begged for a long-distance cure. Barjoseph was impressed by his diplomacy and did his party-piece then and there. The servant was right as rain when Corny got back, probably malingering from the word go. Yet nothing will persuade the old boy that it wasn't one of these 'happenings' everybody talks about. He's financing a new prayer-house for the burgh single-handed, he tells me, as a way of saying thanks."

We've been chatting in the alley out of sight of curious eyes. Now Cass proposes we adjourn to the comfort of a hostelry. I say, "It won't do you a heap of good to be seen with me, Cass, not if it gets to Herod's flapping ears."

He chuckles. "What in hell do I care? I'm not jacking in my favourite gal to please his lecherous majesty who can stare but not dare. Yeah, Miri, I could make a shrewd guess how you fell out with the dirty old peeping Tom."

We go to the Bunch of Grapes, a pub with the sleaziest interior and best wine in town. Cass orders a skin and gets instant service. His uniform commands respect if not popularity. We share the skin as well as all our news since last we were together. He gives me a blow-by-blow account of the campaign and I give him an edited version of my escapades – which brings us back to Yeshua. He remarks pensively, "All these weird goings-on, multiplying loaves, calming tempests and and exorcising demons… You don't credit 'em, do you?"

"It's hard to disbelieve the evidence of my own eyes, Cass."

"O.K. So he's got you hooked on him, ready to swallow his whole bag of tricks. Does that mean what I think it means?"

I've never seen Cass jealous before. It makes him look half his age, a pouting adolescent, and I long to kiss him. "No, my sweet. I do love him but not in that way. He – he's not available. I tried it on, believe me, but no dice…"

He brightens immediately. "So we're still in business even though I can't pull rabbits out of a hat?"

I giggle, relaxed by the booze. "I'll never convince you he's the real thing, will I?"

"I've seen so-called miracle-workers – thaumaturges – perform in Alexandria. They chuck sticks on the ground and turn them into snakes. A dirty-picture merchant there told me how it's done. He said the creatures are paralysed with dope and they come to when they hit the deck. Simple!" He grows serious. "You know why Barjoseph hoodwinks his audiences, don't you? He means to stage a coup – take over the State by force and rule it himself."

"By waving a wand and making you lot disappear in a puff of smoke?"

"I'm not joking, Miri. He's in touch with the Self-rule for Zion brigade – there's a pair of them posing as his followers, so we're informed. I'd hate to see you mixed up in – any unpleasantness."

"How d'you mean?"

"You thought I might be here to arrest Barjoseph. Well, you weren't so far out. The word goes in Tiberias that his H.Q.'s to be raided and he's to be taken in. One reason I came to Capernaum was to tip you off."

Drink clouds the shock of alarm I ought to be feeling: drink and the sheer joy of being with Cass. I tease him: "If you suppose we're plotting revolution, you shouldn't be fraternizing with me, should you?"

"I'm a Roman. He won't shift us with his peasant army. If he tries it on, we'll break him. It's Antipas who has it in for him. He rules by courtesy of Rome yet he knows that if he's toppled by a mass-rising, we shan't come running to pick up the pieces."

"So what d'you suggest we do?"

"I don't give a cuss about your rabble-rouser. If he's wise, he'll go south while there's time and take his chance in Judaea. It's you I'm bothered about. I'd like to take you right out of it."

His arm slides round my shoulders and his blunt fingers explore forbidden territory in the half-light of the saloon. I loosen the collar of my frock to facilitate matters. The wine's releasing stored-up tensions, making me amorous. I want him with an urgency born of sex-starvation yet I can't walk out on my commitment to Yeshua.

"Cass, he won't go – not until he's good and ready. He's said as much. I think he's got some sort of death-wish."

"What's that to us, sweetheart?"

"Don't you see? If I go steady with you again and he's pulled in by your boss, it'd be as if I'm lined up with his enemies. I'd have to watch him go through – God knows what, torture, maybe the chop, like Johanan. I'd be torn apart inside. Don't make me do it."

"You said he meant nothing to you." I open my mouth to protest and he stops it with his own, forcing a rough tongue between my teeth. The big hands stroke my flesh: lover's hands which sense my weakness, the quivering of my desire. "He can't do this for you with all his conjuring, can he?"

"No, Cass, stop it." I wrench myself free from him, sobered by the dilemma that I'm in. "I'll stick to him. I must. I'm bloody fond of you, I need your loving till it hurts. But I can't switch sides. If the worst comes to the worst and Yeshua drops out, we'll think again. You're a great guy, in bed and out of it, and though you're a lousy Alien, I'll take out an option on that offer you once made me, one day... Let's leave it at that."

My voice stays firm, firmer than the rest of me that's crying to be folded in his arms and yield to his passion. Another king-size pout as he glares at me with down-drawn eyebrows. Oh God, do I dig this sullen, overgrown schoolboy! He growls, "You're having it both ways – giving your soul to him and your body to me."

This is remarkably well put, for Cass. He's hit my quandary in one. I don't want to be spread around like a dismembered corpse. I want to be everything to one man alone. But which? I temporise: "Look, Cass, it's out of the question for me to be seen in Tiberias, let alone your barracks. As you said, Herod's after my blood."

"Check. So we get together some place else. Here, for instance. The landlord's bound to oblige a Roman officer paying good Roman coin." He grins. "I'll offer him a few asses for the pleasure of strokin' an ass in a million!"

"Now you're being coarse. So I'm only worth a handful of coppers to you?" I rib him.

"Don't tell me I'm mean – that's a Jewish failing. Heard the one about the Yiddisher momma, by the way?"

"Go on," I encourage him, hoping that his appalling sense of humour will defuse the atmosphere between us.

"She takes little Yacob to the seaside. He gets swep' up by a big wave and she prays for her boy to be saved. Another wave carries him back to shore, alive, and she gives thanks. Then she takes a second look at him and says, 'Lord, one little thing. When he was washed out, he was wearing a new cap. Good 'un, ain't it?'"

"Frightfully amusing..." I judge my moment. "Cass, we're going to call it a day. I'm off home to Migdal and you've got your duties at Tiberias. We'll meet when we meet."

"Whassat supposed to mean? I want it now, Miri!" Drink slurs his speech.

"So do I. Like hell. But the vibes aren't right. This Herod – Yeshua thing: it's got to be sorted out first."

He sneers at me, "You 'fraid Big Brother will smack your wrist for misbehavin' with an Alien?"

"You know I'm not. I've never given a damn what others think of me. Besides, he's broad-minded on the subject of sex, so long as it goes with love, and dead against racialism. I do love you, Cass, but I don't fancy this hole-in-corner stuff. Once the crisis blows over, we'll come out into the open and I'll tell the world that I'm your woman."

He gets heavily to his feet. Thank goodness my head's stronger than his! "Zat your las' word, hun?" Right on, but remember: nex' time I show up, it mayn't be a friendly call. I'm still under Herod's orders an' there's two names writ big at the top of his hit-list."

I watch him stumble out of the saloon. Was he threatening me or merely nursing his manly pride? He's fond of me, that's for sure. Yet he's a soldier first and foremost. Much as he loathes Antipas, he'll put duty in front of personal inclination. I'll take my chance on eventuality – but I must try to persuade Yeshua to give himself a break.

I allow Cass a minute or two to put distance between us, then follow him outside. The open air clears my muzzy head as I walk back to our villa. Thank heaven Mart's taken herself off at last, alarmed by news of Laz's relapse. One whiff of alcohol on my breath and she'd be climbing the wall! I'm worried for my brother too but she refused my company, saying my presence would make him worse. Anyway, something tells me I'll be needed round here – though what help I can give Yeshua in his emergency, I can't conceive. Now that we're free of Mart, we've invited the whole team round for a meal. It's Yeshua's night and he's laying on the nosh; I'd've preferred to leave out two of the guests yet he insists his cousin and Jude must attend. I think he may be meaning to have it out with them once and for all.

I feel almost – guilty as he gives me his unreserved smile and kiss of greeting. My lips still throb with the hunger of Cass's embrace... The others gather round our dining-table as if impatient to get down to the modest feast. Nobody asks where I've been though Jude casts a suspicious glance at me. He keeps a watching brief on troop-movements in the area and might be putting two and two together. Drink and a near-quarrel with my lover have taken away my appetite and I pick at the food while the rest empty their plates. A sit-down meal is a rarity in our lives and they're making the most of it. Autumn's come round again with its abrupt drop in temperature, and Rock kindles a blazing fire in the hearth as we hug it afterwards – almost like the old days when Poppa's friends dropped in for an evening's cosy natter. Yet there are currents of unease stirring and Yeshua's at his most solemn. He sits cross-legged, half in shadow, and stays silent for a time as if rehearsing what he's going to say.

"It must be obvious to you all by now that the Establishment have rejected my mission," he begins. "They won't accept my credentials, they contradict my teaching and now they're warning me off their pitch. You're my friends, my fellow-workers. What would you advise?"

It's a new one for Yeshua to ask our counsel but Si, ever sure of himself, fails to detect any ulterior motive in the question. He steps in with both feet: "I'm glad you've decided to consult us, Master. The situation calls for a cool head and reasoned judgement. Wishful thinking is not going to neutralize the opposition."

"Stampede 'em," puts in Jude promptly. "Rub 'em out if need be. They won't be won over by smart talk."

"A cool head, Jude," Si reproves him. "Our Leader deplores violence, as I do, yet has he considered the advantage of a more sophisticated approach, I wonder? We are not dealing with children."

"You've all heard me commend child-like innocence," Yeshua reples. "Simon and Jude are in favour of a political solution involving bribery, deviousness and the probability of bloodshed. Yet I've told you that only the simplicity of children can gain entrance to my Poppa's kingdom – and mine. How can the two be reconciled?"

Jo says, "No way, Master. We're not politicians planning to take over the government nor trained soldiers who aim to drive out the Aliens. Your rule isn't an earthly one, you've said so more than once; it's to be spread by preaching and prayer."

"Good, Jo, good. A lesson well learnt." Yeshua turns to me. "What d'you say, Miri?"

"You know my opinion, Yeshua. I think Si and Jude will do your cause untold damage. And if your cause suffers, so will you."

"As to suffering, I'm prepared for that. If I teach my little flock to take up their crosses and follow me, I must set the example myself."

I shiver involuntarily. "Why – why do you use that image, Yeshua/"

"I was thinking of a Roman death." His voice is softer than the crackling flames. "No quick, merciful release but a long agony of shame and exposure under the eyes of men."

Jude, needled by his criticism, explodes at this: "What's all this blather about being topped? I'll see to it that no harm comes to you, Boss. It's the oppo that's going to get clobbered – unless they keep their heads down!"

"My friend means," Si interposes smoothly, "that a little diplomacy will offset the possibility of failure. Candidly, Master, I feel you are adopting a thoroughly defeatist attitude. The programme that confronts us is designed to ensure your undying reign as God's Chosen One. All this talk about your premature demise will only cast doubt on your identity."

"He'll be saying next that we can go hang ourselves," grunts Jude, "after all the graft we've put in back-stage."

"Oh no," Yeshua smiles. "I wouldn't dispense with you for the world, Jude. You're cast for a key-role in my Poppa's strategy, did you but know it!"

Jude preens himself, glancing round smugly at those less privileged. Si, none too pleased at his sidekick being singled out, says, "I think you may have misunderstood me, Master. All I'm suggesting is that you – we – should be more discreet in our dealings with the Hasidim. Surely we should look to their support as champions of a free Israel against the adversary within our gates? Yet we appear to do the very opposite. Not only are they branded as 'whitened sepulchres', vipers and other opprobrious epithets, but you – we – extend our evangelization to Gentiles, those outside the Law. This is not part of the Mashiah's brief."

"You're getting a trifle mixed up with your pronouns, cousin, but it's evident whom you hold to blame. If I were to exonerate the Set-aparts, the basis of my teaching would be destroyed. Their false piety and active malice have undermined the religion they profess to be serving. As for your second objection, I freely acknowledge it. When have I ever said my message was confined to Israel?"

Rock gives Si his reluctant backing: "We thought the Mashiah was to be Israel's saviour. Doesn't Scripture make that plain, Master? He's to scatter our enemies like chaff and banish the heathen for their filthy practices and blasphemous idols…"

Jude joins the chorus. "Next thing, you'll be telling us we should love the sodding Aliens." He cocks a wicked eye in my direction, still sore at my remark.

"Is a Roman legionary less worthy of my blessing than a Jew? You take pride in calling yourself a Partisan, Jude, yet God isn't partisan: every act of his creation is an act of love. Not one of his creatures is to be excluded from redemption except those who spurn it of their own free will." Yeshua's face clouds over and he gazes at the burning logs. "What would you say if I told you the day will come when races beyond your ken, in lands you've never heard of, will displace God's chosen people in his service?"

The shocked hush reminds me of our reaction to the offering of his flesh and blood at Gergesa. This time two alone walk out on him – Si and Jude. The rest merely look crestfallen. Jim says in a small voice, "Does that include us, Master? We've given everything up to follow you."

"So you have, Jim. Your reward will be far greater than its initial cost. A man must lose his own life in order to discover it more truly – and you will pay the same price as Johanan, my cousin, did. So will others among you, yet not before they've carried my word abroad to pagan cities. Yes, even you, Rock, with all your prejudice!"

"You know about the Baptist, then?" asks Andy. "We tried to keep it from you... D'you mean we're to die for the cause?" He never wraps things up, old Andy, and his blunt query makes waves.

Yeshua nods. "The thought staggers you now and some will stumble on their road to salvation but believe me, when the moment comes you'll welcome your fate as the passport to Heaven."

Jo says tremulously, "Shall I also be killed for your sake, Master?"

"No, you'll suffer exile and fulfil the visions you dreamed of as a boy, in enforced solitude. That lies far ahead. Your first task will be to care for those most dear to me, my Momma and the girl to whom you owe an unpaid debt..."

Jo looks at me and I return his glance. Neither of us has visualized a future which includes the other, since we drifted apart. Perhaps Yeshua simply means we're to stay good friends, united by our loyalty to him. I can still feel a flicker of resentment at the way he parcels out our lives; if he supposes we're going to patch up the relationship, which he brought to an end, he's right off target... Shut up, Miri, that's your bloody little squatter griping through you.

It hasn't been a light-hearted evening. Yeshua's predictions have put a damper on our get-together and the faithful ten file out quietly with muttered good-nights. He and I are left alone in a room lit only by the dying flames. We both postpone the hour of sleeping because it brings no rest. I'm wakeful these nights with troubles on my mind and he's oppressed by horrible dreams, which rouse him, sweating and white-faced, from his bed. I yearn to comfort him but the only way I know to do that has been proved a washout.

He continues as though the general departure has not disturbed his train of thought. "He's a good sort, Miri, decent and straightforward. He loves you in his way – hasn't looked at another girl since he last saw you. His kiss told you that, didn't it?"

I have a double take. I'd imagined he was going on about Jo until the final sentence. So, not content with telling our fortunes, he's been doing a spot of clairvoyance. The squatter stirs in my bowels but I'll stamp him down for the minute. I'd like to talk about Cass, seeing that Yeshua's already in the know. "Am I wrong to want him so badly?"

"Wrong? Of course not. I'd be bothered if you didn't. Your instinct's perfectly normal."

"I meant wrong to be friends with an Alien?"

"When I spoke of a Roman legionary, who did you think I meant? That should resolve your doubts." He puts his hand on my lap. "One kiss in a public place is no more than a deed of intent. You're longing to go back to him, aren't you, Miri?"

"I – I don't know. Part of me does and it's not just my body; I truly care for him. Yet another part's holding back, telling me I'm bound to someone else." The imp inside me gathers substance, its taloned fingers scrabbling for my brain, my throat, and my limbs. "You've got a stranglehold on me, damn you, you won't let me breathe, live out my life the way I want…" Voice rising, ugly note.

He stares past my eyes straight into the depths of me. "It's time you came out of her, you little pest," he says grimly.

"Let me be. I hate your insufferable holiness, Barjoseph. You stifle me with it. Your friends must face some ghastly death to appease its bloodlust and Miriam must be torn from her lover to be its willing slave!"

"I've made no demands on her."

"Not in so many words. If you had, she'd turn them down. It's because you've wormed your way into the centre of her being that she can't get rid of you."

"Pot calling the kettle black? You've long overstayed your welcome, you nasty – impudent – mischievous – little bugger!"

I fling myself at him, flailing with arms and legs in a transport of fury. The squatter gives me a strength I've never owned – but his is greater. He holds me at arm's length, kicking and screaming, while his grey eyes command. This time I feel no pain, willing him to hold me forever in his firm yet tender grasp, and when I find my real voice, it's that of a small child.

"Help me, Lord." The dusty square in Capernaum swims into memory, a father imploring aid for his tortured son. "Help my unbelief."

"You've no need of help, Miri. Not now. Divinity alone may be addressed as Lord."

He lets me go and I fall at his feet. Time merges to an everlasting moment and I kneel, engulfed in his presence. When I come to, the hearth's black and a pale glimmer from the window stains the wall opposite, Yeshua's sitting bolt upright, awake and very still, I sense that his eyes have never left my face.

"How long, Lord?"

"Five hours or thereabouts, my dear. Compared with eternity, a drop in the ocean."

"You need your rest. I'm sorry."

"Don't be. I've passed my first trouble-free night for many weeks and it's owing to you."

I'm always cold, waking from one of my trances. I tremble and he draws me to him. Now that a barrier's been broken down, we can be intimate without the tension of physical desire. His warmth is comforting, pervasive – not a lover's heat.

"Poor Cass. He needs me."

"Then give yourself to him. Our oneness is on a different level."

"I – I didn't realize I could love you both. I shrugged him off – but you'll be aware of that."

"Yes, it was provisional, wasn't it? You'll meet again and have a chance to finish what you began."

"Could he meet you as well?"

"Herod intends that he should, but the Fox miscalculates as usual. I'll leave the stage to you." He pauses. "I spoke last evening of those who'd suffer in the future for my sake. I didn't mention the one fated to suffer first, before my own ordeal. Yours, dearest Miri, is a very special honour."

TEN

Successive feasts mark the year's progress. Pessach has made way for Shabuoth in mid-summer when we celebrate the harvest, sparse as it is, and Ruth's story is read out in Shul (I've always thought she wasn't quite the little innocent everyone takes her for – she knew darned well what she was doing when she tacked herself on to the gleaners of Boaz and so did Naomi, her mother-in-law, who told her to lie at his feet on the threshing-floor. If only my bid for Jo had worked out as smoothly as hers…). Then there's a five-month gap to Rosh Hoshanah, our new year but not the Romans', the time of penance ending with Yom Kippur. How dreary we kids used to find the endless service on that day, standing with no food in our tummies while the amidah dragged on and the shofar wailed its baby-cry to the heavens. Mind you, it was fun to break the rules if you could get away with it. We'd store goodies beforehand in a neighbouring latrine, ask to be excused one by one then slip out to gorge ourselves in secret!

Yeshua observes these liturgical practices yet he gives each of them a fresh, more personal slant – as he did when multiplying the loaves at Pessach. On the Day of Atonement, for instance, he tells us we must examine our consciences in private instead of just beating our breasts while the Hazan recites his public litany of sins. For once in my life I take a long, hard look at my own past and regret it, realizing how wilful and misguided I've been. Then he talks of the scapegoat led through the City-gates bearing its imaginary load of men's offences and banished to the desert. I've always pitied the defenceless beast unjustly punished for our guilt. He says his poppa is to give us one who'll shoulder our burden of expiation and pay our debts to Him. This would've made no sense to me a while back; now it does – and I'm more than ever determined to prevent Yeshua himself taking on the role!

Many pilgrims have departed for Judaea to spend this sacred season in the City. Others are preparing to leave for Succuoth, the feast of Booths, a week's festival ahead in memory of our ancestors' sojourn in the desert. We beg and bullyrag Yeshua to go south with them but he won't budge, defying Herod's agents. Says it's not ordained by his poppa for him though his followers must go in his place – leaving him here, unguarded. I refuse to abandon him, however, and he seems content that I should remain. Maybe he thinks I'm safe from arrest, being a mere woman… I've a feeling in my bones that Herod is about to strike, now that the majority of his target's supporters have left the coast clear and he can be pulled in without unwelcome fuss.

I'm not wrong. A day or two after Rock and the boys have set off, a deputation from Tiberias shows up in Migdal where Yeshua's known to be staying. He might have stood a chance in Capernaum but not in this back-water region. Oh, it's all very cleverly planned! There's no suggestion of naked force; civilian emissaries inquire as to his whereabouts, saying that His Majesty invites him to the palace as a distinguished guest – but behind them armed soldiers give the lie to their words. Cass's scarlet-crested helmet is conspicuous at their head and beneath it his features are closed, official.

What am I to do? The village males are on their way south, only a few old biddies and small children are about, too ancient or too young for the long journey. I've left Yeshua at prayer in our villa and any attempt to warn him will attract attention. I must put on a bold front, convince them that he's departed with his mates. My persuasion falls on deaf ears, however; I'm as well known to Herod's toadies as they are to me.

"Well, well," remarks their senior spokesman, Phicol, a courtier I disliked intensely for his waspish tongue. "If it isn't My Lord's elusive dancing-girl…He'll be pleased that we've netted one of his game-birds. Don't lie to me, young woman; lead me to your precious Nazirite at once!"

"Look, Sir, take me but leave him alone. He means the king no harm."

Useless ploy, as I knew it would be. Thay lay hands on me at Phicol's orders and I see Cass look mutinous from the rear – but he knows his place. I'm compelled to bring them to the villa, which they break into without ceremony. The diplomatic play-acting is at an end. A few moments later, they emerge empty-handed.

"You've been stalling us," blusters Phicol, "playing for time. While we talked, the quarry's got away. We'll have to chase him down."

He's ignorant, of course, as to Yeshua's streamlined mode of transport. So that's what he meant about 'leaving the stage to me'; my bewilderment is followed by a sense of hurt, then dread as I recall what else he promised for me. The countryside is scoured yet there's no sign of him – Phicol must make do with the bird in hand. His fiction of inviting an honoured guest hardly applies to yours truly. I'm handed over to the patrol, Cass ensuring that they don't handle me roughly but making no demur at my arrest. His covert glances betray concern as we march in silence to the palace yet he can't disguise an air of 'I told you so'. He likes to be proved in the right, even against his own best interests.

I think I can face anything Antipas cares to throw at me except meeting the swine himself. The recollection of his lascivious thirst to feast his eyes on my nakedness is bad enough; far worse the crime gratuitously committed against Johanan. I grit my teeth as we enter the soulless atmosphere of his capital and mount the avenue leading to his domain. Once this seemed my gateway to success, now the spread colonnades look menacing, like colossal jaws about to close on their prey. Friend Chusa awaits us in the sky lit vestibule and as ever, his face gives away nothing though the brows go up a fraction at the absence of the main objective. He exchanges a word with Phicol, and then the patrol is instructed to take me through side-passages to a place of confinement. This is a small chamber I've never seen before, well away from the court's communal living-quarters, thick-walled and windowless. I learn from my captors that it's an interrogation-cell where subversives receive the 'usual treatment' – whatever that might be. Well-suited to El Mashnaka, it seems a tasteless anomaly in urbane Tiberias… At least it's an improvement on the Baptist's dungeon, while Herod's oft-stated dislike of violence may keep him out of the picture.

The sensation of being shut in oppresses me, as always. I've no means of measuring the hours since daylight is denied me; four bare walls, illumined by a flickering sconce, are the limit of my view. My sole distraction is to let a too lively imagination dwell on the prospect before me: not an appealing one! Whatever happens, let's hope Cass won't be involved. I'd rather he's spared than myself. Watching someone you love going through hell must be tougher than the ordeal and I'm scared he might lose his cool. If he tries it on, there'll be two of us in shtook together and our combined future will take a toss. When at length company arrives on the scene, I'm relieved not to identify his craggy countenance. Three guys: a pair of desperate-looking characters, more debased in feature than Jude's crony Yeshua Barabbas (if that's possible) – and Chusa himself.

I detect something more than distaste for his part in this charade, beneath the mask of decorum. I suspect he had a liking for me in former days, influenced maybe by Joanna and their son, Joab, with whom I got on well. I wonder how the lad's faring; if circumstances were other than they are, I'd ask after him – but Chusa makes it clear he's come at duty's call.

"Well, young lady, it appears that you're a party to the escaping of a man His Majesty is most – ah - anxious to meet. I am here to extract information as to where he may be found."

"Since Yeshua's not being taken into custody, Sir, he can't be said to have escaped. He simply went down for the Feast,"

"That's not what My Lord's agents maintain. They say he was with you overnight – conduct unbefitting a man of God, if I may say so. You must be aware of his place of concealment. Not only that, you're also implicated in his activities."

"You know as well as I do that he poses no threat to your master, apart from condemning his conduct."

"That was the Baptist's crime and he paid for it." Chusa gestures at his henchmen. "If you make no answer that satisfies me, I'm instructed to leave you in the hands of these men. Their methods are not for the squeamish."

I'm certain he's bluffing, putting up a stern front to deceive his ruffian assistants who must be informers like everyone else in this dog-eat-dog set-up. No doubt he'd hoped I'd come clean and give away Yeshua's hiding-place plus admitting to some vague conspiracy. Now he can scarcely withdraw from the position he's adopted. The best he can do is to lean over me once I've been strapped into the cell's single chair and whisper, "Miriam, my dear, you're playing into the Tetrarch's hands. He's not forgiven you for digging your nails into him – and he means you to bear the same marks, more deeply incised. He was counting on your refusal to comply."

They haven't gagged me, knowing that my cries will go unheeded. I'm able to answer, "It's no good, Sir. I can't tell what I don't know. He's out of Herod's clutches – and I'm in them. Let him have his petty revenge. But please tell your wife nothing."

He goes out, his urbanity shattered. The zombies close in. They're thugs, hired psychos, and I suspect Antipas has given them free rein to do a thorough job on me, yet they go through the motions of a routine inquiry. It's a double-act: one tries to soften me up with gentle persuasion while the other piles on threats. Then they swap roles – the familiar good guy-bad guy routine. It's said that only those habituated to torture show fear before the event; I mayn't show it but, by Moishe, I feel it. Yet, as they raise their knives and tear down the front of my tunic, I can console myself with the thought that my 'crowning glory' may go unscathed; Jude's would-be assault on my vanity was less bearable than what's to come...

As the first blade caresses the skin of my forehead, I tense at its exquisite pain, coldness like fire. Blood runs down into my eyes and courage deserts me in a rush. Then (from outside or within) some power of endurance surges, blotting out the intolerable present, its shame and its anguish. I watch the knives perform their deft surgery and wonder at the dark runnels staining my white skin. The torturers look baffled, disconcerted. Neither screams nor concessions. It's a letdown for them.

Though my nerves transmit no sensation, my body can no longer take such ill-usage. Half-fainting from loss of blood, I dimly see the door open and Chusa staring, sickened at the sight. He dismisses the knife-wielders, comes over and unties the straps round my wrists and ankles. I fall forward into his arms and he lays me gently on a pallet beside the wall. The ceiling ripples above me. Funny – there's the same spider-shape as in my bedroom at Bethaniah, only now its legs are writhing in a devil's-dance. Chusa's left me once again, don't say he's sending back those brutes to complete their task... No, another face appears in my vague line of vision: Joanna's, Thank God! Tears are running down her cheeks – have I ever seen them look so pale? – And my own are suddenly released, bringing, with the emotion, a surge of agony from brow to groin where the final cut was made.

She has ointment and bandages. She tends my injuries, fuming with a rage I didn't know her to possess. When she sees that I'm climbing back to full consciousness, she looks into my eyes and says, "How could he have done this to you, Miri?"

I mutter feebly, "He's had it in for me ever since I went for him. Kings repay more handsomely than commoners."

"Not Antipas – he's beneath contempt. I meant the Master. Why did he abandon you to answer for him? I don't understand."

I ponder her question dully. "P'raps it has something to do with reparation. The wrongs I've done have to be – requited. Don't reproach him, Joanna. He made it easy to bear."

She smiles with difficulty. "Miri – you're really one of us. No, my dearest, you're further along the road than I am..."

"Will – will Herod want to see the result of his spite, d'you think?"

She shakes her head. "Chusa tells me he's refused to interview in person. I think the mortification you inflicted on him made a deeper wound than any you've endured. These gashes look ugly yet they're only skin-deep, thank God. A little food and drink should restore your strength."

She fetches me nourishment and soon I feel more myself. We talk of old times, of Yeshua's doings and how Chusa forbade her to visit him while the heat's on. "My husband's an upright man," she defends him, "but the King's servant before all. While despising him, he respects his authority."

"Then this cell must be out of bounds for you, Joanna. You shouldn't be ministering to a friend of Yeshua's, surely?"

"Chusa came for me himself. I've never seen him look so angry – and so conscience-stricken."

"It wasn't his fault. He tried to get me off the hook. Tell me, though: how's Joab? Can't I see him, too?

Her face falls. "The poor lamb's been very ill, coughing up blood and suchlike. We had to send him north where they claim the air's purer for his lungs. I've missed him a lot," She brightens. "Still, he's on his way back. He should be home before long and if I can find a way, he'll see his best girl once again!"

"And Salome?"

"The dratted minx! She can wind her stepfather round her little finger these days and we go in fear and trembling of her displeasure. Even the Queen must submit to her least desires." She pauses for my next inquiry. "Isn't there – someone else, Miri?"

"Cass? He brought me here, under orders. Please tell him not to risk his position by visiting me."

"Did you know he's off to the City in a few days? He'll be reporting to Antonia. His second-in-command has already gone."

"I missed Abenadar's nice face in the patrol – he was quite a pal to us at El Mashnaka, wasn't he, Joanna? – More so than he can have realized." I start to yawn and she settles my head lovingly on the pillow.

"You'll sleep, Miri dear. I've put something in your drink to ease the pain. I doubt those fiends will be let loose on you again – not if Chusa has the slightest influence at court."

"Will I be kept here?"

"I'm afraid so. They think the Master may come of his own accord to offer himself as a captive in your place. He's reputed to be your lover, you see…"

"I hadn't considered that possibility. He might just do it, Joanna. Somehow I must get out of here."

"We'll find a way – like last time. Rest now, darling. By tomorrow this horror you've been through will be like a bad dream."

"One thing before I sleep. Please fetch me a mirror…"

She hesitates then, sensing my need, obeys me. It's the same polished copper surface, which reflected my appearance on the morning I charmed Antipas for the first time. Now as I gather courage to look into it, my eyes gaze blearily back from a slashed and mutilated face. Ah well, such marks will heal. My tresses still glow in rich waves from the burnished metal. They salve my woman's pride.

I look forward to a second visit from Joanna, accompanied by young Joab restored to his parents, if not to full health. Instead, an eternity passes in total solitude except for some menial bringing me a plate of scraps and removing the pail provided in a corner of my cell. I feel more myself, my wounds itching but no longer excruciating – she was right, they're superficial and should quickly heal, hopefully leaving inconspicuous scars. When the outside bolt's withdrawn at last and Chusa enters, I shrink from him in automatic dread. He looks remorseful at this reaction yet there's some keener emotion, which is ravaging his features. I never reckoned they could express so much!

He says, "Please don't be afraid, Miriam. I've had my say and Antipas has remitted further – reprisals."

"Very gracious of him."

"He made me describe to him the damage that was done and seems well contented. Had he persisted in his savagery, I should have given notice – and he knew it. I'm no lackey; a nobleman like myself should not be implicated in such sordidness. Besides, I suspect my wife would have left me if I hadn't spoken out!"

"Thanks for letting her come to me."

"She insisted. Joanna can be very strong-willed when her deepest feelings are aroused."

"Won't she come again?"

His look of desperation intensifies. "I – I think not. You see we've had grave news. Joab, whom we thought to be better after a visit to my family-home in the north, has had a serious relapse on his way back. He should be with us by now but it proved necessary to divert him to Capernaum where my personal physician resides. We've had word that there's little, if any, hope…"

My heart bleeds for Joanna – and for the lad who used to make light of his malady. I try to recall my brother at that age, hectic and delicate – yet at least he'd reached full manhood.

"I – I'm so sorry, Sir."

"Some kind folk have taken him in and are tending to his needs. We're about to ride over, though there's nothing we can do."

"Then hurry. You might get there too late."

"Forgive me – a thought occurred. If you could tell me privately where your Master is, he might be able to save Joab's life – for Joanna's sake, not mine."

Is this a trap, a sly ruse to trick me into betraying Yeshua? If so, it's wasted.

"No use, Sir. He's probably in the City. No power on earth could spirit him north in time."

The despair in his eyes is genuine, heart-rending. I think, too, of Joanna, distraught and weeping in her room. No power on earth… Yet Yeshua's power isn't earthly; it transcends both space and time. A scene flashes across my memory – another doomed young body writhing on the ground, my prayer for help winging its way to him, faltering, losing momentum and urgency… Had my faith been stronger then, it might have cured the epileptic without Yeshua's actual presence. I do not doubt him now.

"Bring me something that belongs to Joab, Sir, a garment or some personal possession."

He stares at me blankly then turns on his heel. While he's gone, I kneel, trying to induce a state of mind which has always come to me spontaneously in the past. Yeshua, My Lord, wherever you are, answer me. Make me a channel of your healing to save this needless death… Chusa returns, lays his son's tunic over my outstretched arms. I sink deep, deeper into one of my raptures. A picture forms in my brain: a youngster lying fevered in some fisherman's home, the sheet which covers him bright with arterial blood, adults grouped around impotently, watching him struggle for breath. Gradually his restless movements cease, the brown eyes gazing upward – as the eyes of the convulsed one gazed at me that day.

This time there's no reversion. Joab stays calm, a smile wreathes his lips. The sheet rises and falls to the rhythm of his steady breathing. The greybeard at his side bends over to examine his patient then turns to those behind him; his own features a study in astonishment. To you, Yeshua, the glory of this happening…

I can't get up of my own accord. Chusa helps me to my feet, half-comprehending what I've been about. I tell him, "Your son's well, Sir. He'll be with you soon."

He says nothing, clasping my cold hands in his. Does he believe me? After he's gone from my cell, one thought remains, obliterating the four walls of my prison. My spirit can escape confinement at will from now on and commune with Yeshua's, wherever he may be.

Later, much later, Joanna comes to me. I've seen joy shine like some inner light before – but not as radiantly as hers. She takes me in her arms and holds me to her wordlessly.

"It wasn't my doing, Joanna. Give thanks to the Lord."

"Yes, Miri, I've done nothing else since Joab came back, bragging like a cockerel, He's a changed boy!" She pauses, "I wanted him to show his gratitude in person to the one whose faith saved him but the whole court's fussing over the scamp, even Salome's making eyes at him…. To bring him here might've ruined our plans."

"What plans?"

"Why, to get you away! It's the very least we can do in return for such a deed. When I leave you, my dearest, I shall – forget to draw the bolt. You know your way round the palace as well as anyone. It won't be difficult to avoid being seen in this area. Your boyfriend will be waiting at the west gate, mounted and ready to ride south according to his schedule. As for the sentinel, he won't tell tales on an officer who's highly respected by his men."

"I'd hate to think of your getting into trouble."

"Listen to the child! After what she's put up with… Don't bother your pretty head about us. Antipas is expecting a consignment of Cretan dancing-girls, and I suspect that he's lost all interest in the one who defied him to his face."

"Yes, once he'd disfigured mine… Thank you, Joanna. If things had gone differently, I'd love to stay with you and Joab yet I must return to Yeshua. I've a feeling he'll need all his friends about him before long. Tell Cass I'll be there. What time did he say?"

"Wait for the bugle-call for the first evening-watch, then make your way out. The darkness will conceal you."

A long, tearful embrace and she's gone. I could be following her to freedom through an unbolted door but impatience to get away might spoil everything. Time crawls when you long to end a waking nightmare… As soon as the bugle's blast reaches my ears, I push the door cautiously ajar. An empty corridor looms ahead and I tread it on velvet steps, pausing for any sound of a lurking human presence. At last I find myself in the open air, as relieved as when I once emerged from that claustrophobic tunnel. I linger in the shade of the main block until I'm sure the coast's clear, and then steal across the patio surrounding it.

A guard stands at ease in the arched gateway. He catches sight of me and shifts his ground as though his attention had been drawn elsewhere. I dart between the marble pillars – and my heart stops as a form moves out into my path. So near and yet so far! Two arms thrust forward to seize me, and a voice, half-broken, murmurs its thanks. Joab. Buoyant with released tension and touched by his resolve to see me at all costs, I kiss him fondly and wish him well. Then I'm outside those cold, unfriendly walls and Cass leans down to me from his saddle, within minutes Tiberias is behind us and we're cantering through the dusk towards the frontier of Herod's principality.

We say little to each other on the way. He holds me firmly in front of him with one arm, guiding his mount with the other; his grasp is that of one who fears to lose a prized possession and won't let it go a second time. As hour follows hour and night surrenders to a new day, I revel in my sense of freedom, the thunder of hooves beneath us, which is carrying me far from Herod's tyranny. Please God our paths will never cross again! At this rate, three-days slog by foot will be covered in less than half the time, yet our sturdy horse deserves his rest and eventually Cass reins in at a roadside khan in the badlands of Samaria. No strictly brought up Jew should stop at such a place – but an Alien and an ex-prostitute aren't so choosy. The thought that Yeshua might approve reassures me.

Would he also approve of what I know to be in Cass's mind, and certainly in mine? Fate has at last rewarded us with a chance to be reunited in the truest human sense. He's made no secret of his need and as for me, my flesh has been abused, insulted by Herod's men. Only its proper function can give me back my dignity. Yeshua invited me to offer Cass what he claims by dogged loyalty, and I'll do so with his blessing – offer more than just his claim because I've learnt since earlier days that to give is all that matters.

It's Cass who proves the hesitant one. When the horse has been stabled and fed and we've also dined on good home cooking, he makes sheep's-eyes at me. They say, "I want us to sleep together but I'm not sure how to ask."

I smile at him and speak out loud: "Why the diffidence, Cass? It's not like you to hang back."

"It's your face, Miri. Those bastards sure went to town on you – they'll need their knives when I catch up with 'me! I – I'm wonderin' whether you're up to making love."

"A few cuts here and there plus a little soreness where they tied me down and I fought against the straps won't cramp my style." I nestle closer to him. "My injuries need soothing…"

He pulls away, eyes still on his empty plate. "Look, honey, I'll come clean. I feel – a louse about what happened. I let you down. Should've risked a court-martial and sprung you before they did you over."

"Just what I was afraid of. It wasn't worth it, Cass darling.

Remember, I'm expecting you to pay our household bills."

"You're the tops, Miri." He kisses my cheek, his eyes lifted to the seam across my brow. "By the seven hills, when I get my mits on those sons of bitches! The fact is I was riled by this Yeshua cult of yours. Then, when the steward told me what you'd done for Junior, I hardly knew what to think. Am I going steady with a gorgeous bit of skirt – or some kinda white witch?"

"D'you imagine I'll change you into a toad while you're asleep?" I laugh. "Set your mind at rest, my sweet. First, you only did your duty: second, nobody's taken your place so far as I'm concerned: and third, the boy was cured by means that weren't my own. I was merely an intermediary."

"Barjoseph, you're goin' to say. He's into everything, sod him." The peevish look I find hard to resist. "It's him or me, Miri. We can't both have you - the whole you."

"Two people may be deeply involved with each other yet some part of both will always be separate. That part of me belongs to Yeshua. The rest is all yours."

"Then he's a fool to let you go." The storm clouds blow over and his genial face brightens. "I had a word with the landlord before dinner. He mentioned that he has just one double free overnight. I booked it for us."

"You devil. You've been stringing me along with all this sob-stuff. Well, lead me to it!"

He does. A 'nice' Yehudi girl undresses in the dark but Cass likes seeing his meals served in advance. The lamp shows up my livid scars. I hear his breath sucked in, and then quiet swearing. "I'll hound that pair to death... No, dammit, this was down to me. I owe you. Miri, for every last mark on that perfect skin of yours."

"Right, Cass. I may hold you to that one day. Meanwhile tell me truthfully, do – do they turn you off?"

He yanks me under the sheet with him, holds me as a drowning man clutches a spar and whispers into my ear, "You used to get hopping'-mad when I made fun of your sharp little snout. I told you then I've a fancy for hideous females. Now that you're a regular gorgon, I – simply – can't – resist you."

We've never had it so good. It's as if all our previous love-making has been harvested in one ecstatic night. No future bliss we'll come to share can be more than a memory of this. At last I know what passion really means when all one's longing is to satisfy the other – and Cass, inspired, returns my tenderness. We fall apart once sleep masters us. Of one thing I'm quite certain: in this there was no sin, no taint of sordor. If Yeshua's Heaven excludes the body's sacrament, it must at least contain some echo of its joy.

The final leg of our journey is something of an anticlimax. Last night we reached a high spot in each other's arms; today we face the prospect of yet another separation. Discipline is much stricter in the service of the Roman Procurator, and his cohorts are expected to live in chaste seclusion like those Essenes in their Salt Sea kibbutz. As we draw near the City's battlements and see Antonia rise against the sky, Cass's grip slackens round my waist and I know that military protocol is clamping over him like an iron fist. He's a legionary, bound by his solemn dedication. I, too, am dedicated to a very different cause – one that might so easily clash with his own. We can only trust that once the issue's been resolved, we'll be able to pick up broken threads and weave a pattern for ourselves that will stretch into serene old age.

We part at the Damascus Gate, as formally as when he left me to march against Aretas. He wants to make a firm date ahead but since he has yet to learn his duty-roster and I'm to rejoin a will o' the wisp, this is out of the question. We must bank on good fortune, some chance encounter, to keep in touch. His horse clip-clops up the cobbled slope and its rider's back straightens, his helmet glittering bravely in the sunshine. He doesn't glance backward before wheeling out of sight beyond the Temple's corner. It's like I said: we've each a part the other cannot prise open, an inner world in my case and soldierly ambition in his. What childhood dreams of glory, I wonder, gave rise to that?

The City looks dishevelled, its rooftops and courtyards littered with half-dismembered booths and palm-leaves trodden underfoot in every clear space. Though it's mid-morning, there are few folk about – most will be sleeping off the wild festivities and torchlight dancing of Hoshana Rabbab, the final fling of Succuoth. I feel a nostalgic regret at having missed the feast, even if our private celebration meant a whole lot more to me. We used to love erecting those monster doll's-houses with forked branches and plaited twigs, camping throughout the week in supreme discomfort, which was thrilling for a child. I'm no home-dweller, as you know by now, and our improvised booths were a stage removed from solid walls. When Jo and I fantasized about our future, we said we'd live in such a refuge far away from the world of men.

My first port of call must be the offices of Zabdiah & Sons in Fish Street. It holds its distasteful memories for me yet there's no danger of confronting Jo's poppa since I've heard that declining health has obliged him to take a rest cure in some coastal resort. He's given Yeshua the free run of his premises as a peace offering, Jo told me, and they use the upper floor as a gathering-place when in the City. No doubt they'll be somewhere in the open at this minute but I'll wait for their return.

Business goes on as usual on the ground floor as I enter. Old Oza peers dubiously at me over his dusty ledgers. I put him at his ease, chatting of past encounters as though my previous visit with its dire consequence had never occurred. He shakes his head at mention of his boss's illness and the 'desertion' of his promising younger son.

"He's here now, is Master Jo," he remarks to my surprise. "Up aloft with his friends. Their goings-on are giving us a bad name, you know – they attract unwelcome interest. The tall 'un – him they call master – is setting the City by its ears with his preaching and his cures. Some say he's the Chosen One, others that he's in Satan's employ. As for me, I'm too old for such upsets. All I can do is discourage snoopers and pretend that all's as it should be."

Poor fellow. Yeshua's enterprise belongs to the young who have the eagerness, stomach and idealism for it. The stairway door is bolted on the inside and Oza knocks for me, a summons reminiscent of Jude's three deliberate taps that evening when he lured me to his pad. Can all this subterfuge be necessary for men whose sole crime is their faith? The bolts grind back and Jo himself stands on the bottom step.

"It's you, Miri," he says. "Thanks be! We heard rumours of your arrest. Come up quickly and I'll lock the door on us."

Shadow has obscured my scars from his thankful sight. Jo leads me up the timber staircase and I face a roomful of watchful eyes before recognition dawns and I'm made welcome. There's general consternation at my physical state while they pester me for news of my adventures as if seeking to distract themselves from present fears. My own eyes search for Yeshua as they huddle round me – no sign of him, nor Jude and Si – but a new recruit apparently: a tiny chap with bright eyes and brisk movements like a bird. His unrepressed high spirits bring a ray of sunlight into the assembly's gloom.

"What's going on?" I inquire. "Why all the cloak and dagger stuff – and what are you skulking indoors for when Yeshua's away? Where is he?"

Jim answers sullenly, "Out and about, stirring things up, as usual."

"I don't get it. You've always been at his side in the past. Why aren't you standing by him now? If I can take anything his enemies dish out, surely you can do as much?" By way of shaming them, I outline my experiences as Herod's captive yet despite their sympathy, this has a negative effect.

"If a tin-pot ruler will do that to a harmless girl," Nat points out, "it'll go worse with us down here, what with Temple-police on our tails and Aliens backing them. Stones, scourging, the cross – they're all lined up for law-breakers in Judaea."

"Yeshua's escaped stoning more than once. As for the rest, only common thieves and killers earn such treatment. What've you or he done to deserve it?"

"He's blasphemed, slated the Sads and Set-aparts, chucked the rule-book in their faces. That's all! Take this guy – " he gestures at the bird-man who's been listening intently with his head on one side and staring at me as though my auburn hair and green eyes were some source of huge delight to him. "He's another satisfied customer, healed by the Master. Just one drawback: it was done on the Shabbat."

"Not for the first time," I comment, thinking back to the paralytic at Bethesda. I turn to the little fellow with a smile. "What did he cure you of, pal?"

"Blindness, Ma'am. I've been blind from birth – congenital, they call it. I was in my usual corner with my white stick and my tray of trinkets when I heard these footsteps stopping in front of me. I held out the tray, thinking I'd mebbe get the price of a hot meat pie? I could tell it was a group and they were jabbering on about my parents being sinful folk. That got me steamed up – they're decent, law-abiding mortals, same as me -. Leastways till now that I've ended up on the wrong side of it…

"Well, seeing they weren't going to offer, I pulled my tray back; then one of 'em stepped forward and started smearing some gunge over my eyelids. Here's a liberty, thought I, not only slanging the old folk, but making mock of me into the bargain! I banged down the tray in a rage and went to pick up my stick, but the bloke who'd daubed me said to go and wash my face in Siloam. Something about his voice calmed me down. I put out an arm and he took it, led me to the pool. It's bung-full just now with the autumn rains so I scooped up a handful of water to wipe the muck off." He pauses, looks round at us as if the wonder still overwhelms him. "Any of you tried to imagine what it's like to see for the very first time? See the shapes and colours you've had to guess at all your life? It was – unbelievable! A moment before, my eyes had been as dry as desert wells in high summer – the next I was squatting at the pool's edge and blubbing real tears."

Those waters had been my salvation, too, though they'd led me into darkness.

"I'm so glad for you," I say. "It must've seemed like magic after all those years. But you say you're on the wrong side of the law. Why's that?"

"'Cos I sauced the Holy Joes. After the healer and his mates had left me, they came along and seed me dancing with joy like a loony, naming every blessed thing my eyes fell on to anyone who'd listen. One of 'em asked me what'd happened and I told him. 'Who was it made you well?' he said. 'Describe him.' That wasn't hard, him being the first bloke I'd ever seed. 'Tall beside you,' I said, 'black hair parted in the centre and falling to his shoulders, lean sort of face – plus a look which went right through me.' 'We know him,' he said grimly. 'He'd no right to do this on the Shabbat. He's a violator of the Law, a bad lot.' 'Dunno about that,' says I. 'He made me see, din't he, so he can't be that bad!' 'How dare you contradict me, you little nobody?' he shouted, and he made me take him home to check with my parents that I was reelly blind. Badgered 'em something cruel. I got proper narked and told him to lay off. I said he should be giving thanks like me for the grace of God made manifest – as it says in the Good Book. That put the tin lid on it. He and his gang told me I'd blasphemed and couldn't go to shul any more. So I went to find my fellow-outlaws – and here I am!"

Things have come full circle, I reflect. Yeshua opened his account in the City with a Shabbat healing and now he's repeated his challenge to orthodoxy. On the first occasion I felt he was putting his head into the lion's mouth – today its jaws are ready to close on him.

I say, "We've been through this before. So what's new?"

"The atmosphere, for one thing," mutters Phil. "I felt the change as soon as we arrived south. They were out to get him – and we thanked our stars he wasn't with us. Then, lo and behold, half-way into the feast, he lands here on his magic carpet and all hell's let loose."

Jo's pensive. "The fact is he's a threat to their position. If he turns out to be the true Mashiah, they're in for a raw deal. He's made that pretty clear. If he doesn't, then he's fair game. You know, I think they plug the idea of a saviour simply to keep the people happy and themselves at the top of the pile – they've never for one minute believed in it."

"All of which is no reason for leaving him to face the oppo alone," I retort. "How will you behave if and when things hot up? I never thought to say this, but Si and Jude have more guts than the lot of you."

"Jude's a townsman and a Siccarioth," protests Andy. "He's got buddies who'll close in if the Set-aparts go for him. And Si keeps a foot in both camps. We're mostly yobboes from Galil. They'd stamp on us like beetles. Anyhow, we've taken a vote among ourselves."

"A vote?" I look at Rock for enlightenment.

He clears his throat awkwardly. "The Master asked us for advice that evenin' at your house, Miri. We're going to tell him he should steer clear of the City till the heat's off."

"If that works in with his poppa's plan, he'll agree. Otherwise not. Your opinion won't count either way." I pause. "As for me, I'm going straight out to support him. I've been up against a pair of specialists – and a pack of priests don't scare me!"

The bright-eyed sparrow chirps, "I'm coming with you, Ma'am. Wish I hadn't snapped my bleeding stick in half…"

We clatter down the wooden steps and through the office below. Behind us someone bolts the door. Outside, my companion's gaze darts everywhere. "Look at those pigeons flying from roof to roof – once they were just a whirr of wings to me. And the sunshine catching that gold pinnacle. And that kid playing in the gutter – was he the one who used to help me cross the street, I wonder?" He glances shyly at me. "Watched my first sunset last evening – all shades of red against an apple-green sky. When you came into that dark room and whipped off your scarf, it was like seeing it over again."

For once a compliment doesn't flatter my vanity. I'm only pleased to have given so much pleasure. We set off for the Temple Precinct where Yeshua's certain to be, right in the thick of things. But he meets us halfway. The steep light of midday shadows his cheekbones and deep-set eyes, sculpting the fleshless face. His humour and vivacity have given way to a sombre, tragic mask. He manages a smile of greeting, then focuses on my disfigurement and is grave once more.

"The Fox will answer for that on his death-bed – as his father suffered a terrible fate for child-slaughter in Judaea," he murmurs. "Your pain will be repaid a hundredfold, Miri, my dear."

Si and Jude are trailing in his rear. Before they approach, I whisper to him, "Lord, the others are up-tight about the risk you – and they – are running. They want you to leave the City for the time being – and I think they've got good reason."

"I've stretched their trust to breaking-point in order to test them for the real show-down," he acknowledges. "They're not prepared for it. I'll take them to Perea which is out of range yet far enough from Herod's capital."

"Them – not me?"

"I want you to go home, Miri. My good friend Lazarus is very sick. He needs you, his favourite sister. So does Mart, surprising as it may seem. I'll join you in Bethaniah when the moment's ripe."

"What about me, Master?" pipes up his latest beneficiary. "Mayn't I follow you?"

Yeshua smiles at him. "No, pal, you must stick round and bear witness to God's grace. You're a living reproach to my adversaries: the blind shall see and those who see shall become blind."

Si and Jude catch up with us, exhilarated by the fray. From their angle, presumably, the stage is being set for the breakthrough; a touch more pressure and battle will be joined in good earnest. I bid Yeshua and my sparrow-friend good-bye, wishing our encounter weren't so brief. He must go north and I eastward to a dear invalid's bedside. Recent events have accustomed me to more exciting vistas, yet Yeshua's right. I must be with Laz after so long an absence - and my new self must make the effort to be reconciled with my sister.

ELEVEN

Bethaniah extends no welcome to its erring daughter. It's quiet enough at the best of times: an affluent, well-mannered suburb housing the cream of City-society. I've no doubt our distinguished neighbours have made it a little hell for Laz and Mart on my account, not by outright condemnation but through a policy of pointed disregard. So much more effective! How smug and censorious its hillside villas seem as they overlook my progress – never a face to be seen yet curtains twitching and shutters snapping as I go by. The word will pass from house to house, like borrowed fire: the prostitute's returned. They'll dish the dirt; recount every detail of my downfall and disgrace, until self-righteousness is fully satisfied.

Our own home has a blind look, its shutters closed. This is a place where sickness dwells, withdrawn and melancholy. I hesitate on the threshold yet my sister's antennae have sensed my approach; she darts out and pulls me inside as though to shield us from prying eyes – for her sake, not mine.

"Here you are, Miriam, turning up like a bent shekel yet again! Oh yes, I'd heard about your riding into town on your soldier-friend's pommel, with his arm round your middle. Scandal travels fast in this sanctified district."

"Cass brought me back, true. Without him, I'd never have got have got away from Herod."

"Your usual histrionics… You always were a little liar. Why should you need shielding from the Tetrarch? By all accounts he used to be an admirer of yours – and more beside. I dare say."

"He had a – grudge against me, Mart. Apart from personal motives, he had me pulled in to be questioned as to Yeshua's whereabouts. I was tortured to make me talk…"

"A likely tale!"

"See the evidence for yourself." I remove my headscarf and sweep the hair back from my forehead. She narrows her myopic eyes in the darkened parlour then winces at my jagged scar – but continues to carp, "That could easily have been done in some tavern-brawl, to judge by the company you keep."

"These, too?" I slide my tunic off my shoulders and down to the groin. She stares, traces the marks incredulously with one finger. Her compassion is for Laz alone, I'm sure, yet the nursing habit dies hard. She goes out to the kitchen to fetch water and a cloth.

"Just like the old days when you came back from romping with the boys and I had to tend your cuts and bruises."

As she cleans my wounds, I recall her ministrations; a scolding tongue, but sisterly concern for me beneath the veil of disapprobation. Have I misjudged her all along? There are those whose love and goodness lie hidden under a gruff, ungracious manner. I tell her my story as I told it in Zabdiah's warehouse, omitting the cure of Joab – one day I'll recount that happening to Jo and he can put it in his memoirs so long as he alters details and ascribes all merit where it belongs! She hears me out in silence while her hands betray a softening of attitude.

"You think I've been running after Yeshua like some lovesick adolescent," I conclude. "It's a fact I fell for him and I'm proud to have suffered for his sake, yet now I only want to serve him as you do, Mart. Will you believe me in that, at least?"

She bows her head and I know my words have gone home. I gaze down at her lank hair, already touched with grey, the figure of a woman unblessed by love and drained by the demands of another's illness. I feel remorse, a stirring of long-frozen affection. "Mart, can't we bury the hatchet and be friends – if only for our brother's peace of mind?"

She remains still for a moment, then takes my face between her hands and puts her dry lips to my scarred brow. It's a happening in its own right, this coming together, and I sense a stronger will than ours guiding us. A thin voice from the upper floor calls to her weakly.

"Laz needs both of us with him now," she murmurs. "Let's go up to him."

We mount the stairs together, arm in arm. In the gloomy, stale-smelling sickroom, I make out my bro's face against the pillow, white on white. It's emaciated, skeletal; only the eyes are alive as they focus me with a perceptible effort. I try to conceal my dismay, smiling tremulously. I'm looking at a man in the shadow of death.

"I – I thought I heard a voice that I've been missing badly. Dearest Miri, thank God you're here once more – before too late!"

I take his almost translucent hand in mine. "Yes, thank God," refusing to ponder the significance of his last words. At least he doesn't observe my scars; I mustn't mention what only Mart knows for fear of upsetting him, but he listens to the tale of Yeshua's doings with restive interest. They distract him from his struggle against unremitting odds, I think, yet prompt me to a more constructive purpose. Am I to lean again on Yeshua's distant power, invoke his healing aid for my brother? While Mart descends. leaving us together, I concentrate every fibre of my being to reach him. This time there's no response. The features before me stay unchanged, the fight for breath continues unabated. A phrase of his comes back to me as if his own voice were speaking: 'May your will be done.' Am I being too insistent, imposing my urgency on God Himself?

Laz, with an intuition sharpened by extremity, has understood my aim. "Don't despair, Miri, The Lord's glory will be served as truly by my dying as by some last-minute deliverance. We're all subject to his will."

Yes, he's a dying man and the best we can do is to make his slow decline as painless as possible. Life settles into a groove. Mart and I still have stormy scenes, the overspill of shared anxiety and stress, yet our permanent relationship has altered for the better. We alternate at Laz's bedside, unable to do much more than comfort him with our presence. Not one of his former intimates drops in though his condition is no secret; my being here's responsible for that and conscience pricks me. Out of doors, I move in a zone of isolation - the villagers melting away at my approach to eye me, with horrified fascination, from a safe distance. In Bethaniah, a common whore is as exotic as some legendary courtesan... There are times I'd like to stand at the street-crossing and scream, "I've been a bloody fool but I'm not a Jezebel. If you won't accept my presence among you, don't put my relatives in quarantine as well. Don't let my brother die friendless!" Yet with the passing of my final demon, aggression has gone out of me and been replaced by the strength to endure, not just social banishment, but the loneliness of losing touch with Yeshua. It's as though he's broken contact at his end and I try vainly to find him in my soul's depth. Instead, I'm chained to the monotony of a day-to-day and week-to-week existence without any inward consolation. Sometimes a terror overwhelms me that he's been arrested, killed, his followers scattered. Wouldn't he hasten to his old friend Laz and halt his sinking to the grave, otherwise? The time is so short...

My wordless prayer is answered, yet not by his coming. One evening of late winter, who should turn up in this neck of the woods but Si and Jude, confident as ever of their welcome? It appears they never went with the rest to Transjordan, staying in the City to bring their private schemes to the boil.

"Does Yeshua know what you've been up to?" I ask. A superfluous question!

"Whether he knows or not," says Si haughtily, "the Leader prefers not to be party to our dealings. You heard his criticism at Migdal – lucky for him we decided to see his bid for kingship through!"

"It's all set up," says Jude, smacking his lips over the wine Mart's provided. "Reception-committee laid on, muscle at the ready, an' our take-over schedule timed to the bleedin' second. All we need do is blow the whistle and the whole City will be at his feet."

"You don't say?" Sarcastic. "When I saw them last, your mates were shit-scared he'd be done in before they could pull him out. Scared for their own lives, too."

"They're gutless morons, we know that. One rusty sword between 'em, tucked into Rock's belt. He'll never use it for all his talk of defending the Boss."

"I'm glad to hear it," remarks Si. "No violence unless provoked, I trust you're clear about that, Jude. Miriam has a valid point: the Hasidim were up in arms at his outrageous conduct, and still are. We require some stupendous miracle at this juncture which even they will recognize as worthy of the Mashiah. That should bring them round." He looks keenly at Mart and me. "This is why, in fact, we are here."

"Then it was a wasted journey," she replies dully. "The Master's not deigned to visit us, although a man he loves is on the point of death." She's taken Yeshua's prolonged absence harder than I have.

"Pardon me if I sound somewhat detached about your brother's crisis but believe me, his dying may be our finest chance of winning over the Establishment. Suppose the Leader were to restore him to life, an act which would rival Eliyah's... You follow my meaning?"

Nothing's too sacred for his exploitation. I say tersely, "It's not on. He could have healed Laz by now if that had been his will – or his poppa's. Besides, what you're suggesting must be beyond even his scope."

"Agreed. There were incidents, I recall, in Galil: the son of a widow at Naim and the hazan's daughter at Capernaum – yet death wasn't actually certified in either case. What I had in mind was merely the appearance of death and its subsequent cancellation. If Lazarus is as far gone as rumour has it, we may be able to deceive his mourners."

Can deviousness go further? "You mean that a happening could be – faked?" I ask incredulously.

"Not a bit of it. Your brother would be made totally well – we know the Leader can affect that much - and you'll both be in the seventh heaven as a result. As for the priests and Set-aparts, they'll carry the wonder-worker on their shoulders to his rightful throne, from which he'll serve notice on the enemies of Israel."

"I think you're a great deal too optimistic. Jo, whom you despise for his naivety, grasped the true situation. Once they suspect that Yeshua really has supernatural powers, they'll leave no stone unturned to rub him out – in order to maintain their own authority. The last thing they want is a genuine Mashiah."

Si refuses to be put off his intended scam. Under pretence of concern, he goes up to confirm Laz's precarious hold on life. He'll be well satisfied: my brother's appearance is that of a corpse warmed up, for hours on end, his breathing scarcely perceptible, his form rigid beneath the sheet. When Si comes down, he's rubbing his hands.

"Right," he almost chortles. "Operation Lifewatch is about to be launched. I shall rustle up a number of important witnesses by spreading the news of your brother's decease, while Jude fetches the Leader from his temporary retirement. Oh, and before you make a rather obvious comment, young lady, might I say that I've secured, for a stated sum from our common purse, the – ah – co-operation of a reputable physician who will pronounce death to have occurred."

What can two helpless women with no influence or resources of their own do to deter him? As ever, I fail to allow for the intervention of fate – and within an hour of their departure, poor Laz breathes his last. Our sorrow is mitigated by relief at the ending of his agony, as well as at the foiling of this shoddy subterfuge, so much shabbier than any I once attributed to Yeshua! Now I must stem my own tears and give all my comforting to Mart who's tended her brother so long and selflessly. Grief has knocked her out, and it becomes my task to anoint the cadaver, to swathe it in grave-bands; mine to recite the Shema above it and direct the bearers while they carry it to the tomb where Poppa and Momma already await their final rising...

Yet still no sign of the Master. Jude must have reached him long since and he's had ample time to get here. Of course they hadn't calculated on his seeing through their plot. Presumably he's refused to play it their way – but by the same token, he must be aware of our tragic loss. Is it too much to hope that he should come and share our sorrow? The return of Si, accompanied by the cynical onlookers he's rounded up, is a wretched substitute – though his discomfiture at the news almost makes me smile through my tears,

"So you spoke the truth," says one of the Set-aparts. "Now show us your master and we shall see what transpires."

The voice is Benesdra's. Oh yes, he's on tap to watch Yeshua's humiliation, though conspicuous by his absence at a professed friend's bedside! I haven't told Mart about his contribution to my ruin or his attempt to wipe me out; she circulates among our visitors, pathetically flattered by their condescension after such long neglect. I stay indoors, wrapped in my sadness, wishing the pack of them a thousand miles from here. The noise of their babbling fades as a few drift back to town, bored by this non-event, yet it swells again as a fresh voice makes itself heard. Jo! My heart leaps – not for him, though his arrival pleases me, but for Yeshua who must be at hand. I feel exquisite tension while the minutes slide by, then Mart bursts into the parlour, her face alight.

"The Master's with us again," she exclaims. "He wants you to go to him, Miri."

There's no trace of envy in her tone, only delight. I follow her outside, past the mob of sight-seers to where Yeshua awaits me. I've seen his features eloquent with feeling, but never this degree of grief and pity in them. My tears for Laz flow openly, his within. From the start of his mission, this house has been his refuge from misunderstanding and abuse; he's grown to love those associated with it, as he loves his momma, the memory of his dead poppa... He looks at me and I find myself kneeling as on my vigil that night at Migdal.

"Lord, if you'd been here, Laz would never have died."

"I heard you call me, Miri, but I turned a deaf ear. The trauma you've sustained at your brother's death will steel you for one yet to come. Neither will endure. Lazarus is to rise again."

"Yes, Master, when we all rise on the Last Day," interposes Mart, beside me. (It's a belief I barely credit; she taught me in youth that at the trumpet's sound, our buried corpses would come back to life and roll underground towards the Temple from every point on the compass – the furthest lands where true-born Jews reside – and I found the concept more comical than probable!)

"No, Mart. Now. Today," replies Yeshua. "His death was permitted solely to honour God's Son. D'you have faith that this can be?"

I close my eyes and launch myself into darkness. "I have, Lord."

He helps me to my feet and we walk towards the tomb. His mates follow, uneasy at the sight of his opponents massed together, unsure of his next move. Jude, standing apart, looks as crestfallen as Si at the collapse of their con... Yeshua ignores the crowds, motions Rock and Andy to roll back the big circular golet in its curved groove. Andy wedges it and they draw away from the open sepulchre. Trapped air wafts out, oddly untainted by an odour of decay despite the fact that its occupant has been dead four whole days. The tall figure's back is to us now. He stands as straight as Cass on parade and raises his voice.

"Lazarus, come to me."

For a still moment, all nature seems to draw breath. Then I feel the blast of some gigantic force shake rock and root and subsoil beneath my feet. Its impact stuns me into semi-consciousness, till a gasp beside me restores full attention to the scene. The spectators are on their knees, grovelling among the weeds. One seems to have fainted. Three only stay upright: myself, Yeshua – and the shrouded apparition filling the cavern's mouth.

"Free him from his bonds."

Rock, scrambling to his feet like an automaton, obeys with trembling hands. The arms and legs are freed, the blind face last due to a natural dread. For Jews, dead flesh is anathema. Laz has the air of one awaking from long sleep, dazed and bewildered – yet totally transformed. The evidence of his wasting sickness has vanished, and I'm looking at a man in perfect health. He takes two paces forward as if to test his legs, and then falls into his saviour's arms. For a moment their roles appear reversed: a hale and hearty Laz supports a doomed Yeshua who sways with the draining of his inward power. Yet the latter, as so often, trivializes the marvel he's achieved by uttering a prosaic remark.

"Take him inside and give him something to eat. He must be starving."

Nothing is better calculated to convince those present that Laz isn't a ghost. As I guide him back to the house, Benesdra'a high-pitched drawl offends the ear: "A case of suspended animation – pair of ignorant women – unpardonable error of judgement."

So that's the tale he and his cronies will put about. It's as I suspected. Soon they'll be saying we acted in collusion, an inference which Si's activities have done little to dispel. 'Those who see shall become blind.' Reuben has seen, all right, and therein lies the real danger for Yeshua. The proof of his supernatural claim must seal his fate. Si and Jude, bowled over by their unexpected triumph and impervious to its irony where they're concerned, are unable to grasp that vital fact – nor do they understand that if he's killed, there'll be no one to bring him back to life!

He spoke of bringing honour on himself: another irony, as it turns out, because what follows is a cheap success among spectators who measure status by sensationalism. Suddenly doors are opened to Laz, the revenant, to Yeshua, the man of the hour, and even to Mart whose crustiness is thawed by her borrowed glory. Between the Set-aparts' scepticism and the nine-days-wonder, the spiritual meaning of what's happened goes unobserved – except by the thoughtful few.

I've plenty of time to ponder it since these invitations pointedly exclude yours truly. It seems my notoriety surpasses even so stunning an event! While Laz does the rounds, telling and retelling his memories of the grave, I stay at home absorbed in the marvel of his deliverance from it. I should be overjoyed yet the stink of death surrounds me. It's as though my mind still clings to an earlier despair and can't cope with its happy sequel. The ritual of entombment which I've so recently undertaken weighs on my spirit and while it proved superfluous, a premonition haunts me that I was rehearsing for some drama, hinted at by Yeshua, still to come...

Simon, son of Mordecai, is the king-pin in Bethaniah. Cured of leprosy yet still disfigured by its scars, he's a Set-apart of high standing and an outrageous snob. Needless to say, his mansion is the largest in the village and his banquets put all lesser ones to shame. It's inevitable that he should make the most of our tall headlines. Laz is to be his guest of honour at a slap-up do and Yeshua, normally beyond his pale, is persuaded to attend with his followers. Like all successful hosts, Simon knows the value of religious controversy as a party-booster – and the Nazirite will certainly provide that. Mart is also welcome in the role of a glorified waitress, but I'm conspicuously left out. As usual. Yeshua makes no comment on the guy's discourtesy to me. Laz puts on a display of indignation but celebrity has turned his head a trifle, and he won't refuse his presence at the feast of the season. Mart alone is angry on my behalf.

"I'll help to serve at table," she snorts, "but I'll not sit down with such an arrant tuft-hunter."

They set out for his residence a hundred yards down Bethaniah's single road, leaving me to my own devices. Already the twang of harps and zithers spills out from its dining-hall and I can glimpse the coloured lanterns lighting its porch from my window. Late guests from the City ride along the street, talking and laughing. I don't grudge them their pleasures and I've learnt to ignore the cold-shouldering, which is part of my life, yet solitude intensifies this cloud of ill-omen hanging over me. The house itself seems filled with a stench of graveyard mould. Even my eyes betray me; they keep turning towards an alabaster jar of ointment, which stands, unused, on the shelf opposite. It contains spikenard, costly stuff left over from my anointing of the corpse. (When is a corpse not a corpse? Answer: when it's alive.) Get a grip on yourself, Miri. Think about other things: Cass the unkillable, Yeshua preaching the good news and healing the incurable. Can he be relishing the company of those who plot to destroy him, who'd love to see him safely underground, his limbs constrained by swaddling-bands as Laz's were? This image grows on me as if another brain had planted it, and the memory of his momma's fear accentuates my own. I almost hear her voice reciting prophecy: They shall look on him whom they have pierced and mourn for him as for an only son. What is it that can pierce a man? A sword like the one she was promised at his birth – nails hammered through wrist and foot to fasten living flesh upon a tree – a spear wielded by some indifferent legionary. A Roman death…

My creeping horror finds relief in action. I jump to my feet, grab the ointment-jar and slip out into the dusk. Wild horses wouldn't drag me to the house from which I've been rebuffed, but some influence stronger than myself impels me through its doorway. Ignoring the blank stares and hush of outrage, I single out my Lord, reclining on the left of his host. His long legs rest on a triclinium, sandals removed as etiquette prescribes. I kneel before him, break open the jar's sealed neck and pour its perfumed contents over his feet and ankles. It mingles with my tears as I picture the sweet skin rent by barbed metal. I bow to kiss its surface, my heavy hair falls like a curtain and I use the tresses to wipe away the moisture. They've always been my chief pride – yet what's pride in the face of death's finality?

My outlandish behaviour takes the assembly by surprise. It's Reuben, Mordecai's bosom-pal, who recovers first. He shrills, "We all know this girl, a common tart and adulteress. It astounds me that she has the gall to trespass on us and make an exhibition of herself."

Jo comes to my defence. "You'll take back that last accusation, Sir. I freed her from her vows to me long since. You heard me do so yet you all but had her executed for a crime of which she's innocent!"

Jude, infuriated by the wasting of the valuable nard, is quick to second Benesdra: "She has to be the centre of the stage with her flamin' topknot – why, that amount of ointment must be worth a labourer's yearly screw. I could've traded it and put the shekels to good use."

Yeshua's glance sweeps over the pair of them dismissively. "Let her be. What she's done heralds the future, preparing my body for a fate which most of you already have in mind. Whenever the story of my life is told, from now till everlasting, her deed will be recounted." He turns to his indignant host: "Simon, you've been treating me as a kind of circus entertainer hired out to divert your guests. You didn't direct your servants to wash my feet as they did for your well-connected visitors. This 'common tart' has only put right your negligence."

"I understood you despised such ritual cleansing," splutters Simon.

"I don't despise politeness, merely the presumption that washing justifies a man in my Poppa's eyes. You're so sure of his approval, aren't you? How much does He need to pardon your minor transgressions, would you say?" He holds up forefinger and thumb, a fraction apart. "This much? Whereas, in Miri's case, the margin must be wider…" The gap is extended. "Now, which of you has most cause to show gratitude?"

"The one who owes most to his benevolence, I suppose." Simon is flattered by the contrast.

"Exactly. So she gives thanks and the fullness of her heart to his son – and he returns them in equal measure. The greater the forgiveness, the greater the love." Yeshua leans from his couch and draws me to him. I rest in his arms like a small child while he illustrates his point. "A nobleman had two sons. The elder was dutiful – something of a prig, to be honest – but the younger wanted to sow his wild oats. He asked for his share from the estate then lit out for the bright lights. Only they weren't so bright, as it turned out. Money doesn't last forever when you splash it around on booze and women. He ended up working on a Goy farm, living off husks that the pigs he fed had rejected. Eventually he made up his mind to go home and throw himself on his poppa's mercy. To his astonishment the old man fell on his neck, covering him with kisses, then ordered a banquet such as this one served for his restored child. How about that?"

"A thoroughly pernicious story," comments Reuben the lawyer, glad of an opportunity to put Yeshua down. "A son has no right to squander his inheritance as he pleases; the Law commands him to support a living parent from the interest it accrues. I'm glad that my own progeny aren't here to be corrupted – and I assure you they'd have had the door shut in their faces had they tried it on with me!"

"What about the elder brother?" queries Simon. "He must have felt ill served to see this wastrel feted when his own virtue was taken for granted."

"Indeed he was. He said as much to his poppa who replied that all he possessed was already his, apart from his brother's upkeep. This didn't satisfy him one bit, however; he'd have preferred to see the other punished or thrown out." He pauses. "Just as you'd like me

162

to condemn Miri instead of putting my arm round her."

I look up and catch Mart's eyes as she waits at table. They return my glance with feeling and I realize that Yeshua's tale means more to her than to the rest. Maybe she's thinking of a younger sister who went to the bad and came back to face a very cold reception. Simon, stung by the implied reproof, is predictably pompous: "Neither your questionable narrative nor your present conduct towards a young woman who has disgraced our neighbourhood befits this occasion, sir."

"Very well," says Yeshua impenitently, "Let's try again with a more suitable scenario. Here's you, Simon, sending out invitations to this jolly banquet – or shall we say the one you held not long ago to celebrate your son's wedding? How would you've reacted if your guests had sent excuses not to be there?"

"I should have been exceedingly put out. Apart from the incivility, their coming was required to solemnise the marriage. As it happens," he adds smugly, "they were only too anxious to be asked."

"So you can imagine Miri's feelings when you omitted her name from your list… Supposing, however, that the impossible *had* occurred and your table had been empty. You'd have had a problem on your hands, wouldn't you? Guests there must be at a wedding-feast, as you say. You'd've had no alternative but to send out your servants to scour the district for every vagrant they could find and bring them back to lap up your rich food and toast your son's health."

"The moral of this rigmarole is still more obscure than the previous one. Pray enlighten us!"

"The host is your Father – and mine. Those he first invited – the friends who let him down – are you and your kind. The riff-raff who took their place appear in their own right: the am-haretz, the great unwashed, the sinners and adulterers."

"And the son, one assumes, is your good self," sneers Benesdra, "an ersatz prophet reared by some provincial artisan as the bastard-child of his wife, who bolsters his sacrilegious teaching with faked miracles. No, Barjoseph, you and your regrettable horde of peasants must learn to keep their places in this world, while we shall take our chances in the next."

Yeshua gets up, towering above the prone diners. He addresses Simon Ben Mordecai: "I came here, not because you condescended to invite me but because I foresaw this girl's action and wished to apply a lesson from it. You counted on my provocation to make your dinner-party memorable – I hope I've given you good value, with Miri's help. Good night."

And he leaves his astounded auditors with his arm still round my waist. The sole lesson he's applied so far as they're concerned is the art of making enemies – as if they weren't already that! His mates follow reluctantly, tearing themselves away from a lavish spread, with the exception of Jude and Si who feel obliged, perhaps, to repair the damage done. As for Mart, she makes the bravest gesture of her life by banging down her tray in the table's centre before turning on her heel with Laz in tow. Sick or well, he's still under her thumb!

We return to our humbler abode, depressed and sober despite the wine that's flowed so freely. Yeshua beckons me to sit, cross-legged, at his side and the others make way for me, accepting his preference. They've seen, I suspect, that what I did wasn't of my own choosing; that it formed part of some progression whose purpose is beyond us. There's a general sense that he is truly taking charge from now on; not that he hasn't done so from the start, but in a new and more mysterious way. Yet surely he's more than ever subject to the will of his adversaries? I fill the vacuum in our conversation by relating the ruse proposed by Si – not to slander him in his absence but to warn Yeshua of the pitfalls in his path.

He doesn't respond immediately. (Of course, he knows it all. I keep forgetting!) The rest seem to be in two minds. Rock and Jo are angry, advising him to shake off the inseparables at once. Nat is less positive. He remarks, "It was a low-down scheme, admitted, but they want the same as we do – to put the Master where he should be. We all know what they've been up to and none of us approves yet the guys we're up against wouldn't hesitate to use the same tactics if they were in the minority. A few weeks ago we were scared as all get-out, living on our nerves, and we'd have given all we'd got for a little strong-arm backing. If we mean to reach the top, we'll need some show of force, not to mention a happening or two that'll take the City by storm."

"Like raising the dead?" mocks Jim "No trick about that, was there, for all their stupid antics? And look at the results – a quick cover-up job, damage limitation tactics. All it's done has been to put the Sads and Set-aparts on their guard."

"Be fair, Jim. You're dragging in a side issue. What I'm saying is that good intentions aren't going to topple the Establishment and a magic wand won't make the Aliens vanish into thin air. So how's Scripture to be fulfilled?"

Nobody supplies an answer. In the ensuing silence, Yeshua clears his throat. "The time has come for me to be explicit," he says slowly. "Not one of you has the vaguest idea of my destiny. It's got nothing to do with the sort of triumph Si and Jude envisage for me – and themselves. My every word and deed should have made that clear to you from the beginning. Yet most of you still picture me seated on a golden throne surrounded by my chosen followers and handing out royal edicts to a bunch of cringing Hasidim and Romans."

"You're the Mashiah," stammers Phil, "destined to reign over mankind till the end of time…"

"And you're a parrot mimicking the sayings of the prophets without the slightest concept of their meaning. Are you so simple-minded as to suppose that a wandering lay-preacher with a gaggle of drop-outs at his heels can hope to win political or military supremacy overnight, with or without Jude's terror-squad?"

"But the Chosen One of God – "

" – Is capable of all things? Get behind me, Satan! He tempted me on those lines as I told you once in Yericho. Remember the high hill, the vision of earth's splendour from its summit? He offered it all in return for bending my knee to him – and I refused. Like you, he'd missed the whole point of my enterprise. I must win over my subjects one by one without trumpet or acclaim, establishing my rule of love in their hearts. My kingdom doesn't lie in the future, it's already founded – here in this room within each and every one of my friends – but its gateway to the world has yet to be opened wide. It won't yield to force of arms, only to submission, yours and mine. To germinate and spread its species, a tree must drop its seed. That seed lies buried through the harsh season and when, as now, winter gives way to springtime, it emerges into new birth. My tree will bear fruit in its own kind."

"You used to talk about your kingdom as a mustard-seed," Andy remembers. "Is that what you're getting at, Master?"

"I was thinking of another sort of tree, one fashioned by men…" His voice is very low and the forebodings that have weighed on me since last year's Pessach gather to a head. He adds, "What natural tree could grow on Golgotha?"

"The Place of the Skull? You're joking – it's barren rock!" Jim gasps as Yehua's reference sinks in. "That – that's where the Aliens carry out their executions. You can't mean – "

His protest falls on an awed, incredulous hush. We know he's risked the extreme penalty all along, yet how can we measure the courage or plumb the mind of one who is living the prefigurement of his own most hideous death? Any hope that he's being fanciful is dashed by his next words.

"At this minute one of my flock, somewhat the worse for drink, is weighing up the odds in his fuddled brain. He's asking himself which horse to back before the inevitable occurs: my successful bid for earthly power, or the advantage to be gained by shopping me to my enemies. Little he knows that both are a delusion and that his own soul is being sifted by the father of lies."

I can't help myself exclaiming, "If the devil's using man to plot your downfall, you've a far greater power than his on your side. Won't your Poppa act to prevent harm coming to you?"

He shakes his head. "We're both of one mind, Miri. Indeed, we are one mind. His expectation of my death and my acceptance of it are a single impulse, joyfully shared."

"Joyfully? The prospect of such a horror fills you with joy?"

"Not the horror itself but its outcome. To lay down one's life for one's friends is a matter for gladness – when mankind's saving is at stake, for exultation. Death, not my Heavenly Father, is the tyrant yet his tyranny is a transient one. Your brother escaped it... Tell us your experiences again, Laz."

Laz, well primed in his party-piece, answers: "It's not easy to recall things exactly. When I try to think back, my mind hazes over as if it were telling me to forget and make the most of my good luck. What remains clearest in my memory is the fact that I went on being aware of my existence. Don't those who've lost a limb say they continue to feel it long after it's been cut off? That was how I felt although I had no physical sensation, no consciousness of time or place."

"Yes, transfer isn't immediate. The spirit clings to its earthly dwelling like a child afraid to venture into the unknown. Remember this, all of you: the body dies, yet its essence lingers on and if God permits, may attain to a wholeness undreamt of on this side of the grave. No, I'll explain no further. You must be content to grope at my meaning until all is revealed. Meanwhile, I'm about to set out on the final lap – and you, my friends, are free to choose how far you'll go with me, some part of the way or right to the end if your courage doesn't fail you."

The noise of late-night revelry echoes from Ben Mordecai's domain. My gaffe and Yeshua's rebuke are alike forgotten in the general mirth. Even Jude, the harbourer of grudges, must have got over his anger at my extravagance, his miserly soul calculating how best to improve its fortunes as he rubs shoulders with the wealthy and influential... I can guess who Yeshua spoke of, if the others can't. Somehow I find myself in the centre of this sinister web, caught up in every thread of its complex pattern, a link between dawning treachery and a victim who'll not save himself. Surely Yeshua must be hoping in his heart of hearts for some intervention to reprieve him? Perhaps his last words were meant as a cry for help. No, Lord, my courage will not fail!

TWELVE

Our desolation is shortlived. Two days later, at mid-morning, we're at Bethphage, not a mile from the City, and the greeting of a vast crowd has evaporated Yeshua's gloomy vision. His fans line either side of the road, shouting hoshanas and waving palms as though proclaiming a king's arrival. Many are pilgrims from Galil, come south to celebrate Pessach and camping below the City-walls. We know he's made a hit with these honest folk who believe he's their Mashiah because he says so. Then, too, the news of his most spectacular happening must've leaked out, for all their betters' pooh-poohing. Another sort move among them, however: men of a different stamp, Judaean activists who whip up mass-hysteria. One face I've no difficulty in recognizing; Yeshua Barabbas, the guy whose baleful eyes speak for a tongue torn out by the Aliens. He can't lead the cheering yet his air of brooding menace persuades those round him to redouble theirs.

This must be the reception hinted at by Jude. Its timing is magnificent, I must say, as also its extent, but I welcome it for a different reason. If he's contemplating a sell-out, this indicates that he hasn't committed himself – maybe it's a last throw of the dice and should it fall our way, he'll stick with us. Both he and Si are on top form, the latter checking his greasy scroll for accuracy of detail.

"*Sing for joy, daughter of Zion,*" he reads aloud. "*See your king coming, the just and saviour. He is poor, riding an ass's foal.*" He replaces it in his pouch. "Not at all the scenario I would have devised – a great deal too modest, not to say farcical. All the same, such an animal must be found, and quickly. If we slip up on a single item, the Sephorim will nail us like a flash."

As though on cue, Thaddeus returns from obeying a call of nature, leading a dear little donkey still velvet-soft with its first coat. "Bloke handed me its rope," he explains. "Said my Master would be needing it. Name of Long-ears – the beast, not its owner."

I smile at Si's gaping astonishment and laugh outright at the sight of Yeshua climbing aboard. His long legs trail on either side, feet almost paddling in the dust – yet the colt appears to bear him with ease. My mental picture of a monarch riding in glory on some splendid charger makes a ludicrous contrast! Tom, with a rare burst of humour, suggests the addition of a crown and royal mantle but Yeshua doesn't rise to that. His finger traces the dark cross on the donkey's withers as he murmurs beneath the chanting, "I'll be awarded both in due course – but not from veneration."

The populace enjoys the joke which in no way detracts from their enthusiasm, and they swarm behind us as we proceed towards the Temple's Golden Gate. There are no Sads or Set-aparts to rebuke them; this is the eve of Holy Week, the major religious season of the year, and they'll be busy in God's house supervising the profitable currency-exchange racket, the still more lucrative sale of sacrificial creatures... Our visits to this mercenary scene, when Momma and Poppa were alive, are among my most vivid recollections. Weaving our way through human traffic in the Gentiles' spacious Court, we'd pass under the plaque that threatened death to heathen transgressors. Here, on the threshold of the sacred enclosure, the money-changers' tables were set out, piled with the special coinage which alone could buy each family's Pessach lamb – at inordinate cost, you may be sure! The space remaining was occupied by the dumb victims themselves, oxen tethered to stakes set in the Temple's marble floor, bleating sheep, and squawking birds in their cages. There was always a smell of carnage in the air; hooves pawed the ground and wings fluttered against timber struts as if their owners were struggling to escape the knife. I used to weep for them, knowing what lay beyond the Great Portico with its gilded grape-cluster – nothing more nor less than a slaughterhouse with its altar of sacrifice, its cisterns to drain the evidence of murder. Beyond, the Holy Place was lit by its seven-branched menorah and here incense was offered daily outside the Debir, Holy of Holies, which none bar the current High Priest might enter and that but once a year on Yom Kippur. An empty room – empty as the Ark our ancestors bore across the desert! Why did an invisible deity demand the blood of innocence to slake his thirst? I asked myself. The answer still eludes me...

Yeshua dismounts under Solomon's Porch and tethers Long-ears to a post. It's as well donkeys are valued as beasts of burden or he'd be at risk in this shambles. Nor is he the only one. His rider is advancing on the stronghold of his opponents with Jude and Si purposively at his side and Yeshua Barabbas, his namesake, bringing up the rear. I tremble in anticipation. Is he about to issue some swingeing challenge, backed by his supporters, or propitiate the Sadducees by bowing to their ritual? He takes a long look at the commerce spread before him then, seizing a bundle of cords from one of the Temple-guards, he sets about the traders, overturning their counters and scattering coins in a shower of silver, gold and copper. For a guy who's never lifted his hand except to bless and heal, his performance is impressive. The bankers flinch from his thudding blows while, under cover of the general confusion, bystanders snatch at the fortune rolling between their feet. Flinging aside his instrument, he scourges the offenders with his tongue.

"You've turned my Father's house into a den of thieves. You

Levites who make capital out of taxes, tithes wrung from starving peasants, sin-offerings and this useless slaying of useful animals, then double it by usury, are unworthy to serve Him. To lend money at interest is to grow rich without toil, a scandal in itself. To profit from liturgical exploitation is blasphemy, an abomination." He wheels on those in charge of the livestock: "My Poppa doesn't want blood-sacrifice. Release these wretched victims of your misplaced piety – or I shall!"

Dismayed, they make no move, allowing him to open cages and unloose bound quadrupeds. Darting birds and stampeding oxen add to the turmoil, and I feel my childhood tears avenged.

Lastly, he fixes Jude with a gimlet eye and snaps, "Restore what you've taken – at once! You shame us by your conduct."

Jude's swarthy complexion darkens further and he lets drop the overlap of his tunic above the belt. Gold pieces clatter to the floor amid ribald laughter. His black eyes return Yeshua's gaze with unappeasable rage. At the height of his scheming, the moment that his boss has staged a demo as effective as even he could have wished, he's been shown up for a common thief. I know too well how persistent his rancour can be!

Throughout, the authorities have held back, paralysed by Yeshua's initiative or intimidated by his fans. Now one of the Sads, whose paunch proclaims where some of the profit goes, raises his voice: "By what right have you created disorder in this sacred place?"

"By the right of a son who vindicates his Father."

The other smiles grimly. "I see that your paranoia hasn't deserted you. You still claim what no man – let alone a rustic sawyer – dare call himself, while impugning Yahweh's uniqueness. The Knesset has not been idle during your absence, Barjoseph. I very much fear your days are numbered." He motions to a pair of Temple-police who nod and disappear down a stairway at the northwest corner leading to the bowels of Antonia. Get out of here, Yeshua, I plead under my breath, get out before it's too late!

He holds his ground, unhurried, measuring his reply. "Yet if I am who I say, your days of power are numbered. My kingdom will have priests – but not such as hoard its assets for themselves and defy its master's will."

"We are the Almighty's hallowed representatives, the guardians of his truth."

"No, you're his usurpers. Maybe an allegory will make my meaning clear." While I count the seconds in panic, he glances round the court, the serried faces, upturned tables, empty cages – and his eyes come to rest on the grape-cluster hanging below the archway to his left.

"Israel is named the Lord's vineyard, isn't it? The landed gentry own large properties over which they appoint subordinates to supervise the produce and make due return. It's a standing temptation to cheat and falsify the accounts – so long as their master's at a safe distance. A certain proprietor, not being a total fool, sent his agents to check that all was being honestly conducted. Those who'd been tending his vines and growing fat on the profits they'd held back maltreated them. He sent a second lot who fared no better at their hands. Finally he sent his own son. He at least won't be harmed by them, he told himself. But the swindlers said to one another, 'If we kill the son, we can take over his inheritance.' You can imagine the ending for yourselves."

He's speaking to the assembled priests but a bystander replies: "They clobber him, get clobbered in return by an angry father and their jobs are handed out to blokes he can trust to serve him properly."

The story needs no translating. Like the proprietor, these Sads are no fools; they understand Yeshua perfectly. They've let him rattle on only because it's given their colleagues time to summon help. Their own officials won't nick him while he's backed by his supporters – armed infantry's a different kettle of fish! Already I hear hobnailed boots mounting the subterranean stairs in disciplined unison. He doesn't look round, apparently resigned to his arrest. The patrol ranges itself against the northern wall and their officer marches forward. I glance away, fearing it might be Cass. My averted eyes catch a stealthy movement unseen by those who are watching the central figures in this drama. Barabbas, half-crouched, is edging through the throng behind the officer's back, one fist clasping the haft of a dagger. My scream and pointing finger forewarn his intended prey who pivots round as the killer makes his leap, blade raised to strike. It scythes downward and plunges home before the other can throw up his shield. As he falls, his men pinion Barabbas, while Jude, rushing to free his pal, is roughly thrust aside.

Yeshua can't have envisaged such an atrocity. Shaking at the knees, I join the spectators gathered round a prostrate body. The man lies on his face, a gaping wound between his shoulder blades but very little blood. I know what that means, recalling Susannah's corpse. Someone heaves him over – none too gently for this, after all, is an occupier sent to arrest the people's champion. A blind face stares up at me. Not Cass but some Syrian lesser rank. Relief floods through me like a healing tide. I cudgel my wits and look around for the others. Most have scarpered as I might've guessed, in dread of being implicated. Si, to do him justice, stands his ground and Jo is hugging his Master's shadow. Yeshua's features are withdrawn as he gazes down at the body. His lips form a prayer whose words I faintly hear: "Let those who suffer for me do so by consent, Poppa, yet spare the death of ignorance."

It's time we got out of here. Whether the Romans connect him with Barabbas or not, this disaster must have multiplied his enemies

– and his peril. What started as an insignificant religious dispute, from their point of view, has ended with an act of warfare and they'll be on his tail from today. Should Qayapha, the High Priest, seek an ally to destroy him, they'll be ready to oblige… For once I'm in agreement with his mates; we must lie low, behind bolted doors, in the one safe house at our disposal. We make for Fish Street, almost dragging Yeshua along, yet I'm concerned that Jude's still at large. He's shown himself Barabbas's accomplice and when (if ever) he rejoins us, he's sure to bring down trouble on our heads. Somehow he must be kept at bay – and I, who know his likely whereabouts, must act to stave him off.

Before we reach Zabdiah's premises, I slip away and head towards his hideout. Even by daylight the district has a vicious, secretive appearance. Yes, this is the street he lured me to a year ago and here's the low door with its grating. I give the regular triple knock; the slat is removed on the inside and Si peers out at me. His grey eyes, disembodied, are uncannily like Yeshua's – minus that saving sparkle in their depths. After a pause, the bolts slide back and I'm let in. The room seems much as I recall it: grimy, grease-stained on every surface and sparsely furnished. The fire is out and we're alone.

"Where's Jude?" I ask.

"Out boozing to drown his disappointment, I imagine. Easy way out…" Si's voice has a defeated note as if his life's ambition has deserted him. He stares moodily at the blackened hearth. "I just can't make it out. A happening which exceeded my wildest dreams, a triumphal entry that went without a hitch – then the Leader blows his biggest moment by cracking down on a perfectly legitimate tradition, turning the Temple into a bear-garden and inviting the priests to do their worst."

"It was Barabbas who did the real mischief, surely?"

"He's not – never was – an intimate of mine. Jude's a loudmouth, but he's biddable. Yeshua Barabbas is beyond taming. Violence is a last resort when civilised means fail. I banked on winning round the Hasidim among whom I count some of my closest friends. They'd have made terms with our Leader if he'd behaved more discreetly and left the rest to me."

"How can one who calls himself Mashiah and Son of God be discreet about his claim? It was up to them to knuckle under – or reject him, as they've done."

"I suppose I must concede the point, reluctantly." He fishes the scroll out of his pouch and tears it into shreds, which flutter to the ground. "I never considered the possibility that he might in all truth be the Anointed One. From the start, I saw him as a focal point for Israel's revival, an earthly ruler alone."

"D'you believe now?"

"I don't know. All I'm sure of is that his destiny isn't the one I had in mind. My labours have been totally irrelevant – as you yourself suggested."

"May I make another suggestion, Si? I think it would be as well to keep Jude away from your cousin while the heat's on."

"Yes, I'm with you there. He'll compromise him further by his association and that of his fellow-conspirators. I suspect he might do greater damage, besides." His voice drops. "I think Jude's playing a double game. He's sounded the opposition through contacts made at that banquet in Bethaniah. Now he's hedging his bets; if the Leader pulls it off, he'll take full credit for the fact, and if he goes down – as I'm convinced he will – Jude will be exonerated by his own treachery."

"Have you lost your influence over him?"

"We were allies only because we shared a similar goal. Having put a noose round his neck by trying to rescue that murderous imbecile, he'll play a lone hand henceforth."

"Then I must use whatever means I can to sick him off." I look at Si, not without pity. "What will you do?"

He shrugs wearily. "Yeshua's my cousin, if he's nothing more. He's up against it and I shall stand by him. If he'll have me, I'll go back to him with you."

The door vibrates to a loud tattoo. A drunken voice bawls for Si to open it. He gets up. "Jude. I must let him in and he'll bring the law on us."

He unbolts and the door crashes open. Jude, wide-legged and reeling, staggers into the room. He squints at Si, not taking me in at first. "Shoulda drowned your sorrows like me, ol' man, 'stead of broodin' in this rat-hole. Poor ol' Yesh – we'll have to spring him somehow. Snuffed one o' the bastards, din't he? If it hadn't been for that stupid little slag, he'd've got away with it, and all. By Moishe, when I lay my hands on her... Why, we could've polished off the oppo and taken Antonia before they knew what had hit 'em. As it is, I'm on the run - and he, poor devil, looks likely to be topped."

Jude's fantasy has outlasted his partner's, it would seem. The raw menace in his voice doesn't deter me as it once did. I've a deal in mind – a harder bargain than ever I drove with Herod, and I step forward out of the wall's shadow. His bloodshot eyes, recognizing, fasten on me gloatingly.

"So you've walked right into a trap, slut. Make quite a habit of it, don'cher?" He confronts me, swaying. His wine-soaked breath reeks revoltingly. He twitches off my veil. "This time you won't be so lucky."

"Just a minute, Jude," I say steadily." I came here of my own free will, knowing you've got it in for me. I want to trade my hair for your co-operation."

"My – co-operation?" He stumbles over the word.

"You're to get off Yeshua's back, leave him alone from now on."

He scowls. "No dice. I'll take your hair all right – and improve on those scratches. Why should I make terms?"

I take a risk on Si's change of heart. "Because your buddy won't let you do it otherwise."

"She's joking, ain't she, Si? We agreed she needed to be taught a lesson – all the more, now that she's loused up our plans."

"No, Jude." Si's voice has a fresh firmness. "Violence solves nothing, as we've recently learnt. If you go for her, I'll restrain you."

"Like hell you will! I'll do for the both of you."

"I think not. I'm a man of peace but my training as a militant equips me for self-defence. Besides, you're drunk."

Not so drunk that he can't see sense, however. "So I get even with this bitch in return for laying off the Boss? Suits me. I've wanted to do it ever since you gave me the slip that night, you vicious little slag…" He reaches out with one hand to pluck a crimson strand, scrabbling with the other for his razor. "That head o' hair should fetch a tidy price on the market. There's many might pay dear to flaunt it in place of their own."

"Stop!" Si turns to me. "Miriam, have you made up your mind to this? It's a great sacrifice for a young woman as lovely as yourself."

Sacrifice. That's the in-word nowadays, isn't it? I lost interest in my 'crowning glory' the same evening Jude lost his soul to Yeshua's enemies. I nod dumbly. Relentlessly, Jude's blade begins its work. The silken swathes tumble round me and I gaze at my own abandoned beauty. It seems as if it belonged to someone else, the person I once was: Jo's sweetheart, Cass's lover, prostitute, courtesan…

When he's done, I wrap my veil tightly about my shorn skull. "Let's go," I say to Si. He puts an arm round my shoulders, unable to reply.

Jude blusters, "You're not walkin' out on me, Si? Not after all we've been through?"

Without answering, Si unbolts the door and we go out into the April afternoon. A catspaw of wind penetrates my scarf and I feel its coolness, a new and strange sensation. We start along the shuttered street while an uneven tread dogs us. Dot and carry one. Jude's gone back on his word – and I've given up my hair for nothing!

We relax only when the inner door of Zabdiah's office is shut behind us. And behind Jude. Oh yes, he's clung like a parasite, seeking safety in numbers, no doubt. The mask of toughness has disappeared, leaving the furtive look of some sewer-rat beneath.

It's Jo who's let us in. He takes us upstairs to a room, which smells of naked fear. Yeshua alone preserves his usual calm. He manages a smile for me.

"That veil suits you, Miri," he remarks casually, "Why not keep it on – to please me?"

He knows, of course. I screw up my courage and undo the knot at my throat. There's a general gasp of consternation, quickly suppressed. Jo's stricken eyes survey me – does he still wear my old image on his heart? I say nothing since there's nothing to be said. My gesture has been futile and to explain what's happened would only make Jude's presence more intrusive. If Si was right in his suspicions, it may be wise to bind him closer to us, after all.

Yeshua beckons me, strokes my cropped scalp. "You're lovelier to me than ever you were before," he whispers in my ear. That's good enough! He holds out his arms to Si, and then kisses him on both cheeks, an unaccustomed warmth of greeting which carries its own message. Si bows his head as if in recognition – and abasement. For Jude, Yeshua has no welcome; the dagger-man's face darkens at the snub, as it did this morning when his avarice was exposed.

"We've been discussing our next move, Miri," Yeshua says. "My friends have persuaded me to leave the City for the time being, and I've proposed we camp out during the feast beyond its walls. The Mount of Olives will be pleasant in this fine weather, I think."

Rock says, "We'd rather have made tracks for open country but running for it would be sure to do for us. They'd simply hunt us down. The Mount's too close for comfort, all the same."

"Your fears are groundless, Rock. We'll muck in with the other pilgrims and be inconspicuous. If by any chance I'm taken, you must look to yourselves."

"Not me, Master." Rock half-draws his rusty sword. "I'll be damned if I let you down!"

"No, my friend, not damned. That privilege belongs to someone else." Yeshua doesn't look at Jude, who's following every detail of chat with close attention, for reasons of his own. "Now, let's be practical. We've come to keep Pessach and keep it we shall, despite this morning's episode."

"But that means returning to the City," objects Matt. "We'll have to kill the lamb in the Temple and they'll be on the watch for us..."

"Ah, that's just where you're wrong, Matt. This is our final Pessach together and it's going to be a special one. No lamb."

"No lamb? Then it won't be the real thing," Jim protests. The rest concur with him.

"We must have roasted lamb to eat the Seder," grumbles Tom of the big belly. "I'm lookin' forward to a good meal after living off bread and dried fruit all winter."

"Not if we hold our feasting in advance. Tomorrow, say."

The opening meal of Pessach, without its main course and on the wrong day... This is definitely out of order!

Yeshua continues serenely, "By Friday, the day after, we'll have missed our opportunity. Besides, Tom, when have I ever conformed to the stated rules?"

"Sorry, Master. Forgot you're a law to yourself."

Nat puts in, "Shall we be eating in the open?"

"No, it won't be that informal. We've shared many meals together yet this will be the one I want you all to remember in future. Let's see: Thaddeus and his bro can go back with Miri to the City at midday. They're least likely to be identified, specially Miri with her new hair-do... They'll be met by a young man who'll take them to his parents' place, and there they can prepare and lay out the nosh. We'll follow at dusk."

"How shall we know this guy?" I inquire.

"He'll be carrying a water-jar."

That's a woman's work so he shouldn't be hard to spot. We've long ceased questioning Yeshua's predictions; just as Long-ears was at hand to fulfil prophecy, so we can be sure that all will turn out as he maintains it will. We wait for sundown, and then troop out to the slope rising beyond the eastern wall for a night under the stars. Yeshua's right: in darkness surrounded by these Galilean pilgrims, we're anonymous, while their cheerful chatter lends us an unaccustomed sense of security. How long will it last?

At dawn the three of us appointed by him steal back through the Lion Gate. The sun's just risen over Moab and the trumpets blare out to herald the morning holocaust. Our contact awaits us, complete with his jar perched precariously on his head, a youngster no older than Joab, blushing to be seen in such a task. He leads us to a house in a select quarter of the City – one owned maybe by secret admirers of Yeshua. Has this been planned in advance; and why is the meal so special to him? None of us has an answer as we set the table in an upper room with the food we've bought on our way here: cakes of unleavened bread, sour herbs for the charoseth, vinegar and rough wine. The great platter in the middle, destined to bear its weight of roasted meat, stays empty and Thaddeus, whose appetite like Tom's is large, keeps casting wistful glances at it. They're a quiet pair, these cousins of Yeshua; I've never quite gelled with them and we're reduced to polite, meaningless small-talk. I ask whether their parents will be down for the feast.

"Momma will for sure," answers Jude, so different in appearance and character from his unlovely namesake. "She always brings the Master's momma down with her. We had word a few days back that Poppa's unwell but Aunt Miriam insists on going. She told Momma she mustn't miss this Pessach on any account. She would have gone on her own, it seems, if Momma hadn't obliged."

"Then we'll be three Miriams – your mother, Yeshua's and me," I say brightly, hiding my concern at her insistence. I recall that two-way link between mother and son, which needs no words. She's felt the vibes of his death wish, knows the crisis is upon him, and has resolved to see it through. 'A sword shall pierce your soul...' the old man told her. I must seek her out and offer what human support I can.

The others arrive under cover of darkness. The City's crowding works to our advantage and they're certain they escaped notice as we did. Yeshua comes in last and takes his place at the table's centre with Rock and Jo at either side. Jude is on his own in not jockeying for a position close to the Master; he chooses one of the end-couches, half-lost in shadow. Being the sole female, I'll wait on them with the help of our youthful guide whom Yeshua addresses as Mark. It appears, however, that he's reserved the most menial task for himself. Before the Seder starts, he takes a basin and towel from the corner of the room and proceeds to wash the outstretched feet of his followers. Most of them are thoroughly put out by this honour; Rock all but turns it down, then sees Jude tuck his unwashed legs beneath him and hastily changes his mind. When Yeshua's gone the rounds, he invites me to submit. I hesitate but he says gently, "You alone, Miri, have done the same for me. I must repay the debt." So he does.

We all recite the opening prayer and pass round the first cup of watered wine. Then he says, "It's customary for the youngest present to ask about the meaning of this feast. Last year I reminded you all of our ancestors' escape from bondage, referring to my own predestined role. My words were veiled since none of you was ready for the truth. Today I'll make it plain to you." He pauses, noting hungry eyes directed at the empty platter before him. "You think our Seder incomplete without its principal dish. It isn't so, my friends. I am the Pessach lamb whose blood will save mankind from servitude."

His statement sends shock waves round the board. We've salvaged the faintest hope that what seems imminent and inevitable can yet be prevented by some happy stroke of fate. Hasn't he displayed his power of cheating death, not once but many times?

Jo's voice is tearful: "Yesterday in the Temple, Master, you condemned blood-offerings. You said your Poppa didn't want them, then released the victims."

"I condemned a ritual carried out for personal gain and minus one trace of genuine piety. Sacrifice, in the real sense of self-giving, is most pleasing to my Father."

"Haven't you given up your whole life to Him?"

"Its daytime hours, perhaps. Yet night must fall. My death will point the way for you, my disciples."

"The way," says Tom. "We'll follow your way – if only you'll make it plain to us, Master!"

"I am the way, Tom. I'm truth and life. By clinging to me you'll reach my Poppa's kingdom."

"How can we cling if you leave us in the lurch?"

"I'll never leave you, be assured of that. My present going is the lot of any man yet even when I seem to have deserted you, I'll dwell on in your souls."

"We'll keep your memory fresh, of course, Master," Phil says, "but it's you we need, your guidance."

Yeshua shakes his head. "My being within you will be as real as this my body which is soon to die." He turns to me. "Miri, my dear, pass me the Pessach bread."

Bewildered, I hand him the unleavened cakes.

"Put them on the salver."

I do so. He says, "Once I promised you all you'd eat my flesh and drink my blood. You turned from me in dismay. Believe now that this can be – that as often as you repeat my blessing over bread and wine, they will become myself for your souls' nourishment."

He raises his right hand and makes a cross above the platter. "This is my body." And above the mixing-bowl. "This is my blood of the new covenant to be shed for man's salvation."

Thaddeus's face falls. I'm sure he was expecting the dry cakes to turn – hey presto! – Into lamb's-meat, perfectly cooked and dressed. Yeshua smiles at him. "Taste, cousin, you won't be disappointed."

The other leans forward, takes one of the pieces tentatively and nibbles at it. A slow expression of surprised delight overspreads his face. "This is – terrific, Master! It's like the best meal I've ever tasted, in a single bite…" He sips the proffered wine and smacks his lips over that as well. Is he being ironic or exaggeratedly polite towards a madman? Grinning sheepishly, his mates chew the cakes handed them by Yeshua and show the same reaction. Again, Jude's the exception, waving away the salver and refusing his cup of wine.

"Your turn, Miri."

I pick up the last morsel, swallow the drink. Thad was right. Now I can understand why the vintage at Kana and the loaves beside the Lake went down so well. Yet if I've grasped his meaning, this food isn't what it appears to be. Beneath its outward form it's – himself, whole and entire. For all our communion of spirit, I used to feel cheated of a lover's contact. At this moment, though faith alone sustains it, our contact is complete.

For some of us this strange ceremonial is no more than a piece of magic, an unsuspected treat. Phil returns to his interrupted probing: "You tell us to seek your Poppa's kingdom, Master, but where are we to find it?"

Yeshua's look rebukes him. "Have you been tagging along with me so far, Phil, yet not known me for who I am? Our time together is nearing its close and one last mashal must suffice. There was a guy who set out to discover the goal of existence. He found his route obscured by heavy fog and, like Tom, he was uncertain of the way. His choice of roads seemed endless. Some led him to the brink of precipices, others to impenetrable thickets. Eventually he came to one which wound on without a barrier to stop him, and he thought to himself, 'Why, this must lead me to the truth.' He travelled day and night until the fog lifted one morning and, looking round, he recognized the place from which he'd started. Then he saw it with fresh eyes and knew it for the object of his search." He gazes at our puzzled faces. "My Poppa is already in your midst. We are one; He's in me and I in Him. Yet, though divine, I've assumed man's nature and made myself subject to man's death in order to reconcile humanity with its Creator. My hour is upon me now – and one among you is about to launch me on my final journey."

His mates glance at each other uneasily, restless with tension. One only stays still, his eyes cast down, inscrutable. I watch him from my place behind Yeshua. Jo and Rock exchange a troubled look while the former murmurs, "Tell us who you mean, Master." Yeshua's reply isn't a direct one. He takes a piece of rue from the charoseth we prepared this morning, dips it in vinegar then stretches his arm the table's length.

"You didn't eat the food I blessed for you, Jude. Oblige me by accepting this before we finish our feast."

The black eyes lift, the cracked lips scowl at him. With a bad grace Jude takes and eats the bitter herb. His neighbours pay no heed – maybe they imagine it's a kindly gesture intended to draw him into our spirit of comradeship – yet I know better. It signals Yeshua's awareness of his guilt, as well as his consent to be betrayed.

Rock's also missed the connection. He exclaims, "Whoever the bastard is, it's not me. You know that, Master. I'm going with you all the way."

Yeshua's eyes contemplate him without expression. "Bravado, Rock, bravado. Tell me, what do folk name the bugle-call that sounds from Antonia just before first light?"

"The cock-crow, Master."

"Then I tell you that by the cock-crow you'll have disowned me, not once but three times."

Rock's face reddens in anger. "Are you implying I'm a traitor?"

"No – except to your better self. Cowardice isn't the same as malice. You and your pals mustn't lose heart if you fall at the first hurdle. We'll meet again on this side of eternity and I'll send my Spirit to strengthen your resolve." He laughs at our bafflement. "Just bear my words in mind. The future will unwrap their meaning for you. Shall we sing the Seder hymn and return to Oliver?"

THIRTEEN

We spill out into the dark, Yeshua still talking as though he'd dismissed the threat of Jude's discovered purpose from his mind. I'm not fooled; my own life-wish must offset his death-wish and I'll make one last appeal to his betrayer.

The Siccarioth slips away in the murk, unobserved, as the rest strike eastward for their sleeping-ground. I follow him. If his goal's Qayapha, as Si suggested, he hasn't far to go for the High Priest's palace lies at the exclusive centre of this exclusive district. There's no false modesty about the top brass of Israel's ruling clique! Jude's several yards ahead of me but he's faltering in his uneven stride. It's not his limp alone; I think Yeshua's knowledge has shaken him. To do the dirty on a friend isn't as easy when he states one's intention in advance. Why didn't the Boss prevent me? he must be thinking. Am I exploiting him or is he exploiting me? For all his cynicism, he can't be sure Yeshua's not what he claims to be. To shop an innocent man is one thing – to shop God's Chosen One would be to damn himself.

I catch him up and walk for a while beside him. He darts me a shifty look and limps on as if his path had been predetermined. For once he's stone cold sober and I seize my chance. Abuse will get me nowhere, nor will beating about the bush.

"What's in it for you, Jude?"

He's gone too far to bluff it out. He shrugs: "Thirty shekels."

"The compensation for a murdered slave. You must've done far better out of party-funds."

"I used 'em to promote the cause, didn't I? What a fuckin' waste. A bloke has to recoup his losses somehow. The Sads 've promised me commission on their Temple-trading – if I lead 'em to the goods."

"They'll turn their backs on you once you've done your bit. Probably hand you over to the Aliens as Barabbas's accomplice."

"I can look after myself. Why don't you get back to your superman and leave me be, slag?"

"You swore you'd leave him be. I paid a price for that."

"More fool you. You're a right pair of idgits, you and Barjoseph, trusting a hustler like me. I'm a realist, see? I'm acting smarter than the rest of you. When Rock and his buddies go down, I'll be riding the storm – and it won't be your precious master calling the tune as he did on that perishing lake."

The memory halts him in his tracks. He mutters, "It's funny, all the same. Those happenings knocked me all ends up at the time.

They almost got me thinking there was really something in him…"

This is my opening. I step in front of him and say, "Don't you realize that the man who stood on raging water, healed the incurable and raised a guy to life must be able to change your miserable outlook if he so wished? He's using you to accomplish his own ends, Jude, like some puppet on a string. Admit you're the sucker and turn back before it's too late."

"No one calls Jude the Siccarioth a sucker – and no one takes him for a ride." He peers over my shoulder at the twin residence of Qayapha and his father-in-law Annas, looming ahead in the April moonlight. Temptation reasserts its grip on him. "It's you who's trying to trap me, you little whore. If Barjoseph wants to be a martyr, that's his lookout. He talked some crap about 'turning the other cheek' way back in Galil. Let him turn it now, and take what's coming to him. He showed me up in front of my mates and I've a score to settle with him – same as I did with you."

He shoves me brusquely aside and plods on with fresh determination. I watch him gain entrance at the ornamented gateway. My failure to divert him is disheartening yet not beyond reprieve. By getting in myself, now I'm so near, I might find out enough to warn Yeshua while there's still time. Before the gates clash shut, I run forward and slide between them, unnoticed in the darkness. The great courtyard is empty. I hug its outer wall and work my way round towards the building. Jo, whose family connections opened its doors for him in the past, has described the place to me and I've a fair idea of its layout. Qayapha, Cohen Gardol for this year, lives cheek by jowl with Annas, that wily old wheeler-dealer who's monopolized the religious government of Palestine for half a century. There's an entrance at the rear where Jo, in his apprenticeship days, used to deliver consignments of dried fish to stock the high-priestly larders. I find it without difficulty, neither locked nor guarded, and make my way cautiously through a warren of interior passages. This is the domestic region and if I'm seen, I'll play the part of some minor skivvy hired as an extra for the Pessach celebrations. The servants prove too busy to take notice of a stranger and I'm able to reach the state-rooms at the front, undetected. Ears, rather than eyes, are my guide in these ill-lit corridors; I'm listening for the sound of voices – Jude's which I can't mistake, and the High Priest's which I know from public speeches and pronouncements in the Temple.

Luck's on my side. Beyond a curtained archway leading to the atrium, I hear low-toned conversation – not two, but three men talking. The third, more elderly sounding, must be Annas whose finger is in every pie, however unsavoury. Partially hidden by the curtain's thick folds, I try to make out what they're saying.

"Tonight." That's Qayapha's dry voice. "It has to be tonight. We can't risk an arrest by daylight for fear of rioting, and nothing can be done once the Feast gets under way. Where did you say he could be found, my man?"

"Olivet, Your Worship." A note of unfamiliar subservience in Jude's reply. These are his new masters. "He and his gang are dossing in the olive-grove half-way up the hill, Seems like he's asking to be snatched, don't it?"

"I shall send a detachment of Temple-guards to apprehend him. The others can go free – for the time being. They'll scatter like sheep without their shepherd."

Annas intervenes. "Take my advice, Qayapha, have the Romans in on this one. They know him to be a disturber of the peace, if not a party to yesterday's assassination, and they're sure to co-operate. If his dispatch proves unpopular with the ebionim, they'll also share the blame for it."

"Agreed. I'll go in person to Pilatus and arrange it with him. As you say, Annas, it's best we take no chances. His influence over the commoners is incalculable."

Jude displays alarm. "I'll have no truck with Aliens, Your Worships, and I'll thank you for my cut right away."

"Not so fast. You will be required to identify your leader, and to testify against him at his trial."

"Not me. You swore – "

"I guaranteed you payment on delivery. In view of your reputation, I doubt whether you have much value as a witness but the money binds you to fulfil our stated terms." There's a chinking of coins and a muttered acknowledgement from Jude. Qayapha adds, "What matters more is the immunity from Roman justice which I offer you – for the time being. Continue to serve my interests and it may be extended."

The consultation ends there, apparently, and I'm left to wrestle with my fears for Yeshua. It'll be some time before a posse can be gathered; I'll be able to get back to him, thank God, and pass the message. As I scurry back the way I've come, the words 'dispatch' and 'trial' buzz through my brain. The courtyard's already a hive of activity as Qayapha prepares to set out for the Procurator's H.Q. and lamp-bearers have been summoned. Their flickering torches make concealment impossible – one of them catches a glimpse of me slipping past and seizes me.

"What's this – an intruder?"

I think fast. "I – I came with the informer who's been reporting to the Cohen Gardol. I'm his – woman." The admission almost chokes me.

"We'll check that."

Jude's standing on the edge of Qayapha's escort-party. My captor questions him and he glares at me as if in denial, then grins unpleasantly. "Yeah, sure, she's my gal, all right. Keep a tight hold on her – she'll do my witnessing for me…"

The devil. I'm taken back into the main building and up to a small chamber overlooking the court. In order to ensure my co-operation, I'm locked in. All I can do is watch helplessly as the deputation files through the pillared gateway on its brief journey, first to the Procurator, then to an unprepared and defenceless Yeshua. He has at most an hour of freedom remaining.

My dread of confinement returns although I'd supposed it gone forever. The lifeline which linked Yeshua and myself in spirit when I was Herod's prisoner seems to have snapped. Instead, as I gaze over rooftops to the star-studded sky beyond, a new and terrible sensation overcomes me. I feel the impact of some cosmic doubt, as if mankind's whole future hung upon one wavering resolve, and with this dawns a personal temptation. Jude's satanic mischief has cast me as a witness against Yeshua; very well, I'll be just that, I'll take my oath he's mad - a harmless lunatic whose ravings deserve pity, not condemnation. Sentence of death – if that's what Qayapha has in mind – may give place to mere ridicule and I'll have him to myself ever after…My faith, built up by stages from a groundwork of utter disbelief, of initial antagonism, collapses like a house on shifting sands, and once again I'm the sceptic who refused his claims yet fell for his human magnetism.

At last the courtyard below fills once more. I look down and see a throng, which grows by the minute. Qayapha's raised half the City, it appears, Robed figures cross the paving – members of the Council whose judgement I once faced, while the posse's returning from its assignment. Legionaries; helmets gleam as they lower spears at the command of a voice I recognize too well. So Cass has finally met Yeshua! I could imagine a happier circumstance for their first encounter but there may be cause for a wild hope in my lover's presence… Servants bring out a brazier of glowing embers since the night-air is chilly and all except the prisoner must wait outside for orders. He's led indoors by the rope, which binds his arms.

Almost at once my door's unlocked and I'm released – as far as the courtyard itself. I've some importance now; my testimony may strengthen the High Priest's case: a foolish girl's unguarded prattling. Among the sea of faces, I make out Jo and Rock; they see me and their eyebrows go up. But my query is urgent. Have they. too, been nicked?

"No," answers Jo. "The guards ignored us. We followed them here and the gatekeeper who knows me from the old days let us in. Things look bad, Miri, very bad. Qayapha's trying to pull a fast one with this improvised hearing. I'd say he wants the Master sentenced and seen off before the Shabbat. Postponement could allow for counter-measures by his fans from Galil. He knows, too, that there's more than one Barabbas running loose…"

"Don't be defeatist, Jo. Trial before dawn's illegal, you know that, and the right of execution must be referred to Rome."

"A shyster like the Cohen will bend the law to suit his purposes –

besides which, he's made good and sure that Rome's involved. That's why Rock here's shaking in his shoes."

In fact, Rock has shuffled some paces away from us as though our being together might rouse suspicion. He chafes his hands over the brazier like those around him yet his bulk and rough-hewn features give him away. A servant-girl peers at him then says in broad north-country vowels, "I've seen you before, haven't I? You're one of the Carpenter's mates…"

Rock makes a gesture of denial and the glow of the red-hot embers is mirrored in beads of sweat on his brow.

Jo whispers, "Don't judge him too harshly. He did a stupid thing. When they took the Master, he swiped at one of them with his cutlass – we should've confiscated it long ago. No damage done so far as I could see but it was a nasty moment. If the Master hadn't stepped in and soothed the guy, it might've turned into a straight fight between half a regiment and the four of us."

"Four? Did the rest get away then?"

"It wasn't like that. The Master had taken us – Rock, Jim and me – away from our camping-ground to pray with him in that little garden. Couldn't have been a worse choice, being walled in, but how were we to know they'd come for us tonight? We started to feel sleepy and dossed down, though something told me I ought to stay on the alert. Wished I had – my dreams were something awful! There was horror in them, a tide of blood licking at the edges of my brain and – and a fear that was too dreadful to be borne…"

"I'm with you, Jo. I went through the same ordeal, awake." So that all-consuming terror had not been mine alone. Did I lose touch with Yeshua after all, or was it his own last-minute loss of courage which had infected Jo and myself, his closest confidants?

"We woke a couple of times. His face looked ghastly – dripping with sweat like Rock's, only the drops seemed dark… I guessed he needed our full support for once yet I couldn't keep my lazy eyes open – till the riot-squad hove in sight. That all-time louse Jude was leading the way. He limped up to the Master who'd got to his feet, and I heard him say, "Last time we met, you refused me greeting. Now I'll put you to shame, Barjoseph" and he kissed him on both cheeks. It must've been a prearranged signal because they closed in and ringed him at once. He made no fuss and ticked Rock off for trying to defend him. The soldiers had a mind to rough him up, but their officer kept them on a tight rein. A good disciplinarian and a decent sort, I'd say. That's him over there."

I've no need to look where he points but I can't resist doing so. Cass wears a surly, unforthcoming expression as if, like Rock, he doesn't want to be associated with this affair. He hasn't identified me, veiled and in semi-darkness – even without my scarf he mightn't now! I, on the other hand, must contact him and gain what benefit I can from his unwilling share in Yeshua's custody. The general brouhaha makes it easy to approach him yet almost at once a hand's laid on my shoulder,

"They're asking for you inside, young lady. Look lively."

That's the last thing I want to do, In Yeshua's eyes I'm going to appear a second Jude; far worse, indeed, since he's counting me as his friend. He has access to my inner thoughts, however, and he'll know my only motive is to save his life. I'm ushered into a spacious chamber where a number of po-faced councillors are seated round a richly carved table. Glancing at them, I feel more like a defendant than a prosecution-witness, and I range myself mentally beside Yeshua as he stands, still pinioned, in front of them, flanked by Temple-guards. His trial seems to be holding fire for lack of ammunition, while one of the members argues against its legality. An ally among enemies?

"The Law demands that an accused man be tried by day and in the proper place."

Qayapha at the table's head snaps, "This is an emergency, Nicodemus. Barjoseph has a great deal of popular support, as well you know. Unwelcome publicity on the eve of the Pessach might result in serious disturbance."

"He's also entitled to a second trial before sentence is passed," points out this Nicodemus character – a middle-aged guy with pleasant features and a lawyer's incisive look about him. Not one to be easily overawed.

"He shall have his second hearing – before the City stirs: a full session in the Chamber of Hewn Stone, Does that satisfy you?"

Another voice is heard, an older man's. "It doesn't satisfy me, Qayapha. The evidence we've been subjected to so far is a tissue of contradictions from which a single fact emerges: that the accused claims power to rebuild a ruined Temple within three days. Such a statement may sound absurd yet it's not blasphemous. He's restored health to many and life to at least one – a greater achievement, by far, in my opinion." The speaker looks directly at Yeshua, his sympathy contrasting with the hostile faces on either side. "Why is he not permitted to defend himself, may I ask?"

"Yours is an irregular proposal, Joseph," says Qayapha judicially, "but I'll waive protocol on this occasion. Since his imputed crime is to have uttered sacrilege, let him repeat it if he dares, at this assembly."

Yeshua turns his eyes from his previous advocate to me. "I've taught day after day in the Temple," he says quietly, "and made no secret of the truth about myself. If you wish to hear it, why not question one who's heard me speak?"

The guard on his right swings a fist at him; its smack echoes through the room. "You'll address the Cohen Gardol respectfully, prisoner!" he growls.

Qayapha chimes in smoothly, "Very good. Have the girl brought forward and let her say her piece."

Every eye is on me now, except Yeshua's, yet I feel as much alone with him again as on that night at Migdal when we kept vigil together. I strain to recollect the speech I've rehearsed but it escapes me. I'm possessed once more by an influence stronger than any evil squatter, and the words I speak aren't my own: "He's the Chosen One, Son of the living God, whose mission is to save us from our sins."

The High Priest looks nonplussed for a moment, thrown by the conviction in my voice, then his face clears and he all but smiles. My witness has been more damaging to Yeshua than any betrayal could be.

"You hear her, Carpenter," Qayapha exclaims. "Do you confirm or deny what she has said. Are you the Christ?"

Yeshua's eyes bore into his. "I am – and one day you will see me seated at the right hand of my Father upon the clouds of heaven."

The new confronts the old in this duel between a wandering preacher and the representative of an outworn tradition. Slowly, the Cohen Gardol reaches up and tears his robe from collar to belt.

"He has blasphemed. A vote will no longer be necessary."

The chamber bursts into uproar. But for Qayapha's presence and authority, I'm certain Yeshua would be taken out and stoned to death on the spot. As it is, he makes no move to restrain the violence of his guards who start to strike and spit at their captive, abetted by the judges. My blood boils and I fling myself instinctively between the flailing fists and their helpless target. An arm thrusts me aside like a rag doll and in desperation I rush from the room to seek Cass's aid, as I did on the night of Sue's extremity.

Outside in the torch-lit courtyard, I glimpse Rock's burly shape. He should be using his toil-hardened muscles to shield his Master at this minute. I seize him by the collar and hiss, "He needs you, Rock. The swine are beating him up in there."

He stares at me blankly as if I were a stranger. Others have heard me and they start to question him. He turns away, protesting, "You've mistaken me for someone else. I don't even know the bloke."

I shrug my disgust. Jo's nowhere to be seen though my soldier-boy still stands on the outskirts of the rabble. Thank God. He makes a movement of half-recognition as I approach him.

"Cass, they've set on Yeshua. Can't you make them stop?"

He's not the world's fastest thinker, poor lamb. Perhaps my being here has taken him aback. He scratches his cheek, spits out a dottle of gum. "Orders are to hang around and escort Barjoseph to Antonia at dawn," he says. "This ain't our quarrel, Miri. I can't interfere. Stay cool – they won't go too far at this stage. Your Holy Man wants it done all legal and above-board, an execution signed and sealed by Rome."

"I know." My shoulders sag. I should have remembered that, for

Cass, duty comes first. How far can I rely on his fondness for me? "Look, dearest, you may just be his one hope - and mine. He won't lift a finger for himself, I'm sure of it, but couldn't you do something?"

"Be reasonable, Miri. I'm only a centurion. If the Proc gives the go-ahead, there's damn-all I can do."

"That depends, doesn't it? You might be able to swing it if they leave him in your charge."

"Like springing him under the eyes of a thousand watchers?"

"No. Like turning a blind eye of your own at some convenient moment. His mates'll do the rest."

"And I'll get slung outa the legion or at least reduced to ranks. I'd risk it to save you, babes, supposing it ever came to that, but not for a guy who's bust his chops to cut me out with you."

"You weren't a bundle of help when I was in shtook myself, were you? Sorry. Cass, but you admitted as much. You promised you'd make up for it…"

"Sure I did." He stares pensively at the ground. "Cass ain't the type to renegue on his word. I'll do what I can, Miri, I swear it – so long as your promise stands."

"Of course it does. Once this crisis is past, we'll be man and wife. Yeshua gives his say-so to that, whatever you may think."

There's some disturbance behind me. I turn to see Jo struggling in the arms of Abenadar. He's seen the battered figure of his Master emerge through the stately doorway and he's trying to get to him. Some distance from them, the Cohen's minions are still on at Rock, bullying him to confess his collusion with the prisoner. Frenziedly he throws wide his massive arms and shouts at them but the words are drowned by a bugle-blast echoing from Antonia's parapet. The noise seems to convulse his frame with its shrill challenge. Covering his ears with his hands, he runs through the open gateway, and darkness hides his tears.

As if to reproach man's cruelty to man, the daybreak is immaculate, a ground-haze heralding summer's heat in the midst of spring. The Council-members pottered homeward to snatch some sleep but for the rest of us it's been a fraught waiting-period, anxious for many and wearisome for all. Now we process through empty streets to the Temple, Yeshua already in poor shape yet holding himself as sturdily as ever. He's taken to the chamber, which holds bleak memories for me, while Jo and I are left to kick our heels in the precinct where he chanced his arm two days ago.

There's plenty to hold our interest – if we weren't so distracted by his plight. The moneychangers are setting up their stalls, undeterred by his one-man demo the other day, and the Levites are sharpening their knives. Soon a stream of suppliants will pour in to offer up their yearling lambs. Each wretched creature's throat will be slit, its blood caught in a silver bowl to be sprinkled over the altar, its corpse flayed and entrails burnt, while the right foreleg and cheeks will be removed and set aside for the overfed priests to consume. Incomprehension at this grisly rite surges up in me again, still more vividly as I think of the human victim trapped in their merciless toils. His second trial is being staged as a mere concession to legal form. A majority of two is required to condemn and he has only two to speak in his defence! Almost before the first purchaser has drawn his knife across the first tender throat, the door of the Knesset-chamber is thrown open and a swarm of Sads with Qayapha, their Nasi, at their head, propels Yeshua toward the fortress of Antonia. We follow. There's nothing more we can do apart from showing our fidelity and sharing mentally in his torment. None of his other mates are in evidence – so even if Cass manages to do his stuff and create a diversion, small hope remains of rescuing him. The optimism that has carried me through a series of disasters still buoys me up but Jo is too depressed to speak or to count on a reversal of fortune. This squalid ending bears no relation to his dreams of Mashianic glory.

A lot depends on Pilatus, however. He's played it the High Priest's way so far but will he countenance the killing of a patently guiltless man? Cass tells me he's a jumped-up business tycoon who gained his eminence by marriage. Claudia Procula, his wife, has the ear (maybe more than that!) of Sejanus, the emperor's number one in Rome. No doubt her husband worships wealth and status rather than any god yet he's known to dislike the intransigence of our religious leaders. It would please him to withhold his right of execution, if only to score a point against Qayapha, although he came off worst from his previous clash with our pious tenets and may be wary of offending once again. The situation's finely balanced. What Yeshua really needs is some X-factor in his favour – and I pray that one turns up before too late.

By now the City's filling with its pilgrims and a big concourse stands outside the Place of Judgement fronting Antonia. My heart warms to the many half-familiar folk from Galil – and my spirits rise a fraction. These bluff, good-natured farmers and their comfortable wives will be rooting for the preacher who has taught them simple virtues and healed their neighbours' ills. The sight of their expectant faces reminds me of a custom which may yet deliver Yeshua from priestly vengeance: at Pessach, a single prisoner is given free pardon at the crowd's discretion. Why didn't it occur to me before? Of course they'll pick on him! The other candidate, Barabbas, is no friend of theirs, still less so of Rome, and frankly he merits the law's full weight.

This ray of inner sunshine casts a glow over the scene around me and I survey it with a lightened heart. Sherbet-sellers weave among the jostling, excitable throng and kids play hide-and-seek between a forest of adult legs. News of the day's drama must have spread like wildfire, yet its tragic implications can't dampen the holiday mood. One figure only is noticeable by its stillness and veiled features: a tall woman clothed in black, accompanied by two others whom I recognize, Miriam the wife of Cleophas and momma of Jude and Thad, plus Salome, Jo's momma. The veil conceals a face I know and love, unseen so long. It covers more – the expression of a dread I've also shared, though mine's been a shadow of hers.

I nudge Jo. "There's your momma and Yeshua's. Let's go to them. His friends must stick together."

We thread our way through the milling tourists and greet the three silently. There's no time for dialogue, no need to explain the build-up to this crisis. Our eyes are on the man awaiting judgement as he stands at the centre of Gabbatha, the stone platform before Antonia where his sentence will be passed. His mother never turns her hidden gaze from him but holds out gnarled hands to me. She speaks in a dead tone just audible against the clamour: "You see, Miri, that old man spoke the truth. A sword's already twisting in my heart and I shall bear it till the end..."

"You should've stayed away, Miriam." Fatuous advice, and far too late.

"No, I must offer up my pain alongside his. You too, child. Every tear we shed for him will add its tiny quota to the price of man's ransoming."

Her fatalism is beyond me. Can no one see that we have to oppose this atrocity? The fortress throws its silhouette in blackness across the blazing square, and now the Procurator, a squat, balding man made plumper by his purple-striped toga, descends the stairway. His curule, from which justice is dispensed, is set out to receive him and priests surround the marble chair – as close to a prohibited Gentile building as the Law allows them. Pilatus takes a thoughtful look at the accused while Qayapha lays his charges. After a silence, he bids the guards convey Yeshua to his private apartment for questioning. The delay means an extension of hope for us, impatience for his prosecutors who sense that their Roman adversary's hanging it out in order to tease them.

At length he emerges once more, alone, and announces from the balcony, "I find no fault in this man." His accent is atrocious but his meaning crystal-clear. I breathe again.

Qayapha shouts above the cheering, "He's a blasphemer and by our Law he merits death."

"That is a matter for yourselves," replies Pilatus. "I shall not sanction the extreme penalty because of some petty dispute over your ecclesiastical priorities. The accused may go free."

"He's a seditionary." Qayapha's voice holds an edge of hysteria. "He has won the north to his revolutionary cause. Galil pays homage to him as though he were its king."

"So he's a Galilean?" A smile creeps across the bland, self-indulgent features. "My – ah – friend Antipas is in town, they tell me. Let him judge his would-be usurper!"

Passing the buck – that's always the resort of feeble governors. My soaring spirits take a dive; what mercy can be squeezed from the killer of Johanan? All the same, Pilatus has pronounced and we must follow suit. He clicks his fingers and Yeshua's guards lead him downstairs once more, across the viaduct spanning the Tyropoean Valley towards the palace of Hasmon where Herod resides when he graces the City with his presence. He has no jurisdiction in the south, yet the Procurator has hit on a way to ease their long-standing enmity, with an inoffensive prisoner as his pretext for the compliment. As we trail along in the rear, my arm both guiding and steadying Miriam, the ghost of a plan begins to materialize in my mind. Herod, like Jude, is an obsessive creature who nurses grudges (don't I know it?) but also, I suspect, any yen once formed. He wanted to see and touch me naked. I retaliated, paid the price of doing so with these scars, and now we're quits. If his puerile wish will serve to turn his wrath from Yeshua, I'll give him all the satisfaction which once I refused. For all I care, he can strip me bare in front of his giggling courtiers...

We enter the palace in a body, the Sads determined to force their will on a ruler as indifferent as Pilatus yet one who at least pays lip service to their faith. I contrive to worm my way forward into the royal presence, persuading my companions to stay outside, if I'm to be humiliated, it shan't be in their view. The atmosphere of sensuous luxury brings back the past for me: drapes of velvet and satin, costly fitments, the perfume of joss-sticks mingling with scented flesh whose owners posture and parade in their flaunted garments. Extravagant peacocks. This is the usual panoply of Herod's entourage, wrung out of peasants' taxes. He lounges on his throne, eyebrows raised at our invasion of his privacy. I see no sign of Chusa – does Joanna even know of her Master's arrest? Others, like Phicol, sneer at my showing up yet their eyes are on Yeshua, the King's elusive prey – his self-declared rival.

Antipas listens to Qayapha's charges, then directs a thin-lipped smile at Yeshua. "Forgive me," he drawls. "I'm not sure how to address you: Barjoseph – Carpenter - Mashiah – or Lord God?"

A sycophantic titter from his lackeys. The Tetrarch's opening has set the tone for this interview. Like the Baptist, his cousin is to be fair game for their baiting. Yeshua doesn't answer.

"I've been most eager to offer you my modest hospitality but circumstance has deferred our meeting." Herod's glance flicks lazily over me as I keep my distance. "I had to make do with your charming deputy whose misplaced loyalty resulted in – unpleasantness. I see her concern on your behalf has outlasted that episode and congratulate you on a conquest I signally failed to achieve!"

Another titter. Qayapha has a thwarted look; the reference means nothing to him yet it implies an absence of gravity on Herod's part. His next words confirm the fact: "Now our encounter occurs under different circumstances, I'm being asked to adjudicate on your fate. Were I to do so on my own territory, I shouldn't hesitate to clip your wings – permanently – but since you've made such formidable enemies in Judaea, I feel no urgency. Nor do I wish to abrogate the privilege of Rome in this affair."

Two minds, equal in cunning, are locked in battle. Has Qayapha's scheme backfired on him?

The king's tone sharpens: "Nevertheless, I do not relish insolence. I asked you a question, which you have failed to answer. Let me repeat it in another form. Who do you claim to be?"

Yeshua's mouth stays closed. His eyes look down at the carpeted dais of Herod's throne – not humbly but with barely disguised contempt. I recall Johanan's spitting on the regal slipper.

"Very well. If you find speech difficult in a real monarch's presence, perhaps you'd like to perform some of your party-tricks for us? A little sleight of hand, say, or the displacement of objects by mind-control... No? I warn you that my courtiers don't take kindly to lese-majesty, while my less refined subordinates are only too ready to vindicate my honour,"

I could second that. Two of the ugly group guarding Yeshua scorch my memory as their knives once scorched my skin. I long for Cass but he remained at Antonia when we departed, relieved of duty for the time being. Antipas doesn't need to issue a command; his hint suffices. "This village sawyer calls himself king. Shall we not treat him according to his rank?"

He waves an epicene hand at Yeshua's escort. They grin and shove their quarry out into the barrack courtyard. I hear cackles of mocking laughter, the sound of blows... Minutes later, they return: Yeshua robed in a tattered purple horse-cloth, a circlet of brambles round his scalp, their thorns dug well into the skull, a stave in his right hand for sceptre – the parody of kingship. These courtiers exchange smiles yet his dignity seems undemeaned by the treatment – if anything, Herod is the one who appears deflated, with his flippancy masquerading as lordliness. Real authority comes from within; vulpine eyes fall before his adversary's steady grey ones.

My bile rises. Impetuously, I rush forward and kneel beneath the throne. "Please show mercy, Sir, I – I'll do anything for you if you'll only let him go!"

He holds up his beringed hand and the sledgehammer thudding ceases. "Well, well, the young lady who loves to barter... Last time it was your beauty for another man's release – and I learned the peril of not accepting your stake, Circe. Your skill, in novice hands or rather feet, earned the Baptist a different sort of deliverance for which no doubt he blesses me from Abraham's bosom. I settled my score with you at one remove, yet there's unfinished business between us; you have the power to save his cousin's life, and this time I'll hold to my bargain. Dance for me!"

I've got what I was angling for. Though so much depends on my performance, however, I'm almost mastered by a sense of shame. Don't be a little fool, Miri, you wouldn't have turned a hair in the old days and then you'd no reason except your own advancement. I start to sway my hips without the musical backing to inspire me, my veil and graceless tunic impeding the free flow of my limbs.

Herod raps on the arm of his chair. "This won't do, Circe! How can I appreciate your assets to the full, wrapped in those hideous garments? I named you Daughter of the Sun because your hair entranced me – am I not even to enjoy its sight once more?"

He leans forward and pulls away my scarf. The bored, worldly-wise look he cultivates alters to blank astonishment before he bursts into raucous laughter which rouses willing echoes among the guards and courtiers, as I stand with shaven head in the room's centre. Lifting my eyes, I meet Yeshua's gaze and he smiles back at me. One of my two sadistic pals must have hammered those thorns deep and his own scalp, matted with blood, is a deeper crimson than my vanished plumage used to be.

Herod's fit of amusement is at an end. He says harshly, "I take no pleasure in the gyrations of a cropped scarecrow. Take the girl out of here as well as her rustic paramour."

We're hustled through the ornamented porch, and I see Miriam gasp at her son's disfigurement. This interlude has only increased his anguish – and hers. It's back to Antonia and a long delay while the reluctant Pilatus is recalled. Dramatic tension has given place to suspended interest on the crowd's part during our absence. I watch some youngsters playing Kings on the squares scratched in the judgement-stone of Gabbatha. It's a sport with sinister overtones where the loser pays with his life. The soldiers sometimes force condemned prisoners to play it in all its rigour; these kids content themselves by setting on the unlucky one in fun. Yeshua, too, has striven for kingship and lost by the world's reckoning. How strictly will the rules be applied to him?

The Governor's second appearance is hailed with a mildly derisive cheer. His jaw sets in an obstinate line and he shouts, "Since my colleague won't arbitrate on this issue, I'm prepared to compromise. The defendant shall be scourged by my soldiers, then dismissed."

The Cohen Gardol shakes his mitred head in mute protest, aware that such a penalty may rouse the people's pity without removing the thorn in his own flesh. The habena, a whip of leather thongs studded with teeth of bone and metal, which bite at every stroke, can be a lethal instrument – and not a few have died under its lash. Cass calls it the 'half-way death'. It may be that Qayapha's purpose will be served as well by this as by a cross. His protest is ignored and Yeshua dragged into barracks. What ensues cannot be heard, thank God, yet the woman beside me shudders as if taking every blow on her own body.

I try to comfort her: "It's horrifying, I know, but what they're doing to him might be a good sign. Roman law doesn't allow a convict to be crucified after scourging. These guys aren't animals." I search my mind for some other crumb: "Besides, once he helped me to bear pain, surely he'll do as much for himself?"

She speaks through the hands that clutch her veiled face. "No, no, you don't understand. He's willed this torture, willed himself to endure the worst that men can inflict. No suffering can ever match his own."

I scan the folk around for their reaction. I think they've not realized till now the seriousness of Yeshua's ordeal and a wave of indignation sweeps through their ranks as they rally to his support. Memories of his words and actions pass from mouth to mouth; black looks are flung at the priests in their finery. All this is to the good – yet my eyes, straying beyond, catch sight of one I'd hoped never to see again. Well back beneath the shadow of an archway stands Jude, a cloak wound round his lower features, and by his side a mob of seasoned toughs who can only be the remnant of his 'strike-force'. Why has he – of all men – come here unless to gloat over the sequel of his treason?

A gasp goes up from the assembly, their eyes riveted to the balcony, and I swing round. From the doorway through which a man, injured but erect, was led, a caricature of humanity has emerged, his tunic ripped and slashed with scarlet, face striped with bloody rivulets pouring from the crown of plaited thorn. His wide shoulders are bowed and each step looks a halting agony. I fight back tears of anger and compassion – surely even Jude's shrivelled soul must cringe at the outcome of his malice and greed? Now it's his momma's arm that gives me strength. Pilatus, inured to such sights, barely spares him a glance, but addresses the priests: "Look at the man for yourselves. Hasn't he paid whatever due he owes?"

Qayapha's thin voice almost breaks with fury. "We asked for death, not mere surface abrasion. This miscreant has preached against Rome's oppression. If you dismiss him, you're no friend to Caesar."

It's his trump card, held back till last. He and the Procurator both know it. The old philanderer living in Caprineum, surrounded by his cupids and crocodiles, will boot out any provincial governor who condones, or appears to condone, subversion – yet also one whose error of judgement leads to rioting on Rome's outer frontiers.

"It's a tradition of yours to release one prisoner at this season." Pilatus is playing his final counter-trump. "I offer you, the people, a choice of two: one who has done murder for which the City at large will be penalized, the other whose sole wrong is to claim sonship from a hypothetical god. Which shall I set at liberty?"

A full-throated roar envelops the whole square: "Yeshua – Yeshua – Yeshua!" – the name by which most have known him. The roar turns into a rhythmic chant and my heart sings to its tempo. But then, between repetitions, another name insinuates itself, half-heard at first until the crowd adopts it also: "Yeshua – Barabbas – Yeshua – Barabbas – Yeshua Barabbas…" Many aren't aware of the shared first name nor, if it comes to that, of their Holy Man's patronymic. Now I know the cause of Jude's malign presence (and that of his mates) – to save their partner-in-villainy at the expense of the friend he's deserted, by a simple ruse. What an exchange!

As the chanting dies, the Sads take up the cry: "Crucify the blasphemer! Crucify him!"

Pilatus, a picture of irresolution, calls for a bowl of water and dips his fingers in it. He needn't sully his tongue with the unjust sentence passed on Yeshua. The Jewish act of proclaiming one's personal innocence says it all. If any blame attaches to him, it's small indeed compared with that of Jude and Qayapha. His stubborn championship, the verdict of an outsider and an Alien, almost shines out against the murk of their dishonour. Retreating from the scene of a strategic defeat, he leaves legionaries to select a cross-beam on which their captive will so soon be hung – yet when it's hauled into view minutes later, we see one final spurt of defiance on his part. The titlon telling a culprit's name and offence is scrawled: 'Yeshua of Nazrat, King of the Jews', in Hebrew, Greek and Latin. The Sads go up in smoke about this insult and insist on its being altered, but Pilatus has retired with the last word. For us, the inscription has a bitter irony, brings scant comfort. When the cross-piece has been laid on a bleeding shoulder, an ugly muttering spreads from group to group as spectators wake to the fact that an error has occurred. "It's the wrong bloke" is a phrase constantly repeated roundabout. Already Gabbatha is swamped with legionaries, half a maniple at the very least, and no spontaneous demo could match their expertise. Anger will soon give place to unconcern; nothing, not even a gross miscarriage of justice, must interfere with the festivities. One influential ally might have turned the tide in Yeshua's favour at this point; a mere rabble dissipates its indignation in harmless hurled abuse.

As the cortege of death sets out, my heart drops like lead. The officer in charge isn't Cass but Abenadar. I can't expect to influence his second-in-command in Yeshua's favour. Can he have asked to be relieved and thus shelve an issue, which would strain his twin loyalties to breaking point? It's a question I'll never ask him. He's trapped in a tangle not of his making and to press too hard for motives would be unfair. The sun has reached its zenith, etching the group ahead in light and shade. Its tallest figure bows beneath the cross-beam's weight, ringed by burnished helmets and fenced by spears. We halt at a lock-up where two condemned men join their fellow-sufferer, similarly burdened. They've not been beaten up and scourged, and their step is almost jaunty beside his. He stumbles and falls more than once on the westward march till Abenadar (bless him) commandeers some hefty yokel to carry his burden. It's no great distance from Antonia through the Gennath Gate to the Place of the Skull, a stone's-throw from the City-walls. This outcrop marks the meeting of two roads, one from the north, and the other from Joppa on the coast. Both are dense with pilgrims who pause to stare at the gruesome spectacle with the morbid curiosity of sightseers. The venue's well selected; Rome likes its executions to make maximum impact.

I'm ever conscious of the woman at my side. Miriam has flung back her veil and her features, white as a marble bust, impress me with their stillness. However intense her private torment, she shows no sign of it. Once we're gathered by the fatal mound, Salome hurries forward, producing a flask from beneath her robe. I guess what it contains: drugged wine to ease the victim's pain. With Abenadar's consent, she offers this to Yeshua. He shakes his head. His momma glances at me in reminder of her earlier words – he won't forgo one atom of distress. His companions swig the contents greedily instead, not thanking Jo's momma for her compassion.

The soldiers deal with Yeshua first. The beam is laid behind him and he's thrown on his gashed back, his arms spread-eagled. I turn away instinctively as they prepare to spike his wrists. The hammer-blows sound flat on the breathless air and a moan escapes him as his body's swung sickeningly upward. The beam is locked into its rooted post and his feet are secured by a single nail. Only a block of timber set halfway up relieves the pressure on his pierced extremities. The thieves are treated alike, screaming and cursing – a pair of small-time crooks raised to the level of a Mashiah they don't recognize as such. They merit no attention from the Sads and Set-aparts who've followed us like buzzing hornets and circle the centre-cross on foot or on horseback, mocking the man who hangs from it. The Cohen Gardol hasn't sunk to this level of childish spite but, needless to say, Benesdra's among them. He challenges Yeshua: "If you're the Son of God, then save yourself!"

Stooping, he scrabbles the palm of one hand in mud and smears it over the titlon fixed to the base of the upright shaft. Blood oozing from perforated feet washes it away, leaving the letters to stand out again – as once others stood out in the Temple's dust to mortify him. At length the jeerers grow tired of their sport and abandon us to our silent communion: the three draining their lives out on their trees, our huddle of grieving mourners, and the detachment dicing for the prisoner's garments on Golgotha's naked rock.

A quick death would have been more merciful and dignified. Crucifixion is a long-drawn-out business; its victims often hang for several hours before succumbing. I pray for it to come quickly to Yeshua – and yet, while there's life there's hope… He summons Jo and his momma close to him and speaks to each, so low I can't hear what he's saying at this distance. The anguish in his face is hard to bear and I turn my own to the sky beyond, its pale blue darkening to a deep intensity until it seems we're pinioned under a vast, inverted bowl of lapis lazuli. One of the soldiers glances at the horizon, remarking, "Looks like we're in for a drenchin', mates."

Another says, "No sweat, Marcus. This'll be over by sundown. If the guys are still kickin', we've orders to bust their shinbones. You know the form. There's some Yehudi rule says none must hang on the Shabbat. Ain't that so, sir?"

"Belt up," mutters Abenadar, darting a look at me. "I've no such orders. Anyway the preacher – the bloke they're all so worked up about – is sinking fast. I've never known a guy take so much stick without going under or squawking blue murder like these thieving bastards."

Both observations are true. In contrast to the jabbering robbers, Yeshua wrestles dumbly with his agony. It's terrible to watch him tighten his calf-muscles in order to rise and fill his lungs with air, then slump exhausted – an alternation which resembles some dreadful dance in slow motion. Cass used to say it's lack of breath, not blood, that kills them off in the end. I gaze at the frantic pumping of his rib-cage, the flutter of his heart beneath the stretched and disfigured skin. No man may utter your secret names, O God in Heaven, yet I shall: Yahweh, Eloi, spare your tormented son!

"Eloi, Eloi, lamma sabachthani…" His voice echoes my silent prayer and Miriam at my side continues the psalm: "*My God, I cry by day and you do not answer, by night and I find no rest. I am poured out like water and my bones are out of joint. My heart is like wax, it melts within my breast… They have pierced my hands and my feet, they have counted my bones. They stare and gloat over me, divide my clothing among them and cast lots.*"

He utters one last cry – "It's finished", bows his head and sinks to rise no more. I won't accept this surrender! This is the true blasphemy: that he should submit to death in the midst of life. No one I've ever known has lived to the full as he has or lent so much of his vital urge to others – to Laz and to all those human wrecks he's cured. He can't – mustn't be dead. This is his last delusion and once it's proved so, we'll coax him back to health again, convince him that he must harvest the seed he's sown and die, like the just, in the ripeness of old age… Miriam and her companions are kneeling but I stay on my feet, glaring about me feverishly as if for some happening to intervene, to cheat death of its prey.

During the last half-hour, a steely sky has gradually deepened until the three crosses are black silhouettes against its sombre grey. Now, through the gloom, emerges from the City-gate the indestructible – my battle-scarred survivor. Darling, darling Cass! You've not ducked out of it after all – conscience, or love of me, has brought you here in a bid to redeem what's all but lost. He approaches, not hurrying, maintaining a pretence of official impartiality, accompanied by two robed figures, the men who spoke out on Yeshua's behalf at his trial. By what good fortune have they come together to mount this rescue operation? I run to meet him.

"Cass, it's not too late. Once he's been taken down, I'm certain he'll recover."

His eyes look past me as he chews his eternal gum. "I've got my orders, Miri. None of them says he's to live."

For a moment I refuse to believe my ears. "Look, get him down from that goddam cross and give him to his momma. That's all you need do..."

He brushes me aside, embarrassed by my pleading. "And risk being reduced to ranks for the chancer who's come between us? You can't be serious..."

"It's you who're joking, Cass. You must be! Didn't I offer you my life in return for his?"

He ignores me, examining the crucified. My mind goes back to Herod's twin defections. They were nothing compared with this one. He gestures curtly at a wooden plank propped against one of the posts. Without ado, a soldier picks it up and, swinging back his arm, proceeds to smash the legs of both wretched felons. As they sink, their cries die into silence and the patrol unfastens them from their trees. I shudder in anticipation of two more splintering cracks; haven't they hurt him enough? The soldier questions Cass with his eyes, gets a negative response. A glimmer of hope remains.

Miriam whispers, *"Under the Lord's keeping, every bone of his is safe; not one shall suffer harm."*

Cass takes a spear from one of the infantry, aims its point at Yeshua's left breast. Something inside me snaps and I face defeat for the first time. I watch, inert, as the weapon plunges home. The body doesn't stir, but blood and water gush out as the blade's withdrawn – sign of a life not yet extinct. I know then that I was right – and Cass has killed the one I love and worship. As though to confirm his deed, the earth itself is shaking beneath our feet.

"This was indeed son of the Almighty!" The exclamation is wrung from Abenadar.

"Strange," I hear the guy named Nicodemus murmur, as the Syrian falls to his knees. "The Spirit of God works unpredictably. He told me that himself."

Kneeling, I study those who remain upright: the corpse on its gibbet, Jo Barzabdiah and Caius Cassius Longinus - the three men who've mattered most to me. Only one's survived so far as I'm concerned – the boy who made his vows by the Lake a thousand years ago. The quake moves City-wards, the sky begins to lighten and the tableau returns to life. It seems the elder of Yeshua's supporters, the greybeard who spoke up in his defence and whom Nicodemus addresses as Joseph Ha-ramathaim, has the Procurator's permission to bury Yeshua in his own private tomb set among flowers not far from here. Having hidden his devotion for so long, he wishes to honour him in death. The soldiers wrench out the nails, take the strain, and then lay him over his momma's knees, Jo supporting his head and shoulders. Her strength, physical and mental, has astounded me throughout. Not once have I seen her weep, not once react outwardly to the stages of his passion since a scourging which was concealed from her sight. When he's been disposed, the cross-beams are gathered for future use, the unmourned cadavers placed on field-stretchers, and the detail prepares to march.

Cass, busily directing its bearers, looks everywhere but in my direction. At the last minute, however, he steels himself to meet my eyes.

"It had to happen, Miri," he says, "Sorta straightens things out between us, doesn't it?"

Yes, it had to happen, because an officer's duty comes before emotional commitment. His aim has always been to rank as primus pilus prior, first spear of the Twelth Legion. He's earned that title right enough – and I hope he bloody makes it.

Yes, it does straighten things out, though not in the way that he supposes.

I watch him walking out of my sight and my existence till his party vanishes through the Gennath Gate.

FOURTEEN

The Aliens burn their dead. We bury them in vaults or beneath the soil, It's all the same in the end. What fire does swiftly, decay will do in time. Yet by sweetening and embalming the lifeless flesh, we feed our illusions and shield ourselves from death's finality. Nicodemus has brought with him ointment, spices and grave-bands sufficient for the purpose, yet a lifetime of subservience to the Law makes him and Joseph urge us to scamp our task so that the Shabbat won't be desecrated by an uninterred corpse. Their scruple would have amused – or saddened – Yeshua. No matter: after the day of rest I'll come back and finish the job, as he deserves.

Joseph's tomb is an excavated cave pleasantly bordered by a garden-plot, not unlike my brother's resting-place. Benesdra's jibe returns to me as we anoint and swathe the body: "He saved others but cannot save himself." This won't be temporary accommodation. We hurry his remains into its gloomy depth, laying them reverently on the stone platform, while Nicodemus anxiously watches the sun go down and listens for the trumpet's note announcing the Holy Day and start of Pessach. As Jo pulls away the chock which wedges the golet and it rolls along its groove to close the sepulchre, a joyful blast rings from the Temple's turret and twenty thousand mouths open to taste their first slice of sacrificial lamb. We stand together in front of the rock, collecting our sombre thoughts. I think about that discussion after Simon Ben Mordecai's banquet, trying to recall Yeshua's words: something we were to bear in mind, relating to what Laz had said. Was it the fact that the soul clings to its mortal frame even after death? No comfort there – the fire may flicker on but must expire for want of fuel. He'll go on living, yes, yet only in memory.

"The end of an episode which might have led to Israel's glory," remarks Nicodemus sadly. "I remember his telling me that men must be twice-born. Like a fool I took him literally. How can a man re-enter his mother's womb, I asked. He meant a rebirth of the spirit, of course. Yet isn't there something womb-like about this grave? Maybe I wasn't so far out, after all…"

I can't follow his cloudy speculation. We turn from the loathsome place and wander back to a hostile City. Jo looks suicidal; he needs my moral bracing far more than I need his – or Miriam needs either. I suggest that the three women make for Bethaniah where Mart and Laz can see to their wants and grieve with them over their shared loss, but Jo can't face the company of others and I'll stick with him.

We part with a silent embrace and, before Miriam drops her veil, I surprise a look of – can it be exultation? - In her eyes.

"The bad bit's over," she murmurs to me. "Now my son will prove himself the Mashiah in truth and majesty. You'll see, my dearest,"

A Mashiah eaten by worms in a forgotten spot... I'm glad her faith upholds her. Jo and I trail like orphaned waifs back to the dreary room above Zabdiah's office, which has witnessed our uncertainties and fears. Any expectation I may have had of seeing absent friends assembled here is speedily dashed. They've gone to ground elsewhere or scurried north well beyond Rome and Herod's present reach. My womanly instinct prompts me to put the room to rights and lay the ingredients of a scratch meal. Life must go on. I feel the vibes of Jo's despondency and sense that I'm the stronger at this minute. I must restore his will to survive, by asserting my own.

"You kept faith with him to the end, Jo," I console him. "At least you've no cause for shame."

"You too, Miri."

"The Aliens don't crucify women."

"I meant – you've gone on believing in him. Your trust has outlasted mine."

I used to love kissing his slim brown hands. Now I take them in mine, a gesture of sober comradeship. "I never put him on a pedestal as you did. To me he was simply a man above all others, though there were moments when I thought him to be more... I counted on my own resources to pull him through – and they let me down."

"Poor Miri. You've had nothing but disappointment all along." This is healthier; his reflections are shifting away from Yeshua's fate towards the living. "I was your first, wasn't I? I threw you over for a fantasy that's gone aground and left me rudderless."

"You've got the legacy of his teaching – and a cause to go on fighting for."

"The magic's gone, without him beside me. What did his message amount to in the end? Love: love of God and our fellow men. His own dying was the direct contradiction of that. Telling the world to love selflessly, it's like pissing into the wind. We need to be dragged out of our sewer, delivered from the nature Adam tainted, before that can happen. What chance have we got when even a Mashiah can be destroyed by malice or self-interest? God knows, I'm no Zealot like Si, I never fell for the concept of a warrior-king lording it over subject nations – but I did believe in his immortality, a universe transformed by his saving power."

"Yes, Jo, that vision of paradise on earth has always been more real to you than your actual surroundings, hasn't it? You had me almost subscribing to it once yet I never quite swam out of my depth – which is why I'm ready to pick up the pieces and start again. Women are realists."

"It ever comes back to me, I'll people it with figures of death and destruction, and at its centre, a lamb enthroned, its white fleece stained with blood. The symbol of innocence despoiled by evil... You're right though. Miri, we must make some sense out of what remains to us."

"You said you'd make a book about Yeshua."

"Maybe I will, one day, but not as I meant it to be. The great white hope, which ended in disaster, the story of a flop. A sick joke..."

"Not if we keep his mission alive. D'you remember how he sketched in our futures for us? You and I were to be together again, looking after his momma. I can imagine a worse prospect."

"So can I. You know, he spoke to us from the cross, told us that we should be like mother and son to each other after he'd gone. She has a faith in Yeshua that should strengthen us both, Miri. If only one didn't feel so – helpless without him."

"Be patient, Jo. He'll find a means of putting new heart in you. Didn't he promise he'd stay with us in spirit?"

My question is followed by a hollow tapping on the office-door below. Momentarily we freeze, our sense of danger swamped by a superstitious dread. For some reason, the image of Laz emerging from his tomb invades my brain. Then we laugh shakily at our foolishness and go downstairs, hand in hand. It's Rock. He shoulders past us as if unable to manage a normal greeting, and only once we've settled down does he give us some account of himself. Like Jo, his confidence seems shattered yet it's his own betrayal, not Yeshua's, that's sapped it. So now I've two casualties on my hands! Oddly enough, his coming does us good. Somewhere inside his muddled brain he guards a wistful hope that all is not lost.

"D'you recall that afternoon we spent in Philip's Caesarea?" he asks Jo. "Heathen township stuffed with grottoes and temples to their gods. He made us tell him who folk thought he was. Matt said Eliyah, Phil said the Baptist come back to life. Plain stupid. Then he asked me and, well, it may've been all those shrines and Alien make-believe on my mind, but I heard myself answering that he was truly the Chosen One, Son of the Almighty... So he said, 'That's why I called you Rock, because my Poppa has taught you the truth about me, and your faith is to be the bedrock of my Church that'll never end.'" He pauses in dejection. "Some bedrock! I crumbled at the first breath of real danger, didn't I? Talk about feeling a louse – went and blubbed my eyes out."

"He anticipated that," I remind him gently, "He told you not to despair if you took a tumble."

"Three tumbles. Don't spare me, Miri. Then he said summat about seeing us again this side of eternity. Don't know what in hell he was getting at yet it keeps on ringing through my head and gives me a sort of – certainty."

"Certainty of what?" inquires Jo listlessly.

"Dunno exactly. P'raps that he hasn't really ditched us – that he'll go on being alongside, like he said."

We tire our brains with useless conjecture until the day's traumas catch up with us and we stretch out. The grassy slope of Olivet was bliss compared to this stone floor – although Jo has folded his thick cape underneath me with a tenderness that recalls former days. The hours which follow our rising are among the grimmest I've ever experienced. We're trapped here while the City basks in its festal gaiety – for who knows what further reprisals the authorities may have in mind? We might as well be walled up in Joseph's tomb with Yeshua, dead to the world and clothed in funeral shrouds...

The men take it harder than I do. They're restive, desperate to find out how the land lies. Rock, in particular, wants to prove (to us or himself) that his fit of funk is over. Eventually they risk exposure, and I'm left on my own. I force myself to stop doing purposeless chores and try to pray as Yeshua taught me. It's no good – the contact's simply shut off. When they get back, luckily unapprehended, they've news of Qayapha's latest move.

"He asked Pilatus to have the Master's grave guarded by his troops," explains Jo, "but the Procurator refused."

"Guarded? What on earth for?"

"It seems he's shit-scared we'll steal the body and then declare that it's risen from the dead!"

This would be laughable if we felt like laughter. Only someone as devious as the Cohen Gardol himself could figure out such a possibility.

"Why hasn't he sent the Temple-police?"

"Oh, he has. Doesn't do things by halves, old Qayapha."

"I s'pose the idea might just have occurred to Si and Jude if they'd been running the show."

"Jude," says Rock grimly. "We heard an item about that son of a bitch as well. They say he's gone and hanged himself."

"Never."

"God's truth. The Sads are up in arms – suicide ain't allowed on the Shabbat!"

That puts their whole distorted view of religion into perspective, doesn't it? The despair and self-hatred, which drive someone as low as Jude to take his own miserable life, count for nothing beside the demands of their precious Law. Was it despair? More probably Qayapha withdrew his protection and Jude had no alternative but death by his own hand or Rome's. He, more thoroughly than most, would have known what the latter entailed.

Another prohibition, that of travelling on the Shabbat, has prevented me from returning to the cavern. My determination to pay my last respects is offset by a repugnance to see once again the evidence of a failed cause. I can cope with disillusion, I think, so long as I put the past behind me. While I struggle in vain to force myself to the task, now that the day of rest is over, the sound of a gentle tapping brings me to my feet. The two men are sleeping like logs, after-effect of nervous exhaustion. Cautiously I tiptoe down the stairs and risk a stage-whisper: "Who's there?"

The answering voice is Salome's, and I hear the soft murmur of others. I unbolt the door. The half-light of early dawn scarcely penetrates Zabdiah's office but by the flicker of Salome's torch I can make out Miriam, the momma of Thad and Jude, plus a buxom figure. Can it be – Joanna? We fall into each other's arms and I kiss her quivering cheek, aware that a far deeper tragedy has all but wiped out the memory of my own suffering at Tiberias.

"Joanna! I felt sure we'd meet again."

"I'm so sorry I wasn't able to share in your ordeal, my dearest. I was at Kana, you know, and quite out of touch with these terrible events. As soon as the news came to me, I persuaded Chusa to let me travel to the City. I got here too late – and I'll never forgive myself."

"At Kana? Then your husband's no longer in Herod's employ?"

She shakes her head. "He resigned his stewardship after the treatment you received, Miri. The Tetrarch was mightily displeased, yet Chusa preferred to undergo his displeasure sooner than offend a Power that's not of this earth... Those were his very words."

I beg the three of them to come upstairs, but Salome points to the ointment-jar in Miriam's keeping. She says briskly, "We're on our way to the Master's tomb. The least he deserves is a decent burial – though how we can hope to shift that mill-wheel, I can't imagine."

"Not to mention Qayapha's crowd. Jo found out that he's had guards posted to make sure the tomb's not robbed."

"The wily old schemer," snorts Miriam, "What does he take us for – body-snatchers? Well, they'll hardly suspect four women, if you'll come with us, and maybe they'll roll back the stone."

We journey through slumbering streets under a charcoal sky, only the perpetual flame of holocaust lighting the Temple's phantom pinnacles as we pass. The Gennath Gate is unattended at this hour and we slip through, quickening our pace. For some reason a sense of urgency lends wings to our feet and by the time I reach the Place of the Skull, I'm actually running. How peaceful this deserted spot appears, its gruesome associations overlaid by a virginal calm. Yet we've not come here to indulge our regrets; I skirt the outcrop and race on – until amazement halts me in my tracks.

The cavern's dead in front of me and it yawns open, the golet rolled back and firmly wedged. The guards (if guards there were) have abandoned it. I draw near almost in trepidation and enter the dark interior. The ledge on which we placed Yeshua is untenanted. Odder still, his grave-bands lie, neatly folded, on the floor, I return to the others, in distress.

"They've taken his body, the brutes. We're not even allowed to perform his last rites…"

Slowly we turn about and retrace our steps. Somehow this betrayal feels harder to bear than the drama of Yeshua's execution. Yet it's of a different order: from his arrest to the death-blow of Cass's spear, events pursued an inexorable course as though some Mover, greater than any priest or procurator, had willed what was to be. A divinity or a devil… Now we're confronted by mere human contrivance, a sequel that confirms the half-anxious, half-vindictive cunning Qayapha and his colleagues have displayed throughout. Whatever their aim in stealing Yeshua's corpse, we mustn't let them steal the battered remnants of our dignity as his devoted followers, our dutiful service as his mourners.

We rouse the sleepers and tell them our sorry tale. As I've already guessed, the revelation spurs them first to incredulity then to a hot-blooded indignation. Here's a deed, which calls for instant retaliation, a crisis to drive out all residual fear – but before acting, they must check for themselves. Why rely on the say-so of foolish females? They set out at a pace that only I can match, leaving my friends to brood in the upper room. The heavens already pulse with hidden light awaiting the bugle-call's invitation. My feet lack the impetus of theirs, for I know what lies ahead; from a distance I watch Jo gain over plodding Rock as both approach the cave-mouth. He halts on its threshold as if last-minute superstition has chained him to the spot, while Rock stumbles past him and within. Emboldened, Jo follows and for several moments they are lost to my view. Does it take so long to register the obvious?

When they emerge, their anger seems undiminished. "The bastards," Jo grates. "I know the way their crafty brains are working. If we go round saying our Master's risen, as they think we'll do, they'll be able to produce his body from wherever they're stashing it and prove us to be liars. We'll be nicked for perjury – and they'll have made a clean sweep of the lot of us."

"But why remove it in the first place?" asks Rock.

"Because they aren't sure of our back-up. They imagine guys like Barabbas are in league with us; he'd make short work of their pansy task-force. Then we might've grabbed Yeshua's corpse and claimed the vanishing-act as a miracle. That's why Qayapha wanted Roman sentries."

"Makes sense, that does."

"See here, Rock. I'm going to raise Cain over this. I don't care what they do to me now. I'll pester them into admitting their sacrilege – it'll be some compensation for the Master's death. Coming?"

"You bet I am." At last Rock's chance of making reparation has dawned. "They won't know what's hit 'em once I get started. Just watch me…"

In their transport, the pair has forgotten my existence. I feel their outrage, yet the fire in my guts smouldered and went out two days ago. No reprisal, no belated show of protestation is able to restore the loss or bridge the gulf that Yeshua's passing has made in our lives. They turn back, full of resolution. Poor, lovable idiots... Qayapha and his henchmen will make mincemeat of them. I ought to catch them up and thump some sense into their silly heads yet I'd rather stay here a minute or two, alone at my favourite hour of day, and let my thoughts wander over the past with all its trivial joys and aching sorrows. Alone? It seems that, too, is being denied me. I feel a presence haunting this seclusion. It hovers behind me as I gaze into the sepulchre of our Master and our spent hope. I wheel round in sudden irritation.

Is it a gardener come to tend the flowers, which beautify this solemn place? He's tall, well built, swathed in a linen cape whose hood shadows his face. No, not a gardener... I've got it: one of those guards appointed by the High Priest – left here to watch for Yeshua's accomplices. My heart sinks. Wearily I move towards him, holding my wrists out for the rope. "I'll come quietly," I say.

"Miri."

I know him by the loving warmth in his voice and it sends me to my knees on the sun-baked turf, not daring to lift my eyes. The world's spinning.

"Look at me."

I gaze upward as he flings back his hood. The features that I rinsed of blood have regained their comeliness, the grey eyes sparkle with their roguish glint. This can't be happening...

"Yeshua – Master – Lord!"

"Yeshua will do."

"The spear, Cass's spear. It pierced you to the heart."

He draws open the breast of his robe with one nail-torn hand. The lips of a mortal wound gape wide beneath. Is it hallucination – am I going mad? I must be sure. Crawling forward, I stretch out an arm to ascertain, but he backs a pace, still smiling.

"No, don't touch me. I'm real enough, Miri, a man and no ghost, yet my restoration to the flesh is of a different order. The body that you see is transformed, as one day yours will be, beyond the range of suffering and disease, death or decay. These relics of my passion remain solely to convince the weak of faith that this is truly myself, a dead man risen."

"Let me call back the others, Yeshua. Don't they deserve to know that you've returned to us?"

"They and their friends will know it in good time. Tell them to go north to Galil where I shall be before them. We'll meet there – for a while."

"Only for a while?"

He nods. "I must be with my Poppa. He has first claim on me, now that I've done his bidding. Yet we shan't be separated, Miri. You have the sacrament of my flesh and blood, while our Spirit will watch over you." His eyes linger on me fondly. "Would you like some keepsake - an assurance that this happening is for real?"

"Please, Yeshua."

"Then I'll take away the scars you earned for my sake."

I look at his far deeper wounds and shake my head.

"Very well." He ponders a moment. "I can't have my best girl going around like some badly shorn sheep. My Poppa willed you to be beautiful, a delight for men's eyes – and so you shall be, once again."

His smile lasts on my inward gaze long after he's gone from me. My whirling brain can't comprehend this wonder, the substance of his cloudy prediction: "Destroy this temple and in three days I shall rebuild it." We thought that worldly wickedness overcame him, not knowing that he'd taken on a worthier foe – the last enemy of mankind. I look back on my puny efforts to come between them, to outwit death and salvage a half-life out of total failure; it was he, not Jude's treason or Cass's spear, which foiled me. His mother spoke the truth at Nazrat: "Remember, Miri," she'd said, "whatever the future holds for him, it will happen by his will. His life may be given but not taken."

I recall Jo's words as well: "A sick joke." The joke's on us.

He's convinced that Yeshua gave up his life before the spear plunged home. That may be so, yet the blow was a mortal one in another sense. It killed my love for Cass stone-dead. Poor Cass! He never reckoned on this, his rival returning from the tomb. Fate plays strange tricks. My soldier-boy's a figment of what's passed, yet he who challenged death is now alive to me – alive as no man ever was before.

Slowly I get to my feet and turn to face the day-spring.

I've always liked early morning. Really early, I mean, before the sun came up over the hills, when the sky was a translucent grey and the earth was still asleep. Not a soul in view, just me and an empty world holding its breath, waiting – for what? God knows, but I'd feel it too. Waiting to be born again, the grime and vomit and fag-end of despair cast off as a snake sloughs its skin. A new beginning ahead, not only for me but for everyone and every thing.

Grass sprang under my feet, drenching my ankles in dew. Scented air came to me over flowered fields from a land beyond the furthest range. Nature seemed as it was before men corrupted it, before Eva ate from the tree of knowledge. A linnet's song melted into the harmony of tiny sounds that accentuated this expectant hush. Light rose from its hidden source in the east to flood heaven's immensity with promise, breathing colour into rock and foliage, stringing jewels along the spider's web close to my wondering eyes. I'd pass a hand down my thigh to reassure myself that I was real, all this was real and not some insubstantial dream.

The dawning of a perfect day, a day that would never end. The birth of a perfect self within me who'd never again be touched by pain or evil, who'd love without counting the cost and want for nothing because to be — simply to be — was happiness enough. My heart would grow big, hammer upon my breast-bone, become one with the universe, enfolding all that lived. And I'd ask myself whether one day it would happen...

The sun's disk climbs above the mountains of Moab, dazzling my gaze. A trumpet calls from the Temple's minaret. As I loose my headscarf and newly grown hair (crimson as the new-made wine at Kana) cascades about my shoulders, one question cries out to be answered. Is this the day?